WITHDRAWN
UTSA Libraries

MEMOIR OF THE LIFE OF
JOSIAH QUINCY

A Da Capo Press Reprint Series

THE ERA OF THE AMERICAN REVOLUTION
GENERAL EDITOR: LEONARD W. LEVY
Claremont Graduate School

MEMOIR OF THE LIFE OF JOSIAH QUINCY

By Josiah Quincy

DA CAPO PRESS · NEW YORK · 1971

A Da Capo Press Reprint Edition

This Da Capo Press edition of
Memoir of the Life of Josiah Quincy
is an unabridged republication of the
first edition published in Boston in 1825.

Library of Congress Catalog Card Number 78-146274
SBN 306-70098-0

Published by Da Capo Press
A Division of Plenum Publishing Corporation
227 West 17th Street, New York, N.Y. 10011
All Rights Reserved

Manufactured in the United States of America

MEMOIR OF THE LIFE OF
JOSIAH QUINCY

MEMOIR

OF THE

LIFE OF JOSIAH QUINCY JUN.

OF

MASSACHUSETTS:

BY HIS SON,

JOSIAH QUINCY.

———————— Breve et irreparabile tempus
Omnibus est vitæ ; sed famam extendere factis,
Hoc virtutis opus.

BOSTON:
PUBLISHED BY CUMMINGS, HILLIARD, & COMPANY.
1825.

DISTRICT OF MASSACHUSETTS, TO WIT:

District Clerk's Office.

BE IT REMEMBERED, that on the twenty-first day of May, A. D. 1825, in the nineteenth year of the Independence of the United States of America, Cummings, Hilliard, & Co. of the said district, have deposited in this office the title of a book, the right whereof they claim as proprietors, in the words following, to wit:

"Memoir of the Life of Josiah Quincy Jun. of Massachusetts: by his son, Josiah Quincy.

——————— Breve et irreparabile tempus
Omnibus est vitæ; sed famam extendere factis,
Hoc virtutis opus."

In conformity to the Act of the Congress of the United States, entitled, "An Act for the encouragement of learning, by securing the copies of maps, charts, and books, to the authors and proprietors of such copies, during the times therein mentioned:" and also to an Act, entitled, "An Act, supplementary to an Act, entitled, 'An Act for the encouragement of learning, by securing the copies of maps, charts, and books, to the authors and proprietors of such copies, during the times therein mentioned;' and extending the benefits thereof to the arts of designing, engraving, and etching historical, and other prints."

JNO. W. DAVIS,
Clerk of the District of Massachusetts.

University Press.—Hilliard & Metcalf.

TO THE

CITIZENS OF BOSTON,

This MEMOIR of one, who, in times of great peril and oppression, was among the most strenuous assertors of the rights of the inhabitants of this metropolis, is respectfully dedicated,

By their fellow citizen,

JOSIAH QUINCY.

Boston, April 26, 1825.

PREFACE.

By the lapse of half a century, the actors in the scenes immediately preceding the war of the American Revolution, begin to be placed in a light and at a distance, favourable at once to right feeling and just criticism. In the possession of freedom, happiness, and prosperity, seldom if ever before equalled in the history of nations, the hearts of the American people naturally turn towards the memories of those, who, under Providence, were the instruments of obtaining these blessings. Curiosity awakens concerning their characters and motives. The desire grows daily more universal to repay, with a late and distant gratitude, their long neglected, and often forgotten, sacrifices and sufferings.

Among the men, whose character and political conduct had an acknowledged influence on the events of that period, was Josiah Quincy Jun. The unanimous consent of his contemporaries has associated his name, in an imperishable union, with that of Otis, Adams, Hancock, Warren, and other distinguished men, whose talents and intrepidity influenced the events which led to the declaration of Independence. This honour has been granted to him, notwithstanding his political path was, in every period of its short extent, interrupted by intense professional labours, and was terminated by death at the early age of thirty-one years.

The particular features of a life and character, capable, under such circumstances, of attaining so great a distinction, are objects of curiosity and interest. Those who recollect him, speak of his eloquence, his genius, and his capacity for intellectual labour; of the inextinguishable zeal and absorbing ardour of his exertions, whether directed to political or professional objects; of the entireness with which he threw his soul into every cause in which he engaged; of the intrepidity of his spirit, and of his indignant sense of the wrongs of his country.

It is certain that he made a deep impression on his contemporaries. Those who remember the political debates in Fanueil Hall, consequent on the Stamp Act, the Boston Massacre, and the Boston Port-Bill, have yet a vivid recollection of the pathos of his eloquence, the boldness of his invectives, and the impressive vehemence with which he arraigned the measures of the British ministry, inflaming the zeal and animating the resentment of an oppressed people.

These recollections, however, are evanescent. The peculiarities of tone, gesture, and turn of thought, which distinguished the orator, perish with him, and with those who were witnesses of their effect. It is among written memorials that the historian must look for those traits of virtue and talent which fix the destiny of character, and by which the false is detected and the true established.

The chief memorials of Josiah Quincy Jun. belonging to this class, were, by his last will, bequeathed to his son, the editor of this work. They have frequently been solicited for publication, but, with the exception of the few extracts which Gordon made and inserted in the first volume of his History of the American Revolution, no part has before been submitted to the press. They are now given to the general eye, not so much because they belong to that individual, as because his memory, from the circumstances of his life, death, character, and labours, is inseparably identified with the times in which he lived, and with the fortunes of his country.

A memoir of this kind has been often urged on the editor as a duty. But it is difficult for a son to execute such a task, without being suspected of undue bias, or of motives different from those which are avowed. Obstacles of this character have deferred until the present time, and would have postponed until a still more distant period, this publication, had they not been overcome by considerations arising from the uncertainty of life, from the accidents to which all manuscripts are exposed, and from a sense of duty as well to the individual as to the public. The few facts known concerning his life, extracts from his writings, and original letters, to and from distinguished men of his time, will be inserted in chronological order, and selected exclusively with reference to the light they throw on character, motives, and principles.

His pamphlet on the Boston Port-Bill will be subjoined. Although temporary in its object, it is among the best remaining evidences of the spirit and political principle of the period in which it was written. Nor can it fail of permanent interest from its connexion with the history of this metropolis, and with that most oppressive measure of the British ministry, which, more than any other, precipitated the crisis of the American Revolution.

Of all monuments raised to the memory of distinguished men, the most appropriate, and the least exceptionable, are those, whose foundations are laid in their own works, and which are constructed of materials, supplied and wrought by their own labours.

MEMOIR.

JOSIAH QUINCY Jun. was a descendant from one of those pilgrims, who, in the reign of Charles the First, sought, in these western regions, an asylum from civil and religious persecution. His ancestor, Edmund Quincy, came from England with the Rev. John Cotton, and arrived at Boston in the month of September 1633. In November following, his name and that of his wife are mentioned on the records of the First Church. He was elected the succeeding May, by the town of Boston, one of its first representatives to the first General Court held in the Colony; and it appears by the records of that town, that "on the tenth day of the ninth month, 1634, Edmund Quincy and others were appointed to make and assess a tax of thirty pounds to Mr Blackstone," to purchase his right and title to the peninsula of "Shawmut," now Boston.

In 1635, the town of Boston granted lands at Mount Wollaston to William Coddington and Edmund Quincy; who took possession of them in the following year. Edmund Quincy died soon after, at the age of thirty-three.

His only son, Edmund Quincy, was born in England, in 1627. He inherited and settled on his father's estate at Mount Wollaston, afterwards Braintree; was a magistrate of the county, and Lieutenant Colonel of the Suffolk regiment. He died in 1697, having had two sons, Daniel and Edmund. Daniel, the eldest, died before his father, leaving one son, John, born in 1689.

John Quincy was an inhabitant of the town of Braintree, and was one of the most distinguished public characters of that period. He held the office of Speaker of the House of Representatives, longer than any other person, during the Charter of William and Mary; and served as representative from the town of Braintree, and as member of the Executive Council of the Province for forty successive years. His paternal estate (Mount Wollaston), on which he resided during his whole life, is now the property of his great grandson, John Quincy Adams.

Edmund, the youngest son of Edmund Quincy, was born in Braintree, in October 1681; was graduated at Harvard College in 1699; and entered early into public life, as representative of the town of Braintree, and afterwards as member of the Executive Council. He held the commission of Judge of the Supreme Court of the colony, from the year 1718, to his death. A controversy having occurred between the province of Massachusetts Bay and that of New Hampshire, relative to their respective boundary lines, he was appointed by the General Court of Massachusetts, their agent at the Court of Great Britain. In December 1737, he embarked for England, on that mission. Soon after his arrival in London, he died of the smallpox, February 23, 1738, at the age of fifty-seven. His death was deeply lamented by his countrymen. The General Court of Massachusetts, as an acknowledgment of his worth, and considering that his life had fallen a sacrifice in the public service, made a donation to his heirs, of one thousand acres of land, in the town of Lenox, in the county of Berkshire; and caused a monument to be erected over his grave in Bunhill-fields, London, at the expense of the colony.

This Edmund Quincy left two sons, Edmund and Josiah. Edmund, the eldest, was born in Braintree, in 1703, was educated at Harvard College, and received his degree in 1722. He was many years a merchant in Boston. Afterwards he resided on his paternal estate in Braintree; was author of "A Treatise on Hemp Husbandry," published in 1765, and died an acting magistrate of the county of Suffolk, in July 1788, at the age of eighty-five.

Josiah, the youngest son of Edmund Quincy, was born in Braintree, in 1709. He was graduated at Harvard College, in 1728, and entered into business as a merchant in Boston. In 1737, he accompanied his father to England, passed several years in Europe at different periods of his life, and finally returned to America in 1749. He was appointed in 1755, by Governor Shirley, joint commissioner with Thomas Pownall, afterwards Governor Pownall, to negotiate with the colonies of Pennsylvania and New York, for assistance in erecting a frontier barrier against the French, at Ticonderoga. In this mission he availed himself of the influence of Dr Franklin,* and was successful. The particular circumstances of this negotia-

---

* See Appendix.

tion are related in the Memoirs of that great man, written by himself.

Josiah Quincy retired in 1756 from business, and resided in Braintree, on his portion of his paternal estate, until his death, in 1784. His latter years were embittered by the loss of his youngest son, the subject of these memoirs, with whose zeal in the cause of American liberty, he cordially co-operated ; and whose reputation for genius, and rising promise of future usefulness and distinction, he had cherished as the hope and solace of his declining years. He was in friendship and correspondence with Washington, Adams, Franklin, Bowdoin, and other distinguished characters of that period.* His first wife was Hannah Sturgis, daughter of John Sturgis Esq. of Yarmouth, by whom he had three sons.

Edmund, the eldest, was born in Braintree, in October 1733. He received his degree at Harvard College in 1752, entered into business as a merchant in Boston, and visited England in 1760, and 1763. He was the intimate friend of Dr Mayhew, and a correspondent of Thomas Hol-

---

* As the letters of such men cannot fail of being interesting to their countrymen, a few of those, found among the papers of Josiah Quincy, are inserted in the Appendix.

lis Esq. of London.* Being a zealous whig and a political writer of that period, he would have probably taken an active part in the American Revolution, had his life been spared. But his health declining under a pulmonary complaint, he sailed, by the advice of his physicians, to the West Indies, and died at sea in March 1768, at the age of thirty-five years.

Samuel Quincy, the second son, was graduated at Harvard College in 1754; engaged in the study of the law, and became eminent in that profession. He was appointed Solicitor General of the province, under the crown, and held that office until the revolution. Influenced by his official duties and connexions, his political course was opposed to that of the other members of his family. On the termination of the siege of Boston in 1776, he left this country with other loyalists. He was appointed attorney for the crown in the island of Antigua, which office he held until his death in 1789.

The youngest son of Josiah Quincy, having died in the lifetime of his father, was known to his contemporaries by the name of Josiah Quincy Jun.

---

* A letter from Mr Hollis is inserted in the Appendix to this work.

He was born in Boston February 23, 1744. The delicacy of his constitution, during his infancy and childhood, excited the anxiety of his friends. As he advanced towards manhood their apprehensions were increased by the extreme sensibility of his temperament, and the ardour and industry by which, even in youth, he was distinguished.

These qualities characterized him through life, and being brought into strong activity by the political excitement of the period, caused the early termination of his career.

Josiah Quincy Jun. acquired the rudiments of a classical education at Braintree, under the tuition of Mr Joseph Marsh, who was for many years master of a highly respected private school in that town. In 1759, he entered Harvard University, where his industry, zeal, and unconquerable thirst for learning, were conspicuous. His taste was refined by an intimate acquaintance with the ancient classics, and his soul elevated and touched by the spirit of freedom they breathe. His compositions during this period also prove, that he was extensively conversant with the best writers of the French and English schools. Above all, the genius of Shakspeare seems to have led captive his youthful imagination. In his writings, quotations, or forms of expression, modelled upon those of that author, perpetually recur. There still exists among his papers, a manuscript of the date of 1762, he then being in the junior class of the college, of seventy closely and minutely written quarto pages of extracts from that writer.

He was graduated in 1763, with unblemished reputation. Three years afterwards, on taking the degree of Master of Arts, he pronounced the English oration, at that time a new thing in the exercises of the University, and considered its highest academic honor. His subject was " patriotism," and it appears by the periodical publications of the day, that he acquired, both on account of the composition and delivery, great reputation.

From the University, he passed in 1763, into the office of Oxenbridge Thacher Esq. in Boston, one of the most eminent lawyers of the period, and entered upon the study of the law with that intense ardour and industry, which were his distinguishing characteristics. Mr Thacher died in July 1765. Mr Quincy remained in the office during the residue of his student's term, took a general oversight of its concerns, and on entering his professional career, succeeded to an extensive practice, which his talents, diligence, and fidelity, in a great measure, secured to himself. His industry while a student, and during the first years of his profession, is proved by several manuscript volumes, in his own hand, consisting of " Reports of cases, and points of law, solemnly adjudged in the Supreme Court of the Province," part of which are original, and part copied from the minutes of eminent lawyers.

The arguments of Auchmuty, Thacher, Gridley, Otis, Adams, and other distinguished lawyers, with the cases cited, in various important questions, are here abstracted and preserved.

On commencing the practice of the law, he early became distinguished for the zeal with which he engaged in the service of his clients, and the learning and eloquence of his arguments both to the court and jury. Otis, Adams, Sewall, and the other great luminaries of the bar at that period, were by many years his seniors. His practice, however, soon became extensive, and his high rank as a lawyer was acknowledged by his contemporaries. Although his attachment to professional pursuits was strong, and his attention to his business unremitting, yet the political circumstances of the times were of a character to call into immediate action that love of country, which was the deep-seated passion of his soul.

Notwithstanding the repeal of the Stamp Act, in March 1766, the avowal contained in that repeal, " of the absolute right of Parliament to bind the Colonies, in all cases whatsoever," had excited great alarm, and just discontent, among the friends of liberty in America. The course of measures adopted by the British ministry towards the town of Boston, tended to quicken those fears, and extend that discontent. In the autumn of 1766, the companies of Royal Artillery, then stationed at Castle Island in the harbour of this town, were augmented. In the June following, additional reinforcements arrived. In July 1767, the British cabinet resolved upon new restrictions on American commerce. It was determined to raise a farther revenue by imposts, additional to those already existing, and which were, in themselves, sufficiently obnoxious and oppressive. The number of the officers of the customs was to be multiplied. The governor, judges, and revenue officers, were to be paid by the crown, without resort to the colonial legislature. The military force in the colonies was largely to be increased, and the power of the military commanders to be augmented, so as to make them more effective instruments in putting down opposition.

The knowledge of this revived scheme of oppression, reached America in the September of that year, accompanied by letters from the friends of American liberty in Europe, stating that it was the intention of the administration to cause the authors of the riots, and the writers of the seditious pieces in America, to be arrested and sent to England to be tried for high treason. This news rekindled the flame which the repeal of the Stamp Act had, in some degree, allayed. The public prints became immediately the vehicles of the boldest language, and the most vivid excitement. At this time, Mr Quincy, as far as can be gathered from his papers, first commenced his political animadversions on the times, and their resulting duties. Two pieces, signed Hyperion, were published by him in the Boston Gazette, in the latter end of September, and the beginning of October, 1767. The following extracts will show both the temper of the times, and the spirit of the writer.

"It cannot be
But we are pigeon-livered, and lack gall
To make oppression bitter."

"When I reflect on the exalted character of the ancient Britons, on the fortitude of our illustrious predecessors, on the noble struggles of the late memorable period, and from these reflections, when, by a natural transition, I contemplate the gloomy aspect of the present day, my heart is alternately torn with doubt and hope, despondency and terror. Can the true, generous magnanimity of British heroes be entirely lost in their degenerate progeny? Is the genius of Liberty, which so late inflamed our bosoms, fled forever?

"An attentive observer of the deportment of some particular persons in this metropolis, would be apt to imagine that the grand point was gained; that the spirit of the people was entirely broken to the yoke; that all America was subjugated to bondage. Already the minions of power, in fancy fatten, and grow wanton on the spoils of the land. They insolently toss the head, and put on the air of contemptuous disdain. In the imaginary possession of lordships and dominions, these potentates and powers dare tell us, that our only hope is to crouch, to cowl under, and to kiss the iron rod of oppression. Precious sample of the meek and lowly temper of those, who are destined to be our lords and masters!

"Be not deceived, my countrymen. Believe not these venal hirelings when they would cajole you by their subtleties into submission, or frighten you by their vapourings into compliance. When they strive to flatter you by the terms 'moderation and prudence,' tell them, that calmness and deliberation are to guide the judgment; courage and intrepidity command the action. When they endeavour to make us 'perceive our inability to oppose our mother country,' let us boldly answer: In defence of our civil and religious rights, we dare oppose the world; with the God of armies on our side, even the God who fought our fathers' battles, we fear not the hour of trial, though the hosts of our enemies should cover the field like locusts. If this be enthusiasm, we will live and die enthusiasts.

"Blandishments will not fascinate us, nor will threats of a 'halter' intimidate. For under God, we are determined, that wheresoever, whensoever, or howsoever, we shall be called to make our exit, we will die freemen. Well do we know that all the regalia of this world cannot dignify the death of a villain, nor diminish the ignominy, with which a slave shall quit his existence. Neither can it taint the unblemished honour of a son of freedom, though he should make his departure on the already prepared gibbet, or be dragged to the newly erected scaffold for execution. With the plaudits of his conscience he will go off the stage. A crown of joy and immortality shall be his reward. The history of his life his children shall venerate. The virtues of their sire shall excite their emulation."

Other political essays, breathing the same spirit, and tending to rouse the indignation of his countrymen, at the measures of the British cabinet, were published by him in the Boston Gazette, in the course of the ensuing year. A letter written about this time to one of his friends, strongly depicts his feelings, and indicates the absorbing influence, with which the enthusiasm of the period had possessed his heart and understanding.

TO THE REV. JOHN EAGLESON.

"*Boston, Sept.* 15, 1768.

" Respected Sir,

" Your friendly letter came to hand a few days since, and a leisure moment now presenting, I with pleasure seize the opportunity of writing to you. The rights and liberties of Americans become every day more and more the serious object of attention. As political disputation increases, a settlement of the point in question removes farther and farther from the design of both parties. Private pique, envy, and personal resentment soon preclude a fair and candid discussion, and intemperate passions will forever prevent any equitable decision.

" The present aspect of the day is gloomy indeed, yet we are far from despair. Though the clouds, full charged, rise thick and fast, the thunders roll, and lightnings play, nay, it is said, are just within striking distance, there are not wanting those among us, who believe that proper conductors will safely carry off all the political fluid, the clouds disperse, and the sky soon become calm and serene. Visionaries, you know, are credulous, enthusiasts are bold and enterprising; many such, Mr Eagleson is sensible, inhabit these northern regions.

"We Americans have a righteous cause. We know it. The power of Great Britain may oppress, nay, for a time apparently subdue us. But, before all the freeborn sons of the north will yield a general and united submission, to any tyrannic power on earth, fire and sword, famine and slaughter, desolation and ruin, will ravage the land. When thus I venture, without any pretence to the spirit of prophecy, at a hasty prediction, you will probably smile at my reverie. But you know, political dreamers are the most obstinate, and incorrigible, of all sinners. You will see, by our public prints, the late transactions of this town, and the situation that we are in at present. Daily in the expectation of troops: some say three regiments, and three ships of the line. Opinions differ respecting what ought, and what will be, the deportment of this people. On the one hand, a swarm of court dependants, and a standing army in the bowels of a state, have been in all ages, and nations, thought, and found to be, the bane of civil freedom. On the other, an open rupture with Great Britain (I had like to have said *mother* state), is a dreadful alternative.

"But our all is at stake! The pulse of the people beats high, and it may well be imagined, that in our present state, all ranks among us are much agitated. This therefore may apologize for my not being in a facetious, and proper frame of mind, to answer some parts of your entertaining letter. To see the daily blunders which are committed, and the deep tragedy which is now acting, on the political theatre, and not to be moved, is to be an unfeeling wretch indeed. If the contempt and indignation of every sensible and humane man in Christendom, were sufficient to explode a political system, there would be some hopes of seeing 'Venice Preserved and the Plot Discovered.'"

About the last of September of this year, two British regiments, the 14th under the command of Colonel Dalrymple, and the 29th under that of Lieut. Colonel Carr, arrived in Boston from Halifax. They were landed from fourteen ships of war, which lay with their broadsides towards the town, with springs on their cables, and their guns ready to fire, in case of the least opposition. With muskets charged, bayonets fixed, drums beating, fifes playing, and a complete train of artillery, the troops took possession of the common, the state-house, the court-house, and Faneuil hall. The main-guard, with two pieces of artillery, was stationed at the state-house, with their guns pointed towards it. The town wore the aspect of a garrison. Counsellors, as they entered the council-chamber, citizens, as they passed and repassed on their private business, were challenged by sentinels.

It was at this moment, and under such a state of terror and danger, that Mr Quincy published " Hyperion " in the Boston Gazette of the third of October. As it is strongly indicative of the temper of that most eventful moment, as well as eminently characteristic of the mind and feelings of the writer, it will be here published entire.

" ' The aggregated judgment of the common people,' says an eminent writer, ' discerns most truly the errors of government, forasmuch as they are the first to be sure to smart under them. In this only they come to be shortsighted ; that though they know the diseases, they understand not the remedies, and though good patients, they are ill physicians.'

" What are the present sentiments of the inhabitants of North America ? Discern they not most truly, and smart they not most severely under the errors of government ? The disease is known and felt; but where is the remedy,—where is the physician ? For the people to ask counsel is deemed treasonable; to assemble themselves to consult, is denominated rebellion. Thus would some potentates terrify mankind with a few sounding, technical expressions. It has been found in all ages difficult to persuade men, by the most refined court-chicane, out of their reason; and tyrants have ever found it impossible to argue, sooth, or frighten the common people out of their feelings. It is truly strange to hear the arguments, and see the parade of some at this day. One would from their conduct be induced to imagine, they thought it the most likely way of dispiriting the people, to render their case irremediable. Certainly such politicians have little studied the volume of nature. A nation, not as yet entirely enervated by luxury, not wholly depressed by slavery, when reduced to despair, are invincible to a proverb.

"After what has been said and wrote on both sides of the Atlantic, upon colony-affairs; after the most perspicuous demonstration of the illegality and ill-policy of the measures pursued against this continent; it would be an affront to the understanding to attempt setting the matter in a clearer point of view. The meanest capacity must perceive, the remotest peasant in the wilds of America must feel, the consequences.

"British taxations, suspensions of legislatures, and standing armies, are but some of the clouds, which overshadow the northern world. Heaven grant that a grand constellation of virtues may shine forth with redoubled lustre, and enlighten this gloomy hemisphere!

"If ever there was a time, this is the hour, for Americans to rouse themselves, and exert every ability. Their all is at a hazard, and the die of fate spins doubtful! In vain do we talk of magnanimity and heroism, in vain do we trace a descent from the worthies of the earth, if we inherit not the spirit of our ancestors. Who is he, who boasteth of his patriotism? Has he vanquished luxury, and subdued the worldly pride of his heart? Is he not yet drinking the poisonous draught, and rolling the sweet morsel under his tongue? He, who cannot conquer the little vanity of his heart, and deny the delicacy of a debauched palate, let him lay his hand upon his mouth, and his mouth in the dust.

"Now is the time for this people to summon every aid, human and divine; to exhibit every moral virtue, and call forth every christian grace. The wisdom of the serpent, the innocence of the dove, and the intrepidity of the lion, with the blessing of God, will yet save us from the jaws of destruction.

"Where is the boasted liberty of Englishmen, if property may be disposed of, charters suspended, assemblies dissolved, and every valued right annihilated, at the uncontrollable will of an external power? Does not every man, who feels one ethereal spark yet glowing in his bosom, find his indignation kindle, at the bare imagination of such wrongs? What would be our sentiments, were this imagination realized?

"Did the blood of the ancient Britons swell our veins, did the spirit of our forefathers inhabit our breasts, should we hesitate a moment in preferring death, to a miserable existence in bondage? Did we reflect on their toils, their dangers, their fiery trials, the thought would inspire unconquerable courage.

"Who has the front to ask, Wherefore do you complain? Who dares assert, every thing worth living for is not lost, when a nation is enslaved? Are not pensioners, stipendiaries, and salary men, (unknown before,) hourly multiplying on us, to riot in the spoils of miserable America? Does not every eastern gale waft us some new insect, even of that devouring kind, which eat up every green thing. Is not the bread taken out of the children's mouths and given unto the dogs? Are not our estates given to corrupt sycophants, without a design, or even a pretence of soliciting our assent, and our lives put into the hands of those whose tender mercies are cruelties? Has not an authority in a distant land, in the most public manner, proclaimed a right of disposing of *the all* of Americans? In short, what have we to lose—what have we to fear? Are not our distresses more than we can bear; and to finish all, are not our cities, in a time of profound peace, filled with standing armies, to preclude us from that last solace of the wretched—to open their mouths in complaint, and send forth their cries in bitterness of heart?

" But is there no ray of hope? Is not Great Britain inhabited by the children of those renowned barons, who waded through seas of crimson gore to establish their liberty; and will they not allow us, their fellow men, to enjoy that freedom, which we claim from nature, which is confirmed by our constitution, and which they pretend so highly to value? Were a tyrant to conquer us, the chains of slavery, when opposition should become useless, might be supportable; but to be shackled by Englishmen,—by our equals,—is not to be borne!

"By the sweat of our brow, we earn the little we possess; from nature we derive the common rights of man;—and by charter we claim the liberties of Britons! Shall we,—dare we,—pusillanimously surrender our birthright?. Is the obligation to our fathers discharged, is the debt we owe posterity paid? Answer me, thou coward! who hidest thyself in the hour of trial! If there is no reward in this life, no prize of glory in the next, capable of animating thy dastard soul; think and tremble, thou miscreant! at the whips and stripes thy master shall lash thee with on earth,—and the flames, and scorpions, thy second master shall torment thee with hereafter!

"Oh, my countrymen! what will our children say, when they read the history of these times, should they find we tamely gave away, without one noble struggle, the most invaluable of earthly blessings? As they drag the galling chain, will they not execrate us? If we have any respect for things sacred; any regard to the dearest treasure on earth;—if we have one tender sentiment for posterity; if we would not be despised by the whole world;—let us, in the most open, solemn manner, and with determined fortitude, swear,— we will die,—if we cannot live freemen!

"Be not lulled, my countrymen, with vain imaginations, or idle fancies. To hope for the protection of Heaven, without doing our duty, and exerting ourselves as becomes men, is to mock the Deity. Wherefore had man his reason, if it were not to direct him? Wherefore his strength, if it be not his protection? To banish folly and luxury, correct vice and immorality, and stand immoveable in the freedom, in which we are free indeed, is eminently the duty of each individual, at this day. When this is done, we may rationally hope for an answer to our prayers; for the whole counsel of God, and the invincible armour of the Almighty.

"However righteous our cause, we cannot, in this period of the world, expect a miraculous salvation. Heaven will undoubtedly assist us, if we act like men; but to expect protection from above, while we are enervated by luxury, and slothful in the exertion of those abilities with which we are endued, is an expectation vain and foolish. With the smiles of Heaven, virtue, unanimity, and firmness will insure success. While we have equity, justice, and God, on our side, Tyranny, spiritual or temporal, shall never ride triumphant in a land inhabited by Englishmen."

The following extract from a letter, written to his father, in December, 1768, on a subject of personal interest, marks how deeply the love of independence was impressed upon his heart; and how consistent were the principles of his private and public life.

" An independency, in the strict sense of the word, I know is not the lot of man; but to restrain, to a certain degree, the instability of fortune, is much in our power. So far then, an independence is attainable. Let those, who will, laugh at the paltry certainty which is to be gained. Surely, it would be some alleviation under the pressure of misfortune, to think, that our own folly and rashness contributed in no part to the heavy burden. Alas! how few of the sons of men have this happy consolation. Hence, most of those idle and vague declamations, which we so often hear, upon the fickleness and inconstancy of fortune. When thoroughly examined, the grand source is found in the hasty presumption of a foolish vanity, or the weak irresolution of a vicious heart. To apply for assistance, where my own foresight might have prevented the necessity, would be to me worse than death. Early in life, I was fixed; experience has confirmed me, to suffer every stroke of adversity, let it be as severe as even imagination can paint, ere I would implore any earthly relief from distress, against which my own prudence might have armed me. To ask assistance, where, if it were declined, your redoubled efforts would supply your exigence, is the daily course of human affairs; but to seek relief, where a denial reduces you to despair, would be torment beyond expression.

" Through your watchful care of my education and your kind munificence, I am out of a temptation to the meaner vices, and in that state, which to one of my temper, is the happiest human nature can boast, an independency, save on God and myself, for a decent support through life, and the hope of quitting the stage with that best human standard of true worth, the general approbation of my countrymen. How deeply my heart is affected, by those invaluable favours, is not for profession to convince you, but will be, I trust, best manifested by the uniform tenor of my life."

The political course of Mr Quincy having rendered him obnoxious to the Supreme Court of the province, he was omitted in the distribution of the honours of the gown, which was due to his rank and standing at the bar. This circumstance is thus noticed in the fourth volume of his manuscript Law Reports.

"August 1769. At the last sitting of the Supreme Court in Charlestown, I argued (for the first time in this Court) to the jury, though not admitted to the gown; the legality and propriety of which, some have pretended to doubt. But as no scruples of that kind disturbed me, I proceeded (maugre any) to manage all my own business (for the first time also in this county,) though unsanctified, and uninspired by the pomp and magic of——the Long Robe."

At this period his professional engagements became so extensive, as often to preclude him from any particular oversight of the publication of his political essays. A direction to the printers, which appears on some of his original manuscripts, —" Let Samuel Adams Esq. correct the press,"— indicates the mutual respect and intimacy, which subsisted between them, and which continued uninterrupted until his death. Notwithstanding the multiplicity of his professional avocations, and his ardent zeal in exciting and directing the political energies of his countrymen, his literary pursuits were never relinquished. His manuscripts and common-place books prove how deeply he was imbued with the love of letters. His library, which was extensive for that period, was destroyed by fire, about ten years after his death; a loss the more to be regretted, as the few volumes which escaped, show that his practice was to read with his pen in his hand, and to record in the margin or blank pages, by way of reference, or remark, either his own thoughts, or the parallel thoughts of other writers, which reading recalled to his memory.

In October 1769, he married the eldest daughter of William Phillips Esq., at that time one of the most eminent merchants in New England; and who, in the crisis of the country, which succeeded, was distinguished by the readiness, and the amount, with which, in the most perilous and dubious periods of the controversy, he contributed to its support. In this connexion, the result of an early attachment, Mr Quincy found a companion, possessed of an intellect and spirit, capable of appreciating and supporting his own character and virtues. During his life she was the confidant of his noble views, and entering, with like ardour, into his political course, cheerfully submitted to the privations it induced, encouraging him with all her influence to risk the perils to which his open, undisguised zeal in the cause of his country, at that time, were thought to expose him and his family. She survived her husband three and twenty years; his fame and memory being the chief solace of her life; and the perfect fulfilment of parental duty to their surviving child, its only object.

Among his original papers for the year 1770, are " An address of the merchants, traders, and freeholders of the town of Boston, assembled at Faneuil Hall, January 23, 1770, for the purpose of enforcing the non-importation act:" two essays, signed, " An Independant," published in the Boston Gazette on the 12th and 26th of February 1770: another signed " An Old Man," published in the Boston Gazette of August 6,

1770 : and the "Report of a committee appointed to draw up instructions, for the representatives of the town of Boston, and which was unanimously accepted by the inhabitants, 15th May, 1770." The original draft of this report in the hand writing of Mr Quincy, signed by Richard Dana, and attested by William Cooper, town clerk, exists among his papers.

The boldness of his political course may be estimated by a single paragraph extracted from one of the above mentioned essays, styled " The Independant," and published on the 12th of February, while Boston was in a state little short of a garrison, and only twenty days previous to the Boston massacre.

" In answer to the question, ' What end is the non-importation agreement to answer ?' I give the following reply.

" From a conviction in my own mind, that America is now the slave of Britain ; from a sense that we are every day more and more in danger of an increase of our burdens, and a fastening of our shackles, I wish to see my countrymen break off,——*off forever!*—all social intercourse with those, whose commerce contaminates, whose luxuries poison, whose avarice is insatiable, and whose unnatural oppressions are not to be borne. That Americans will know their rights, that they will resume, assert, and defend them, are matters of which I harbour no doubt. Whether the arts of *policy*, or the arts of *war* will decide the contest, are problems, we will solve at a more convenient season. He, whose heart is enamoured with the refinements of political artifice and finesse, will seek one mode of relief; he whose heart is free, honest, and intrepid, will pursue another, a bolder, and more noble mode of redress. This reply is so intelligible, that it needs no comment, or explanation."

It was scarcely to be anticipated that one, who could discern thus clearly, and display thus boldly, the inevitable crisis which ensued, should be one of the selected judicial defenders of those, who were the instruments in shedding the first blood, that flowed in the contest which terminated in American Independence.

The tragedy of the 5th of March 1770, denominated, in the language of that period, " The Boston Massacre," had wrought the whole people of Massachusetts, and above all the inhabitants of

Boston, to the highest pitch of rage and indignation. The populace breathed only vengeance. Even minds better instructed, and of higher principles than the multitude, in the excitement of the moment, could not endure the doctrine, that it was possible for an armed soldiery to fire upon and kill unarmed citizens, and commit a crime less than murder. Political animosity and natural antipathy to troops stationed in the metropolis, sharpened this vindictive spirit. The friends of the government were either silent, or only expressed regret and lamentation at the event. The friends of freedom were loud in their indignation, and clamorous for that justice which declares, that " blood shall be the penalty for blood."

Among those, who sympathized most deeply with the mass of his fellow-citizens, in their hatred of the instruments of their oppressions, and in their detestation of the principles they had been sent hither to maintain, was Josiah Quincy Jun. No one had more openly, or pathetically than he, appealed to his fellow-citizens, or had more studiously excited their resentment, both in the gazettes, and in Faneuil hall, against the troops and their employers. What then must have been his surprise, to find that Captain Preston, and the accused soldiers, had selected him as one of their defenders! On the day of Captain Preston's imprisonment, that officer sent for him to the jail, and solicited his engagement in his own behalf, and in that of the soldiers. To understand the difficulty of Mr Quincy's situation, it is necessary to realize the exasperated state of public feeling. The spirit of revenge glowed with a fervour almost universal. On the one hand were the obligations of humanity, official duty, and the strong desire that justice should not fall a sacrifice in her own temple, to the passions of the moment. On the other hand, the confidence of political friends, popularity, and that general affection which his public course had attained for him, in so remarkable a degree, among his fellow-citizens, were to be hazarded. These difficulties and dangers he shared with his intimate friend and copatriot, John Adams, who, being several years his senior, both in age and at the bar, was joined with him as elder counsel. Their mutual friendship, cemented by professional and patriotic labours, terminated only with life. After deliberation and consultation with each other, and their friends, both of these patriots yielded all personal considerations to the higher obligations of humanity and official duty. They braved the fury of the moment; and interposed their learning, talents, and well-earned influence, to that torrent of passions, which, for a time, threatened to bear down the landmarks of justice.

Gordon states, that " they offended several of their own party by undertaking the defence of the prisoners." * This, however, gives but a faint idea of the actual state of feeling which these two gentlemen had to encounter on the occasion. The following extracts from a correspondence, which parental affection and anxiety induced Mr Quincy's father to commence, will indicate the nature and extent of the sentiment prevalent at that period on the subject.

TO JOSIAH QUINCY JUN., BOSTON.

"*Braintree, March* 22, 1770.
" My dear Son,
" I am under great affliction, at hearing the bitterest reproaches uttered against you, for having become an advocate for those criminals who are charged with the murder of their fellow-

---

* History of the American Revolution, vol. i. p. 291.

citizens. Good God! Is it possible? I will not believe it.

"Just before I returned home from Boston, I knew, indeed, that on the day those criminals were committed to prison, a sergeant had inquired for you at your brother's house,—but I had no apprehension that it was possible an application would be made to you to undertake their defence. Since then I have been told that you have actually engaged for Captain Preston;—and I have heard the severest reflections made upon the occasion, by men who had just before manifested the highest esteem for you, as one destined to be a saviour of your country.

"I must own to you, it has filled the bosom of your aged and infirm parent with anxiety and distress, lest it should not only prove true, but destructive of your reputation and interest; and I repeat, I will not believe it, unless it be confirmed by your own mouth, or under your own hand.

"Your anxious and distressed parent,
"JOSIAH QUINCY."

TO JOSIAH QUINCY ESQ., BRAINTREE.

"*Boston, March* 26, 1770.

"Honoured Sir,

"I have little leisure, and less inclination either to know, or to take notice, of those ignorant slanderers, who have dared to utter their "bitter reproaches" in your hearing against me, for having become an advocate for criminals charged with murder. But the sting of reproach when envenomed only by envy and falsehood, will never prove mortal. Before pouring their reproaches into the ear of the aged and infirm, if they had been friends, they would have surely spared a little reflection on the nature of an attorney's oath, and duty;—some trifling scrutiny into the business and discharge of his office, and some small portion of patience in viewing my past and future conduct.

"Let such be told, Sir, that these criminals, charged with murder, are *not yet legally proved guilty*, and therefore, however criminal, are entitled, by the laws of God and man, to all legal counsel and aid; that my duty as a man obliged me to undertake; that my duty as a lawyer strengthened the obligation; that from abundant caution, I at first declined being engaged; that after the best advice, and most mature deliberation had determined my judgment, I waited on Captain Preston, and told him that I would afford him my assistance; but, prior to this, in presence of two of his friends, I made the most explicit declaration to him, of my real opinion, on the contests (as I expressed it to him) of the times, and that my heart and hand were indissolubly attached to the cause of my country; and finally, that I refused all engagement, until advised and urged to undertake it, by an Adams, a Hancock, a Molineux, a Cushing, a Henshaw, a Pemberton, a Warren, a Cooper, and a Phillips. This and much more might be told with great truth, and I dare affirm, that you, and this whole people will one day REJOICE, that I became an advocate for the aforesaid "criminals," *charged* with the murder of our fellow-citizens.

"I never harboured the expectation, nor any great desire, that all men should speak well of me. To inquire my duty, and to do it, is my aim. Being mortal, I am subject to error; and conscious of this, I wish to be diffident. Being a rational creature, I judge for myself, according to the light afforded me. When a plan of conduct is formed with an honest deliberation, neither murmuring, slander, nor reproaches move. For my single self, I consider, judge, and with reason hope to be immutable.

"There are honest men in all sects,—I wish their approbation;—there are wicked bigots in all parties,—I abhor them."

"I am, truly and affectionately,
> your son,
> "JOSIAH QUINCY JUN."

The trial of Captain Preston commenced on the 24th of October 1770, and was concluded on the 30th of that month, with his acquittal. Of this trial it is not known that any minutes exist. When that of the soldiers commenced, a short-hand writer was employed, from whose notes an account of that trial was published. As this volume has recently been republished, and is of easy access, no other extracts from it will be here inserted, than such as tend to throw a light on the mind and character of the subject of these memoirs. Not only for this purpose, but also as one of the best indexes to the state of the public mind, at that time, in relation to this trial,—the whole of his argument, so far as it is connected with general topics, and indicative of the particular excitement existing at that period, will be extracted. What is relative only to the evidence, will be omitted. This course will at once explain and exhibit the nature of the popular passion, against the influence of which, the advocate deemed it necessary to guard the jury, and the address with which the topics were selected, and pressed upon their understandings and hearts.

After the counsel for the crown (Samuel Quincy Esq. Solicitor General) had closed the opening of the trial, Josiah Quincy Jun. addressed the court and jury.

" May it please your Honors, and you, Gentlemen of the Jury.

" The prisoners at the bar stand indicted for the murder of five of his Majesty's liege subjects, as set forth in the several indictments, which have been read to you. The persons slain, those indictments set forth, as ' being in the peace of God, and our lord the king, at the time of the mortal wounds given.

" To these indictments, the prisoners have severally pleaded Not Guilty: and for their trial have put themselves on God and their country, which country you are. And by their pleas, thus severally pleaded, they are to stand, or fall, by the evidence which shall respectively apply to them.

"By their plea of not guilty, they throw the burden of proof, as to the fact of killing, upon the crown; but, upon which being proved, the matter they allege, to justify, excuse, or extenuate, must be adduced by them, and supported by legal evidence. The truth of the facts they may thus allege is your sole and undoubted province to determine, but upon a supposition that those facts shall appear to your satisfaction, in the manner we allege, the grand question then to be determined, will be, whether such matters, so proved, do, in law, extenuate, excuse, or justify. The decision of this question belongs to another department, namely, the Court. This is law, so well known, and acknowledged, that I shall not now detain you by a recital of authorities, but only refer you to Judge Foster's Crown Law, where this point is treated with precision, and fixed beyond controversy. It may not be amiss, however, to assure you, that as certain as the cognizance of facts is within your jurisdiction, as certain does the law, resulting from these facts, in cases of the present kind, seem to reside solely in the Court: unless cases where juries, under the direction of the Court, give general verdicts, may be denominated exceptions.

"In the cause now before us, it will not be contested, that five persons were unfortunately killed, at the time the indictments charge; and this case will naturally enough divide itself into three main divisions of inquiry.

First. Whether any homicide was committed?

Secondly. By whom was it committed?

Thirdly. Is there any thing appearing in evidence, which will justify, excuse, or extenuate, such homicide, by reducing it to that species of offence, called manslaughter?

" Before we enter upon these inquiries, permit me, gentlemen, to remind you of the importance of this trial, as it relates to the prisoners. It is for their lives!—If we consider the number of persons, now on trial, joined with many other circumstances which might be mentioned, it is by far the most important, this country ever saw. Remember the ties you are under to the prisoners, and even to yourselves. The eyes of all are upon you. Patience in hearing this cause is an essential requisite, candour and caution are no less essential. It is tedious and painful to attend a trial of such length; but remember the time which has been taken up by the Crown in the opening. By every bond of humanity and justice, we claim an equal indulgence; nay, it is of high importance to your country, that nothing should appear on this trial to impeach our justice, or stain our humanity.

" And here let me remind you of a notion, which has certainly been too prevalent, and guard you against its baneful influence. An opinion has been entertained by many among us, that the life of a soldier was of very little value: of much less value than others of the community. The law, gentlemen, knows no such distinction; the life of a soldier is viewed, by the equal eye of the law, as estimable, as the life of any other citizen.

" I cannot any other way account for what I mention, but by supposing that the indigence and poverty of a soldier,—the toils of his life,—the severity of discipline to which he is exposed,—the precarious tenure by which he is generally thought to hold his life, in the summary decisions of a court-martial, have conspired to propagate a sentiment of this kind; but a little attention to the human heart, will dissipate this notion.

" The soldier takes his choice, like all others, of his course of life: he has an equal right, with you, or me, so to do. It is best we should not all think alike. Habit makes all things agreeable; what at first was irksome, soon becomes pleasing.

But does experience teach, that misery begets in general a hatred of life! By no means: we all reluct at death; we long for one short space more; we grasp with anxious solicitude, even after a wretched existence. God, and nature, have implanted this love of life. Expel therefore from your breasts an opinion so unwarrantable by any law, human or divine; let not any thing so injurious to the prisoners, who value life as much as you; let not any thing so repugnant to all justice, have influence in this trial. The reputation of the country depends much on your conduct, gentlemen; and, may I not add, justice calls aloud for candour in hearing, and impartiality in deciding, this cause, which has, perhaps, too much engrossed our affections; and, I speak for one, too much excited our passions.

" The law, by which the prisoners are to be tried, is a law of mercy,—a law applying to us all,—a law, Judge Blackstone will tell us, ' founded in principles that are permanent, uniform, and universal, always conformable to the feelings of humanity, and the indelible rights of mankind.' Sec. 4, 13. Cap. 3.

" How ought we all, who are to bear a part in this day, to aim at a strict adherence to the principles of this law : how ought we all to aim at utterly eradicating every undue bias of the judgment : a bias subversive of all justice and humanity.

" Another opinion, equally foreign to truth and law, has been adopted by many. It has been thought, that no possible case could happen, in which a soldier could fire, without the aid of a civil magistrate. This is a great mistake,—a very unhappy mistake indeed ! one, I am afraid, that had its influence on the fatal night, which we all lament. The law, as to the present point, puts the citizen and soldier under equal restraint. What will justify and mitigate the action of the one, will do the same to the other. Let us bear this invariably in mind, in examining the evidence. But before we proceed to this examination, let us take a transient view of some occurrences, preceding, and subsequent to, the melancholy fifth of March.

" About some five or six years ago, it is well known, certain measures were adopted by the British Parliament, which gave a general alarm to this continent. Measures were alternately taken in Great Britain, that awakened jealousy, resentment, fortitude, and vigilance. Affairs continued long fluctuating. A sentiment universally prevailed, that our dearest rights were invaded. It is not our business here to inquire touching these delicate points. These are concernments, which, however interesting or important in themselves, we must keep far away from us, when in a court of law. It poisons justice, when politics tincture its current.

" I need not inform you, how the tide rose, as we were advancing towards the present times. The general attention became more and more roused,—people became more and more alike in opinion and practice. A vast majority thought all that is dear was at stake,—sentiments of liberty,—property,—ignominious bondage,—all conspire to increase the ferment. At this period the troops land. Let us here pause, and view the citizen, and the soldier.

" The causes of grievance being thus spread far and wide, the inhabitants viewed the soldiery as called in, foreign from their prime institution, to force obedience to acts, which were, in general, deemed subversive of natural, as well as constitutional freedom. With regard to the universal prevalence of ideas of this kind, it does not fall within our present plan, to give you direct, positive evidence. It would be too foreign to the present issue, though pertinent enough, when considered as a clue to springs and motives of action, and as an additional aid, to form a just judgment in our present inquiry. You, gentlemen, who come from the body of the country, are presumed to know these facts, if they are true; nay, their notoriety must be such, provided I am not mistaken in my conjecture, that the justness of my observation on this matter must be certainly confirmed by your own experience. I presume not in this, or any other matter of fact to prescribe to you: if these sentiments are wrong, they have no influence: if right, they ought certainly to have their due weight.

" I say, gentlemen, and appeal to you for the truth of what I say, that many on this continent viewed their chains as already forged; they saw fetters as prepared; they beheld the soldiers as fastening, and rivetting for ages, the shackles of their bondage. With the justness of these apprehensions, you and I have nothing to do in this place. Disquisitions of this sort are for the Senate, and the chamber of Council,—they are for statesmen and politicians, who take a latitude in thoughts and action; but we, gentlemen, are confined in our excursions, by the rigid rules of law. Upon the real, actual existence of these apprehensions, in the community, we may judge; they are facts falling properly within our cognizance, and hitherto may we go, but no farther. It is my duty, and I ought to impress it on your minds, and you, gentlemen, ought to retain the impression. You are to determine on the facts coming to your knowledge; you are to think, judge, and act, as jurymen, and not as statesmen.

"Matters being thus circumstanced, what might be expected? No room was left for cordiality and friendship. Discontent was seated on almost every brow. Instead of that hospitality, which the soldier thought himself entitled to, scorn, contempt, and silent murmurs were his reception. Almost every countenance lowered with a discontented gloom, and scarce an eye, but flashed indignant fire. Turn and contemplate the camp. Do we find a more favourable appearance? The soldier had his feelings, his sentiments, and his characteristic passions also. The constitution of our government has provided a stimulus for his affections:—the pride of conscious virtue, the sense of valour, the point of honour. The law had taught him to think favourably of himself;—had taught him to consider himself as peculiarly appointed for the safeguard and defence of his country. He had heard, that he put not off the citizen, when he entered the camp; but because he was a citizen, and wished to continue so, he made himself, for a while, a soldier. How stinging was it to be stigmatized, as the instrument of tyranny and oppression? How exasperating to be viewed, as aiding to inthrall his country? He felt his heart glow with an ardour, which he took for a love of liberty and his country, and had formed to himself no design fatal to its privileges. He recollected, no doubt, that he had heretofore exposed himself for its service. He had bared his bosom in defence of his native soil, and yet felt the smart of wounds, received in conflict for his king and country. Could that spirit, which had braved the shafts of foreign battle, brook the keener wounds of civil contest? The arrows which now pierced him, pierced as deep and rankled more, than those of former times.

"Is it rational to imagine much harmony could long subsist? We must take human nature as we find it, and not vainly imagine, that all things are to become new, at such a crisis. There are an order of men in every commonwealth, who never reason, but always act from feeling. That their rights and liberties were filched away one after another, they had often been told. They had been taught by those whom they believed, that the axe was now laid to the root of the tree, and one more stroke completed its fall. It was in vain to expect to silence or subdue these emotions by reasons, soothings, or dangers. A belief that nothing could be worse than the calamities, which seemed inevitable, had extended itself on all sides, and arguments drawn from such sources had little influence. Each day gave rise to new occurrences, which increased animosities. Heartburnings, heats, and bickerings became more and more extensive. Reciprocal insults soured the temper, mutual injuries imbittered the passions. Can we wonder, that when every thing tended to some important action, the period so soon arrived? Will not our wonder be increased to find the crisis no sooner taking place, when so many circumstances united to hasten its approach? To use an allusion somewhat homely, may we not wonder that the acid and the alkali did not sooner ferment?

"A thought here imperceptibly forces itself on our minds, and we are led to be astonished that persons so discordant in opinion, so opposite in views, attachments, and connexions, should be stationed together. But here, gentlemen, we must stop. If we pursue this inquiry, at this time, and in this place, we shall be in danger of doing great injustice. We shall get beyond our limits. The right of quartering troops in this province must be discussed at a different tribunal. The constitutional legality, the propriety, the expediency of their appointment, are questions of state, not to be determined, or even agitated by us, in this court. It is enough for us, if the law takes notice of them when thus stationed, if it warrants their continuance, if it protects them in their quarters. They were sent here by that authority, which our laws know; they were quartered here, as I take it, agreeably to an act of the British parliament; they were ordered here by your sovereign and mine.

"Let me here take a method very common with another order of men. Let me remind you of what is *not* your duty.

"Gentlemen, great pains have been taken by different men, with different views, to involve the character, the conduct, and reputation of the town of Boston, in the present issue. Boston and its inhabitants have no more to do with this cause, than you, or any other members of the community. You are, therefore, by no means to blend two things, so essentially different, as the guilt, or innocence, of this town and the prisoners together. The inhabitants of Boston, by no rules of law, justice, or common sense, can be supposed answerable, for the unjustifiable conduct of a few individuals, hastily assembled in the streets. Every populous city, in like circumstances, would be liable to similar commotions, if not worse. No rational or honest man will form any worse opinion of this metropolis, for the transactions of that melancholy night. Who can, who will, unnecessarily interest themselves to justify the rude behaviour of a mixt and ungovernable multitude? May I not appeal to you, and all who have heard this trial thus far, that things already wear a different aspect from what we have been heretofore taught to expect? Had any one told you, some weeks ago, that the evidence on the crown-side would have appeared in the present light, would you have believed it? Can any one think it his duty, to espouse the part acted by those assembled in King street? I think not; but lest my opinion should not have any weight, let me remind you of an author, who, I could wish, were in the hands of all of you ; one whom I trust you will credit. I am sure you ought to love and revere him. I wish his sentiments were engraven in indelible characters on your hearts. You will not suspect him of being unfriendly to liberty ; if this cause and its events must be interwoven with a matter so foreign to it. I allude to the third letter of the 'Farmer of Pennsylvania,' to his countrymen.

" ' The cause of liberty,' says that great and good writer, ' is a cause of too much dignity to be sullied by turbulence and tumult ; it ought to be maintained in a manner suitable to her nature. Those who engage in it, should breathe a sedate, yet fervent spirit, animating them to actions of prudence, justice, modesty, bravery, humanity, and magnanimity.' What has there transpired on this trial, savouring of any of these virtues? Was it justice, or humanity, to attack, insult, ridicule, and abuse a single sentinel on his post? Was it either modest, brave, or magnanimous, to rush upon the points of fixed bayonets, and trifle, vapour, and provoke, at the very mouths of loaded muskets? It may be brutal rage, or wanton rashness, but not, surely, any true magnanimity.

" ' I hope,' says the same eminent writer, ' my

dear countrymen, that you will in every colony be upon your guard against those, who at any time endeavour to stir you up, under pretence of patriotism, to any measures disrespectful to your sovereign, and our mother country.' By this it should seem, as though the 'Farmer' never expected any period would arrive, when such measures would be warrantable. Now what more disrespectful to our parent country, than to treat with contempt a body of men, stationed, most certainly, by the consent of her supreme legislature, the parliament of Britain? What more disrespectful to our common sovereign, than to assume the sword of justice, and become the avengers of either public or private wrongs? Though the soldiers who appeared in the earlier part of the evening, in Cornhill, acted like barbarians and savages, they had now retired, and were now confined in their barracks; what though an impertinent boy had received unjustifiable correction from the sentinel; the boy, and the persons in Cornhill, must have recourse only to the law for their redress. Courts of law are styled 'vindices injuriarum,' the avengers of injuries, and none others are to assume this prerogative. The law erects itself as the supreme, dernier resort, in all complaints of wrong; and nothing could more essentially sap our most important interests, than any countenance to such dangerous encroachments on the domains of municipal justice.

"But finally, to finish with the justly celebrated 'Farmer.'—'Hot, rash, disorderly proceedings injure the reputation of a people, as to wisdom, valour, and virtue, without procuring the least benefit.' Thus have you the sense of this great authority, with us. And let me ask all those, who have thought the cause of this country connected with the agents of the assembly in King street, whether the proceedings of that unhappy night were hot, rash, or disorderly? If they were, have they not, in the opinion of this great friend of liberty, injured our reputation, as to wisdom, valour, and virtue; and that too, without procuring the least benefit? Who then would sacrifice his judgment, and his integrity, to vindicate such proceedings?

"To what purposes the soldiers were sent; whether it was a step warranted by sound policy, or not, we shall not inquire; we are to consider the troops, not as the instruments for wresting our rights, but as fellow citizens, who being to be tried by a law, extending to every individual, claim a part in its benefits,—its privileges,—its mercy. We must steel ourselves against passions which contaminate the fountain of justice. We ought to recollect, that our present decisions will be scanned, perhaps through all Europe. We must not forget, that we ourselves will have a reflective hour,—an hour, in which we shall view things through a different medium,—when the pulse will no longer beat with the tumults of the day,—when the conscious pang of having betrayed truth, justice, and integrity, shall bite like a serpent, and sting like an adder.

" Consider, gentlemen, the danger which you, and all of us are in, of being led away by our affections and attachments. We have seen the blood of our fellow men flowing in the streets. We have been told that this blood was wrongfully shed. That is now the point in issue. But let it be borne deep upon our minds, that the prisoners are to be condemned by the evidence here in court produced against them, and by nothing else. Matters heard or seen abroad, are to have no weight: in general they undermine the pillars of justice and truth. It has been our misfortune, that a system of evidence has appeared in the world against us. It is not our business to blame any one for this. It is our misfortune, I say. It should be remembered, that we were not present to cross-examine; and the danger which results from having this publication in the hands of those, who are to pass upon our lives, ought to be guarded against. We say we are innocent, by our plea, and are not to be denounced guilty by a new species of evidence,—unknown in the English system of criminal law.

"But as though a series of *ex parte* evidence was not enough, all the colours of the canvass have been touched, in order to freshen the wounds, and by a transport of imagination, we are made present at the scene of action. The prints exhibited in our houses, have added wings to fancy, and in the fervour of our zeal, reason is in hazard of being lost. For as was elegantly expressed, by a learned gentleman at the late trial, 'The passions of man, nay, his very imaginations are contagious.' The pomp of funeral, the horrors of death have been so delineated, as to give a spring to our ideas, and inspire a glow incompatible with sound deliberative judgment. In this situation every passion has been alternately predominant. They have each in its turn, subsided, in degree, and then have sometimes given place to despondence, grief, and sorrow. How careful should we be, that we do not mistake the impressions of gloom and melancholy for the dictates of reason and truth. How careful, lest, borne away by a torrent of passion, we make shipwreck of conscience.

"Perhaps you may be told, gentlemen, as I remember it was said, at the late trial, that passions were like the flux and reflux of the sea, the highest tides always producing the lowest ebbs. But let it be noticed, that the tide, in our political ocean, has yet never turned; certainly the current has never set towards the opposite quarter. However similes may illustrate, they never go for proof. Though I believe, that it will be found, that if the tide of resentment has not risen of late, it has been because it had reached the summit. In the same mode of phraseology, if so homely an expression may be used; perhaps, as the seamen say, it has been high-water slack,—but I am satisfied the current has not yet altered its course, in favour of the prisoners at the bar.

"Many things yet exist sufficient to keep alive the glow of indignation. I have aimed at securing you against the catching flame; I have endeavoured to discharge my duty in this respect. What success will follow those endeavours, depends on you, gentlemen. If being told of your danger will not produce caution, nothing will. If you are determined in opinion, it is vain to say more; but if you are zealous inquirers after truth, if you are willing to hear with impartiality, to examine and judge for yourselves,—enough has been said to apprize you of those avenues, at which the enemies of truth and justice are most likely to enter, and most easily to beset you.

" Gentlemen of the Jury,

" I shall now, for argument's sake only, take it for granted, that the fact of killing had been proved upon all the prisoners: you are sensible this is not really true, for as to this point, there are several of the prisoners upon whom this fact is not fixed. But as I shall hereafter take occasion to consider the distinct case of each prisoner, as he is affected by the evidence, I at present choose to avoid confusion, and apply myself to the full strength of the crown; and, upon a supposition, that all the prisoners were answerable for the act of any one, see how the prisoners are chargeable, by the evidence already offered, with the crime of murder :—or rather endeavour to point out to you those facts, appearing by the evidence on the crown side, which will amount, in law, to a justification, an excuse, or at least, an extenuation of their offence. For we say, that give the evidence for the king its full scope and force, and our offence is reduced, at least to manslaughter: in which case, we claim the privilege of that law, by the sentence of which, if guilty, we must suffer the pains of death ; a privilege, we can never again claim, a privilege, that by no means implies exemption from all punishment: the offender becomes liable to imprisonment for a year, incurs a forfeiture of all goods and chattels, and, till he receives the judgment of law, is to all intents a felon, subject to all the disabilities and other incidents of a felon. Without taking up time, in attending and discussing points, no way pertinent to the present issue ; without a tedious recapitulation of circumstances with which, I take it, we have no more concern, than either of you, gentlemen ; I say, passing over all these matters as foreign to this trial, let us state evidence appearing even from the crown witnesses."

Mr Quincy then proceeded to examine the evidence for the crown, and afterwards adduced the witnesses for the prisoners. This examination, with his comments, occupied four days, when he concluded his argument for the prisoners, as follows.

"May it please your Honours, and you, Gentlemen of the Jury.

"I have now gone through those authorities in law, which I thought pertinent to this trial. I have spoken at so much length, not for the information of the court, but to satisfy you, gentlemen, and all who may chance to hear me, of that law, which is well known to those of us, who are conversant in courts, but not so generally known, or attended to, by many, as it ought to be. A law, which extends to each of us, as well as to any of the prisoners; for it knows no distinction of persons.

"The doctrines, which have been thus laid down, are for the safeguard of us all;—doctrines which are founded in the wisdom and policy of ages; which the greatest men who ever lived, have adopted and contended for. Nay, the matter has been carried by very wise men, much further than we have contended for. And that you may not think the purport of the authorities read, are the rigid notions of a dry system, and the contracted decisions of municipal law, I beg leave to read you a passage from a very great theoretic writer, a man whose praises have resounded through all the known world, and probably will, through all ages; whose sentiments are as free as air, and who has done as much for learning, liberty, and mankind, as any of the sons of men. I mean the sagacious Mr Locke. He will tell you, gentlemen, in his Essay on Government, p. 2, c. iii, 'That all manner of force, without right, puts man in a state of war with the aggressor: and of consequence, that, being in such a state of war, he may lawfully kill him, who puts him under this unnatural restraint.' According to this doctrine, we should have nothing to do, but inquire whether here was 'force without right;' if so, we were in such a state as rendered it lawful to kill the aggressor, who 'put us under so unnatural a restraint.' Few, I believe, will say, after hearing all this evidence, that we were under no unnatural restraint. But we do not wish to extend matters so far. We cite this author to show the world, that the greatest friends to their country, to universal liberty, and the immutable rights of all men, have held tenets, and advanced maxims favourable to the prisoners at the bar. And although we should not adopt the sentiments of Mr Locke, in their most extensive latitude, yet there seems to be something very analogous to this opinion, which is countenanced in our laws.

" There is a spirit, which pervades the whole system of English jurisprudence, which inspires a freedom of thought, speech, and behaviour. Under a form of government like ours, it would be in vain to expect that pacific, timid, obsequious, and servile temper, so predominant in more despotic governments. From our happy constitution then results its very natural effects,—an impatience of injuries, and a strong resentment of insults :—(and a very wise man has said, ' He who tamely beareth insults, inviteth injuries.') Hence, I take it, that attention to the ' feelings of humanity,'—to ' humanity and imperfection,'— ' the infirmities of flesh and blood,'—that attention to the ' indelible rights of mankind,'—that lenity to ' the passions of man,'—that ' benignity and condescension of the law,'—so often repeated in our books. And, indeed, if this were not the case, the genius of our civil constitution, and the spirit of our municipal law would be repugnant ;

that prime defect in any political system,—that grand solecism in state policy.

" Gentlemen of the Jury,

" This cause has taken up much of your time, and is likely to take so much more, that I must hasten to a close : indeed I should not have troubled you thus long, but from a sense of duty to the prisoners ; they, who in some sense may be said to have put their lives in my hands ; they, whose situation was so peculiar, that we have necessarily taken up more time, than ordinary cases require ; they, under all these circumstances, placed a confidence, it was my duty not to disappoint ; and which I have aimed at discharging with fidelity. I trust, you, gentlemen, will do the like ; that you will examine, and judge with a becoming temper of mind ; remembering that they, who are under oath to declare the whole truth, think and act very differently from bystanders, who, being under no ties of this kind, take a latitude, which is by no means admissible in a court of law.

" I cannot close this cause better, than by desiring you to consider well the genius and spirit of the law, which will be laid down, and to govern yourselves by this great standard of truth. To some purposes, you may be said, gentlemen, to be ministers of justice; and 'ministers,' says a learned judge, 'appointed for the ends of public justice, should have written on their hearts the solemn engagements of his Majesty (at his coronation), to cause law, and justice, in mercy, to be executed in all his judgments.

> 'The quality of mercy is not strained;
> It droppeth like the gentle rain from heaven—
> ———— It is twice blessed;
> It blesses him that gives, and him that takes.'

"I leave you, gentlemen, hoping you will be directed in your inquiry and judgment, to a right discharge of your duty. We shall all of us, gentlemen, have an hour of cool reflection, when the feelings and agitations of the day shall have subsided; when we shall view things through a different and much juster medium. It is then, we all wish an absolving conscience. May you, gentlemen, now act such a part, as will hereafter insure it; such a part as may occasion the prisoners to rejoice. May the blessing of those, who were in jeopardy of life, come upon you,—may the blessing of him who is not faulty to die, descend and rest upon you and your posterity."

John Adams Esq. then closed the defence, in an argument admirable for its learning, acuteness, and strength. The result of their exertions was the complete acquittal of six of the soldiers, and the conviction of the remaining two of the crime of manslaughter only.

Thus terminated, in a manner forever honourable to the character of the American people, this most solemn and eventful trial. In other countries, soldiers, who, in subduing popular tumults, have killed unarmed citizens, have been sacrificed at the instant, to the public indignation. Trial, in such cases, has been often only a mockery; the sovereign himself having been compelled to yield his own instruments, as victims to appease the rage of the people. Even the walls of prisons have been no security against the vengeance of an excited multitude; but amidst the most violent effervescence of the American revolution, respect for the ancient institutions of the country maintained, at all times, the ascendency of the judicial tribunal. Notwithstanding the metropolis of Massachusetts had witnessed five of its citizens publicly slaughtered in its streets by the military arm, and notwithstanding curses, and execrations, and clamours for vengeance were loud, and deep, and almost universal, yet justice maintained the strength and integrity of her temple. The passions of the moment, restrained in her courts, waited patiently for her decision, and submitted to a judgment, in which neither the feelings nor the sentiments of the time acquiesced. The multitude was silent, though not satisfied, under the authority of the laws.

These are triumphs of principle, worthy of record, both for the honour of the fact and the influence of the example. In the language of the subject of this memoir, for the result,—" this whole people have reason to rejoice."

During the years 1771 and 1772, Mr Quincy was actively engaged in the labours of his profession. He now entered upon an extensive field of business, which his singular powers of eloquence opened for him, and which his unwearied diligence and fidelity secured. Although his professional occupations were of the most constant and engrossing character, he found time to employ his pen in the cause of his country.

Among his original manuscripts there still remain many essays published in the Gazette of this period. In one signed " Mentor," published February 11th, 1771, he laments " hearing so little discourse relative to a decent, manly, and instructive commemoration of the melancholy tragedy of the 5th of March, 1770," and urges the discreet, as well as zealous friends of liberty and mankind to form a regular plan for that purpose, to the end that there may be an annual development of the " fatal effects of the policy of standing armies, and the natural tendency of quartering regular troops in populous cities in time of peace." His labours in the papers of those years appear to have been incessant, and on various topics. His manuscripts, which remain, show that during these years he wrote, among other essays, those under the signature of " Callisthenes," "Tertius in nubibus," " Edward Sexby," and " Marchmont Nedham," "Draught of instructions to the Boston representatives in May 1770," and a " Report of a Committee chosen by the Inhabitants of Petersham, in the county of Worcester, 4th of January 1773." These all breathe that bold, ardent, and vehement spirit, which characterized his life, speeches, and writtings. For the most part they relate to temporary topics, and are directed to expose the character or to unmask the design of the British ministry, or their agents. An extract from the essay signed

"Callisthenes," published in Edes and Gill's Gazette, September 28th, 1772, on the subject of the grant of salaries to the judges, from the crown, will show the current and temperature of his mind.

"In your Gazette of the tenth of February last, I took occasion to deliver my sentiments on the imprisonment of Ebenezer Richardson. A truth, I there delivered, give me leave to repeat. 'No tyranny so secure,—none so intolerable,—none so dangerous,—none so remediless, as that of Executive Courts.'

"This is a truth all nations bear witness to,—all history confirms. So sensible are all tyrants of the importance of such courts, that to advance and establish their system of oppression, they never rest until they have completely corrupted, or bought, the judges of the land. I could easily show that the most deep laid and daring attacks upon the rights of a people, might in some measure be defeated, or evaded, by upright judicatories,—that bad laws, with good judges, make little progress. 'Let me make the judges,' said the pedant King James, 'I care not who makes the laws.' And this was very far from being the worst speech of that vainglorious monarch. How would that silly tyrant have hugged himself, in fancied bliss, if he had been gratified with making laws, judges, lawyers, sheriffs, &c.; and with paying and displacing them at pleasure! Could a Nero wish more? The people then would have no more real life, than might be extinguished with one single stroke.

" My countrymen, Great Britain, with legislative solemnity, has told you, she can bind you and yours, by her laws, when the parliament please. The parliament have so bound, and are still so binding you. Who appoints,—who displaces our judges,—we all know. But who pays them? The last vessels from England tell us,—the judges, and the subalterns, have got salaries from Great Britian!

" Is it possible this last movement should not rouse us,—and drive us—not to desperation—but *to our duty* ?

" The blind may see,—the callous must feel,—the spirited will act."

For the two last years, Mr Quincy's constitution, naturally feeble, and susceptible to a very extraordinary degree, began to yield to the continued current of his professional and political occupations. It was his nature to engage, in whatever he undertook, with an earnest, indefatigable endeavour, which absorbed his whole mind, and exhausted his entire strength. In the latter end of 1772, his complaints assumed a decided pulmonary character, and it became necessary for him, according to the opinion of his physician, to lay aside all cares, except those which had for their object his life and health. The following letter written by him to his father, about this time, is in reply to his parental inquiries on this subject.

TO JOSIAH QUINCY ESQ., BRAINTREE.

"*Boston, Thursday,* 2 *o'clock.*
"Honoured Sir,
"I thank you very sincerely for your solicitude and good wishes. My fever the last two days and nights seems almost wholly to have left me; my slumbers are sound and undisturbed, and the light of the morning finds me refreshed. I find my bodily health less impaired than I could expect. Indeed I have perceived of late no propensity to that fainting and languor, which the last year troubled me so much. Dr Warren thinks that my symptoms are favourable, and my

prospect of health (humanly speaking) certain. * * * * * * Thus much to gratify you, sir, with particulars, and to do it, has been as much my pleasure, as my duty. A little now to gratify myself. The science of giving advice is one of the most difficult of any; yet both the male and female world think themselves adepts in it. But of the few who are any way skilled in this nice art, how few know the mode of application, and the time to administer. But of the empirics in this mystery, with which the world swarms, how few are truly solicitous about the real welfare of the pretended object. How many are actuated by the felicity they feel, from gratifying the pride of their own hearts? This may not be any justification of an obstinate mule, but it may serve as some palliation for the conduct of those who feel, and those who can see. There are those who have the gift of prophecy, and many who have the gift of tongues, but alas, how few have the gift of persuasion.

"With my best wishes for the family, and a grateful remembrance of your attachment and goodness to me,

"I am your very affectionate son,

"J. QUINCY JUN."

The encouragement thus given him by his physician, however, proved delusive, and in February 1773, it was decided that his only hope of life depended upon an immediate change to a more southern climate. He accordingly on the eighth of that month took passage from Boston for Charleston, South Carolina, with the intention of returning from thence by land, to Massachusetts. This journey, in the state of intercourse which then subsisted between the colonies, was considered in the light of a visit to foreign lands, concerning which it was becoming the adventurous traveller to bring home, for his own benefit, or for the instruction of others, whatever knowledge his rare opportunities permitted him to collect. His journal, although written under great disadvantages from ill health, and composed of sketches made necessarily in haste for the purpose of aiding his own recollections, rather than of being subservient to the information of others, contains many important facts and interesting anecdotes. It throws also a strong light upon the state of manners and political sentiment, which at that period existed among the colonies.

Some of his particular observations, from the familiarity of our present intercourse, might appear trite and uninteresting, and will be omitted, as also will be, for the most part, all those particuular strictures on the nature and effect of that portion of the population of the southern colonies, which was most likely to make the deepest impression on an inhabitant of the northern, and by which a stranger, of his turn of mind, could not fail to be peculiarly affected. With these exceptions the journal will be published entire.

JOURNAL OF A VOYAGE TO SOUTH CAROLINA, &c.

" The design of the ensuing Journal is, among other things, to gratify one, who has a right to a very large share of my thoughts and reflections, as well as to participate, as far as possible, in all my amusements and vicissitudes. To be a memorial of my thoughts as they rise, and to remain a future witness to myself of the changes of my own sentiments and opinions.

"To record those kindnesses, and little civilities, which might otherwise imperceptibly fleet from the memory, but which ought nevertheless to be held in remembrance, till we shall embrace an opportunity fully to return them.

" To those therefore, into whose hands this Journal, either before or after my death, may chance to fall, the foregoing considerations may serve as some excuse for those trifles, I foresee it will contain, and shall not strive to avoid.

"JOSIAH QUINCY JUN.
"*Boston, February 8th,* 1773."

" 1773. February 8th. Sailed in the Bristol Packet, John Skimmer commander, for South Carolina, with the design of taking the tour of the southern provinces for my health. The 'Nos patriæ fines, et dulcia linquimus arva,' of Virgil was uppermost in my mind, and when I came in sight of my father's dwelling, ' Tu, Tityre, lentus in umbra,' seemed the sweetest harmony I ever carolled. * * *

" A more disagreeable time can hardly be conceived, than the season of my first days and nights. Exhausted to the last degree, I was too weak to rise, and in too exquisite pain to lie in bed. Unable to take any manner of food, I remained wholly confined to my state-room, till pain forced me to make one effort to get fresh air. Assisted by two people, I reached the foot of the companion stairs, but was not able to proceed further. The fresh air, instead of refreshing, at first overcame me, and after several fainting turns, I was carried back to bed. My sickness came on with redoubled violence, the night passed heavily away, and my cabin was so sultry and hot, that to rise or perish seemed the only alternative. I knocked for the watch upon deck, and with the assistance of two of them, was seated on a hencoop, by the side of the binacle. Scenes altogether new and surprising presented themselves to my view. I had not been on deck, since passing the light-house, and had never before been out of sight of land. The heavens were overcast with black and heavy clouds, with here and there a light, flying, wild cloud, interspersed. A hard northeast wind, the weather extremely close,— and distant flashes of lightning gleamed all around the horizon. The waves seemed to curl with flames, just sufficient to make the darkness visible; and successive peals of distant thunder—all conspired to make deep impressions and fit the mind for meditation. To know how all this affected me, a person must consider my weakness, my situation, and cast of mind.

" What a transition have I made, and am still making! was the exclamation of my heart. Instead of stable earth, the fleeting waters,—the little hall of right and wrong is changed for the wide, expanding immeasurable ocean. Instead of petty jars and waspish disputations, waves contend with waves, and billows war with billows; seas rise in wrath, and mountains combat heaven; clouds engage with clouds, and lightnings dart their vengeful coruscations; thunders roll, and oceans roar:—all ether flames, and distant shores, sea, air, and heaven reverberate the mighty war, and echo awful sounds.

> 'The sky it seems would pour down livid flames,
> But that the sea, mounting to the welkin's cheek,
> Dashes the fire out.'

Vast field for contemplation! riches for mind and fancy! astonishing monuments of wisdom! magnificent productions of power! The ingenuity, the adventurous spirit, the vast enterprise of man, next succeed to employ reflection. A little skiff, scarce a speck in this wide expanse, flew through the waves, and plyed this angry flood;—braved the threatening dangers, this world of night and chaos.

"While thus surprised and gratified, I rejoiced to think of my undertaking; and was pleased with the hopes of being wiser and better for my eccentric motion. Suddenly the weather changed, became doubly inclement, and cold, rain, and sleet threatened my health, if I remained longer upon deck. But to go, in my enfeebled state, to a hot cabin, was intolerable. Rain and cold appeared less dreadful than heat and bad air. I sent for my cloak, which, with my surtout, was to fit me for a companion to the sailor at the helm till sunrise. The weather increased in badness; I became fretful;—'twas death almost to retire to my cabin,—an exclamation escaped me,—I repined, I murmured,—I exclaimed again,—when (I shall never forget the sensation) the seaman at the helm carolled, with his marine pipe,

> 'How little do these landmen know,
> What we, *poor sailors*, undergo!'

"The best divine, moralist, or philosopher could not have devised a better cure for my spleen and vexation. Upon comparison, how little reason had I for complaint! How much ground of gratitude to Heaven! The honest tar continued his carols, and his notes were truly music to my ears,—

> 'A concord of sweet sounds.'

I was persuaded the fellow chanted his naval tune to divert me, but whether he expected to do it by the harmony of sounds and numbers, or by the sentiment of his song to alleviate my afflictions, in calling me to consider those of others, I doubted. But it was wholly immaterial to me; either way, I was equally obliged to him. My hand mechanically went to my pocket, but searched in vain for my purse. This was deposited in my sea-chest the day before I sailed. Luckily a small remnant of my last fee was in the lining of my pocket.—I threw it to the helmsman, who, in endeavouring to catch it, struck it half through one of the scupper holes. It was now out of his reach; he could not leave his helm to get it; I could not rise from my seat without help, and no one was on deck but us two. The witty, careless, good-humoured fellow looked a little chagrined at first (for every roll of the sea threatened its loss), but with great ease and indifference, turning upon his heel, he warbled with ineffable harmony,

' Ah! why should we quarrel for riches,
Or any such glittering toys;' &c.

To know how this turn of the sailor was relished, to realize the pleasure it gave me, one must know every circumstance of my situation, and every feeling of my heart. * * *

" Days of heat, cold, wind, and rain now rolled on. Confined to my cabin almost wholly, I became pale, wan, and spiritless; and, as I have since learned from my servant, every person on shipboard gave me over, and concluded I should never reach land. I was perfectly sensible of my danger, but by being carried upon deck, night and day, when it did not storm violently, my spirits revived, but my appetite never. My second week at sea was now passing, with only little incidents, perhaps no more worthy of recording, than those, which, for want of better materials, have engaged my idle time, and found a place in the preceding pages. With us, came passenger, one Mr ———, late a purser on board his Majesty's twenty-gun ship of war, lying in Boston harbour;—a gentleman lately obliged to ask leave to quit the service, for following the practices and examples of his superiors, which in them escaped with impunity. ' See little villains hung by great.'

" Mr ——— was one day uttering his complaints, when, among other things, an expression escaped him, remarkable as coming from one, who had been fifteen years in the crown service, and retained much of the peculiar sentiments and manners of such an employ. He was speaking of the partiality of a court of inquiry, which had sat upon him, and the little reason to hope for justice in a court martial, with which he was threatened, unless he would ask leave to quit his birth.

" ' Good God!' cried he, ' why do I complain? What reason had I to expect any thing better. *A government that is arbitrary is always unjust. A tyranny in one, or more, is always cruel and unrighteous.*' Such sentiments from him surprised me. I was impatient to know whether these reflections were founded in his heart, or were only the overflowings of spleen, disappointment, and revenge. For great is the sense of wrong, when oppression touches ourselves; weak, weak indeed, when we are exempted from all apparent danger of a like misfortune.

" Mr ―――― was a man of good natural powers, considerably acquainted with essays and the belles-lettres, though not learned, or conversant with the severer studies. I took this opportunity to start the controversy between Great Britain and the colonies. I spoke of the conduct of both, of present measures, and of the probable consequences. I hoped hence to draw the general opinions of his corps, and also, what must have frequently transpired in his company, for the last seven years. 'Very true,' said he, 'Mr Quincy, we all know this. Great Britain has no right to tax you. The ministry know it as well as you, but money must be had somewhere. Every thing is strained to the utmost at home. The people of England see as well as you, that North America must one day be independent, and it is her interest, and most certainly that of the present administration, to prevent this, as much as possible; and they will prevent it, for a much longer time than you imagine. For you can't contend with the power of Britain, whose navy conquers the world; and your first men are all bought off, and will be more and more so, in proportion as the ministry are wise and well informed. Who can blame them for it? They are in the right of it to do it, and you are in the right of it, to make opposition; but all will not do; you must submit for a great while yet to come. Why, all the world are slaves, and North America cannot hope to be free.'

"A train of conversation of this kind, pleased and exasperated. I reasoned, spoke of facts, of history, of human nature, of glorious sacrifices—

till from inveighing, I almost stormed. The agitation did my health good, if nothing more; for I wanted my blood to circulate. Upon my telling him, that the present steps of the British government were to the last degree iniquitous, repugnant to the first notions of right and wrong,—' Oh, Mr Quincy,' he replied, ' what do you tell of that for ? there can be no government without fraud and injustice. All government is founded in corruption. The British government is so. There is no doing without it in state affairs.' This was a clencher. ' Well, I hope, Mr ———, you will never more complain of arbitrary proceedings, and wrong, and cruelty, seeing such is the government you have served, and are now raging to be employed by.' ' Yes, yes, when it touches *one's self*, we have a right to complain. Was any one ever served as I have been ? Admiral ——— has himself, to my knowledge, done ten times as bad, and yet the scoundrel persecuted me with unrelenting, brutal cruelty.' Here I let matters drop, making only a few natural reflections on the character of man. * * * * In the course of this time I had a good opportunity of discovering the great corruption of administration, and the gross frauds of the servants of the crown. Mr ——— frequently owned to me, that his salary and birth were only worth £45 sterling a year, but that the year before last he made £300, and the last six months, at the rate of £400 sterling a year. And this will not seem at all incredible to those who are informed of the ways and means of doing it, and the sharers and connivers at it.

"February 21, 1773. This morning we were within thirty leagues of our port, which we should have probably reached the preceding day, had we not been becalmed twenty-four hours. At about seven o'clock, A. M. a black cloud hung over the northeastern part of the horizon, and at ten, the winds rose extremely high, at N. N. E. Before night, the wind blew a hurricane. Every thing threatened a terrible tempest. We were in the latitude of the Bermudas; a latitude remarkable for storms and whirlwinds. The hurry, noise, and confusion of preparing for the storm, was astonishing to one, never in a like situation. Rain, hail, snow, and sleet descended with great violence, and the winds and waves raged all night. About four in the morning Captain Skimmer called to me, saying, 'Mr Quincy, come and see here; you may now say you have seen a storm at sea. I never saw so dismal a time in my life.' The scene beggars all description. As the day advanced, at times light openings in the clouds gave a view of the horrors all around us; such apertures were ever attended by a tenfold gust of wind. The waves rose in mountains on each side, and we were alternately elevated to the clouds, and sunk in the deep. I frequently saw the yards plunged in the waves, and was often sent by force of the motion, across the cabin. I used to keep myself in bed, by throwing my left arm over my right shoulder, and then twisting a cord, fastened to the side of the vessel, round my wrist; I thus prevented my being pitched out of bed. It was so dark, by reason of thick fogs, that at mid-day you could not see the end of the bowsprit, and often scarce discern the yards. The exhalations from the water resembled, in density, and much in smell, the vapour from a burning lime kiln. In short, horror was all around us. Our Captain had been thirty years a seaman; Mr ——— had been on all the coasts of Europe and America; and the mariners had, one or other of them, visited most parts of the ocean, but none of them had seen so terrible a time. Seas struck us repeatedly, with terrible concussions, and all seemed to expect instant death. In this manner day succeeded day, and night closed upon night; here a gleam of hope, and then anon a bitter disappointment. In vain did we look for change; tempest and whirlwinds seemed to have attained stability.

> 'In every place
> 'Flamed amazement.——Not a soul
> 'But felt a fever of the mind.'

"On Wednesday night (February 24th), the rain much abated, but the clouds did not disperse, nor the winds lull. I put my head out of the companion-door, in order to take a view, and could not help repeating those beautiful lines of our poet:

> 'Unmuffle, ye faint stars; and thou, fair Moon,
> That wont'st to love the traveller's benison,
> Stoop thy pale visage through an amber cloud,
> And disinherit Chaos, that reigns here.'

"February 25th. On Thursday things remained much as they were; towards night the clouds were dispelled, stars were here and there to be seen, and every thing seemed to promise better times; but our hope was 'as the morning cloud, and evening dew.' Before daylight, seas, winds, snow and rain, raged more than ever. All matters had, previous to this, been disposed to encounter the worst. Every thing was either lashed upon deck, or removed from it. Axes had been delivered out, and all was prepared for cutting away the masts; which we expected to be obliged to do, every minute. We had long lain under bare poles, except what is called a balanced mainsail, to keep her head to the winds and seas as far as possible. All now retired to the steerage or cabin; none remained upon deck. We drew towards the shore with incredible swiftness, considering we carried no sail. Seas broke over us often; now and then one would strike with enormous force. The whole of this night (after eight o'clock), I believe every soul on board expected to perish. We were now in that latitude, in which the remains of my elder brother were deposited in the ocean, and probably very near the spot where the ship, with Mr John Apthorp and lady on board, foundered. It was impossible at this season to exclude this from remembrance. The mind dwelt upon it. Especially, as in case of our loss, there would have been a like ignorance of our fate, and length of expectation of friends, as in the unhappy case of Mr Apthorp and his lady. To consider, to ruminate, to waver, to despond, to hope, and ponder anew, was natural to the scene.

> 'A thousand fantasies
> Begin to throng into the memory,
> Of calling shapes, and beckoning shadows dire,
> And aery tongues, that syllable men's names
> On sands, and shores, and desert wildernesses.'

"Providence now gratified a frequent desire of my heart,—that I might be in a situation, so circumstanced, as to be fully convinced of a speedy departure to that 'bourn,' from which 'no traveller returns;'—that I might have the exercise of my understanding,—time to examine my heart,—to reflect upon the past,—look forward to the future,—weigh and consider whether I leaned upon 'the pillared firmament,'—or 'rottenness.'

"To notice the operations of the mind, and observe the emotions of the spirits at such seasons, is certainly a duty, and a very profitable employ. The justness of our sentiments, opinions, and judgments concerning all subjects, is here brought to the test; and the propriety, right, and equity of our past lives, must stand an audit. We hence are powerfully taught, what is folly, what wisdom,—what right, and what wrong;—the duties we have omitted, and those we have performed;—a reflection upon the one is pungent, a review of the other exquisitely joyous.

"Experience gives weight and energy to what before was fluctuating and feeble.

"I had often in past life expressed my creed, that every man died a hater of tyrants, an abhorrer of oppression, a lover of his country, and a friend to mankind. My conviction upon this head now received confirmation. I hope I shall never forget the resolutions I then formed, the sentiments I then entertained. I make this minute I am now writing, as a memorial of the past, and a memento for the future; to aid me in engraving them on the tablet of my heart. At the making of this minute I have not yet reached the land; the day is more cheerful, but dangers not at an end. I pray God to seal instruction at this instant;—that every thought and sentiment which is just and true,—that every resolution which is good and noble, may not be shipwrecked in the future whirl or tempest of tumultuous passions,— become the fleetings of a bird of passage,—'the baseless fabrick of a vision,'—but stable as the 'pillared firmament,' and influential as the midday sun.

"February 26th. Upwards of an hundred hours had now passed without sight of the sun; the wind had set almost wholly from N. N. E.;

the gulf-stream (said to run along the Carolina shore upwards of five knots an hour) directly opposite. All of a sudden the water changed colour; we threw the lead and found soundings;—the terror and confusion on shipboard was now great indeed. Whether the land was off the bar of Carolina, Roman shoals, or the Bahama sands, was altogether uncertain to every person on board. New dangers now stared us in the face. Necessity compelled us to venture upon deck, and to hoist a reefed fore-sail; for the wind set violently on the shore. At this time it was about eight in the morning. In the afternoon the clouds seemed again to scatter, and though we flattered ourselves less than before, yet the signs of better weather worked forcibly on our hopes. At night however, new clouds arose, with redoubled heaviness and blackness, and our captain said he believed we should have a harder time than ever. The winds changed almost every minute, and what is very extraordinary considering their violence, these variations were to directly opposite points of compass. We had the greatest reason to fear the consequence; but the rain falling in incredible floods imperceptibly allayed the seas, and assuaged the storm.

" After a very trying night to those sailors who kept the deck, the morning broke with signs of fair weather. At twelve o'clock (February 27th), we had a tolerably good observation, and found ourselves to the southward of our port. Our crew were spent, pale, and spiritless. The pleasures of a returning sun are not to be conceived but by those who have been in like jeopardies and trials.

" We had once during the storm discovered a ship near us; we now again saw her. Each made a signal to speak together, and each bearing down upon the other, we met just at twelve o'clock. It proved to be a ship from St Croix. She had scarce a rag of sail standing; most of her running rigging gone; her hands alternately at the pump. She looked distressfully enough.

" Each one on board our brig began now to compare our own case with that of our fellow voyager, who appeared bound to the same port with us;—all were moralizing on the scene;— for we had comparatively suffered no such damage in the storm. Extreme precaution, watchfulness, and steadiness in our master, great activity and courage in our crew, all knowing and willing to do their duty; with extremely fine sails, rigging, &c., had saved us from much injury, which we should otherwise certainly have suffered. The captain of the ship told us that he had been a seaman twenty-one years, and never had seen ' such a time in his days.' No person on board our vessel had ever been to Carolina, which occasioned our captain to ask the master of the ship, whether he had ever been the like voyage before; to which he answered, ' Yes, about twenty-one years ago.' On our replying that we had never been there, the hearty fellow commanding the ship cheerfully said,—' Give us this sun, and this breeze, and we'll soon be better acquainted with the way.' I could not help being surprized with this sort of ease and jollity, immediately after such hair-breadth 'scapes, and in such a shattered condition. Our crew were mightily pleased with his courage,—and a horse laugh, ' brave fellow,' &c. re-echoed through our bark.

" This interview, also, was one of those we must experience, before we can form a true idea of its pleasure. It was far beyond what a mere landsman would suppose. We soon outsailed the ship, but before we had gone far, our captain on a sudden seemed very angry with himself. No one knew the cause of his agitation, when he ordered the peak of the mainsail dropped, and to bear down again on the ship; which being done, we all waited to know the cause of it. Every countenance seemed to express wonder, at what it could mean, and the hurry of executing the orders of the master prevented us from asking questions. While we were thus waiting with expectation, the speaking trumpet resounded, 'Do you want any thing that I have got;—provisions, water, canvass, or rigging?' What were the sensations of my heart at this question? and how were my spirits moved, when the hoarse reply was;—'No, no, plenty, plenty here yet, thank God! Who is the commander of that brig?' 'John Skimmer.' 'God send you well in!'

"This scene almost overcame me, for I was weak and feeble. Here was a most beautiful assemblage of sympathies and virtues, and my mind was so softened by disease and misfortune, that it was well fitted to feel the energy of such an union. Humanity and benevolence, gratitude and thankfulness, were shown reciprocally in the offer and return, and vied in lustre;—a similitude of calamity had inspired friendship and charity. It has been said, that 'necessity is the mother of invention,'—may we not also say, that misfortune is the parent of virtue?

'What sorrow is, thou bid'st us know,
And from our own, we learn to melt at others' woe.'

"February 28th. We now were off Charleston Bar, and the wind being in our teeth, we were the whole day beating up. Just before sunset we passed the fort. Charleston appeared situated between two large, spacious rivers. The number of shipping far surpassed any thing I had ever seen in Boston. On landing on Sunday evening, the town struck me very agreeably; the number of inhabitants, and the appearance of the buildings far exceeded my expectations." * * *

The following letter of this date is found among Mr Quincy's papers.

TO MRS QUINCY, BOSTON.

Charleston, S. C. March 1, 1773.

The first emotion of my heart is gratitude to Heaven;—the second, love to my friend nearer than a brother. How much we owe to God, can only be known by reflection on the imminent dangers, from which I have been delivered. A voyage more disagreeable, dangerous, and terrible, perhaps was never passed, than that which landed me upon this distant shore. * * * * *

* * * * I omit lesser hardships, disappointments, and afflictions. I cannot say that I was ever well at sea, although I was not always very ill. What cause have we for thankfulness. I had not the least expectation of ever seeing you, or my dear boy, again; I was fully convinced that we must perish. Heaven has gratified a frequent desire of my heart,—that I might once see death before my eyes, as if striking his dart; —that I might know, if possible, the stability of what I lean on;—whether 'the pillared firmament,' or 'rottenness.' How often did I rejoice that ignorance freed my first and best friends from pain on my account; and that long expectation of hearing from me, would lessen the weight of what length of time must convince them of. How often did I feel the pang of separation, and look forward to that 'bourn,' from whence 'no traveller returns.' How frequently clasp my dear boy, and view him in a wide, corrupt world; —destitute of the instruction, vigilance, care, and protection of a father.

"You will doubtless wish to know what real damage our vessel sustained, and when I tell you but a very trifle to her rigging, you may be surprised. But the wonder will cease when I inform you, that our brig was remarkably well found : new sails, rigging, and in very fine order, active and good seamen, and a most incomparable commander. Such precaution before danger, such vigilance, activity, and firmness in it, were truly astonishing; we passengers almost idolized him. But before the storm was over, all were nearly beat out,—master and mariners, as good as ever stepped between stem and stern of a ship. But I must have done. Last evening at dusk I landed here, in better health than could be expected, especially when you are told, that the wet of the cabin, and dampness of my bed, were so great, that the one was flowing, and the other might have been wrung. This town makes a most beautiful appearance as you come up to it, and in many respects a magnificent one. Although I have not been here twenty hours, I have traversed the most populous parts of it. I can only say in general, that in grandeur, splendour of buildings, decorations, equipages, numbers, commerce, shipping, and indeed in almost every thing, it far surpasses all I ever saw, or ever expected to see in America. Of their manners, literature, understanding, spirit of true liberty, policy and government, I can form no adequate judgment. All seems at present to be trade, riches, magnificence, and great state in every thing; much gaiety, and dissipation. * * *

"There are such a multitude of ghosts and shadows here, that I make not so bad a figure on comparison. I shall give you an account of my health, when I can with certainty; every thing looks favourable at present that way." * * *

JOURNAL CONTINUED.

"February 28th, 1773. On landing on Sunday evening I proceeded to the coffee-house, where was a great resort of company, busy and noisy. I here met with Mr Lavinus Clarkson, to whom I had letters, who much befriended me in getting lodgings, which we were put to great difficulty to obtain. By ten o'clock, however, we procured one near the statehouse, and this night I had the most refreshing slumber I ever enjoyed. In the morning the same gentleman politely attended me to introduce me to those to whom I had letters of recommendation.

"March 1st. This and the next day, I spent in traversing the town and viewing the public buildings and the most elegant mansion houses.

" March 2d. This day I was visited by several gentlemen, to whom yesterday I had delivered letters. Received a ticket from David Deis Esq. for the St Cecilia concert, and now quit my journal to go.

March 3d. The concert-house is a large, inelegant building, situated down a yard, at the entrance of which I was met by a constable, with his staff. I offered him my ticket, which was subscribed by the name of the person giving it, and directing admission of me by name. The officer told me to proceed. I did, and was next met by a white waiter, who directed me to a third, to whom I delivered my ticket, and was conducted in. The music was good,—the two base viols and French horns were grand. One Abercrombie, a Frenchman just arrived, played the first violin, and a solo incomparably better than any one I ever heard. He cannot speak a word of English, and has a salary of five hundred guineas a year from the St Cecilia Society. There were upwards of two hundred and fifty ladies present, and it was called no great number. In loftiness of headdress, these ladies stoop to the daughters of the north,—in richness of dress, surpass them,—in health and floridity of countenance, vail to them. In taciturnity during the performances, greatly before our ladies; in noise and flirtation after the music is over, pretty much on a par. If our ladies have any advantage, it is in white and red, vivacity and spirit. The gentlemen many of them dressed with richness and elegance, uncommon with us: many with swords on. We had two macaronis present, just arrived from London. This character I found real, and not fictitious. 'See the macaroni!' was a common phrase in the hall. One may be styled the bag, the other the queue macaroni. Mr Deis was very polite, and introduced me to most of the first characters:—among the rest to Lord Charles G. Montague, the Governor, who was to sail next day for London,—to the chief justice and two of the assistant judges, and several of the council. Spent this day, March 3d, in viewing horses, riding over the town, and into the vicinity, and receiving formal compliments.

"March 4th, Thursday. Dined with David Deis Esq. with four other gentlemen,—good wines, and festivity. The first toast, ' The King;' the second, a lady; the third, ' Our friends at Boston, and your (meaning my) fireside.' The master of the feast then called to the gentleman on his right hand for a lady. This was done to every one at table, except the ladies, who were called on for a gentleman, and gave one with ease. No compulsion in drinking, except that a bumper was called for at the third toast. Politics an uninteresting topic.

March 5th, Friday. Dined at a very elegantly disposed, and plentiful table at the house of John Mathews Esq. in company with the chief justice of St Augustine, and several other gentlemen. No political conversation.

March 6th. This day was to have been spent with T. L. Smith Esq. at his country seat. Bad weather prevented, and I took what is called a family dinner with him in town. Before dinner a short account of the late disputes with the Governor, Lord Charles G. Montague, and the state of matters at present. No politics after dinner.

"Sunday, March 7th. Went to St Philip's church—very few present, though the first part of the day is the most full. A young clergyman read prayers, with the most gay, indifferent, and gallant air imaginable. A very elegant piece of modern declamatory composition was delivered by another clergyman by way of sermon from these words in Job:—' Acquaint now thyself with God: that good may come of it.' Having heard a young church clergyman very coxcomically advance a few days before, that no sermon ought to exceed twenty-five minutes, I had the curiosity to see by my watch, whether our clerical instructer was of the same sentiments, and found that he shortened the space above seven minutes and a half. This divine, after showing that avocations, business, &c. precluded a certain species of acquaintance with God, very sagely said, 'I come now to show that there is a certain allowable acquaintance with God.' *Qu.* What kind of acquaintance can the creature have with the Creator which is not allowable? This church is the most decorated within, though not the most splendid without, of any in the place. I find that in the several places of public worship which I have visited, a much greater taste for marble monuments prevails here, than with us to the northward. A majority of both sexes at public assemblies appear in mourning, and I have been told, that mourning apparel at funerals is greatly in fashion.

"March 8th. Dined with a large company at Miles Brewton's Esq. a gentleman of very large fortune,—a most superb house, said to have cost him 8000£. sterling. Politics started before dinner: a hot, sensible, flaming tory, one Mr ———, a native of Britain, advanced, that ' Great Britain had better be without any of the colonies : that she committed a most capital political blunder in not ceding Canada to France: that all the northern colonies to the colony of New York, and even New York also, were now working the bane of Great Britain : that Great Britain would do wisely to renounce the colonies to the north, and leave them a prey to their continental neighbours, or foreign powers : that none of the political writings or conduct of the colonies would bear any examination but Virginia, and none could lay any claim to encomium but that province :'—strongly urged, ' that the Massachusetts were aiming at sovereignty over the other provinces, that they now took the lead, were assuming, dictatorial," &c. &c. ' You may depend upon it,' added he, ' that if Great Britain should renounce the sovereignty of this continent, or if the colonies shake themselves clear of her authority, that you all (meaning the Carolinas and the other provinces) will have governors sent you from Boston. Boston aims at nothing less than the sovereignty of this whole continent—I know it.' It was easy to see the drift of this discourse. I remarked that all this was new to me; that if it was true, it was a great and good ground of distrust and disunion between the colonies; that I could not say what the other provinces had in view, or thought, but I was sure that the inhabitants of Massachusetts paid a very great respect to all the sister provinces ; that she revered almost, the leaders in Virginia, and much respected those of Carolina. Mr ——— replied, 'When it comes to the test, Boston will give the other provinces the shell, and the shadow, and keep the substance. Take away the power and superintendence of Britain, and the colonies must submit to the next power. Boston would soon have that. Power rules all things; they might allow the others a paltry representation, but that would be all.' The company seemed attentive, and incredulous,—were taking sides, when the call of dinner turned the subject of attention. ——— seemed well bred and learned, but very warm and irascible. From his singular looks and behaviour, I suspected he knew my political path. A most elegant table, three courses, &c. &c.

At Mr Brewton's side-board was very magnificent plate. A very fine bird kept familiarly playing about the room, under our chairs and the table, picking up the crumbs, and perching on the window and side-board.

"March 8th. Received complimentary visits from Charles Cotesworth Pinckney Esq., Messrs Bee, Parsons, Simpson, Scott,—all gentlemen of the bar. I was much entertained with Mr Pinckney's conversation, who appeared a man of brilliant natural powers, and improved by a British education at the Temple. This gentleman presented me with the only digest of the laws of the province, made some years since by Mr Simpson, late Attorney General (in the absence of Sir Eagerton Leigh). This present was the more acceptable, as there is no collection of the laws of this province in a book, to be had.

"March 9th. Spent all the morning in viewing the public library, state-house, public offices, &c. Was accompanied by Messrs Pinckney and Rutledge, two young gentlemen lately from the Temple, where they took the degree of Barrister at law. The public library is a handsome, square, spacious room, containing a large collection of very valuable books, prints, globes, &c.

I received much information and entertainment from the above gentlemen. Mr ——— informed me of an anecdote to which he was personally knowing, which I desired him several times to repeat, that I might be the better able to relate it. He said, that two gentlemen playing at a tavern, one of them gave the pretender's health, the other refused to drink it: upon which he who gave the toast threw his glass of wine in the refuser's face. For this an action of trespass was brought, and Sir Fletcher Norton closed the cause in behalf of the plaintiff, before Lord Mansfield, at Nisi prius. His lordship, in summing up the case, told the jury it was a most trifling affair, that the action ought never to have been brought, and they ought to find the offender *not guilty.* Sir Fletcher, after his lordship had sat down, rose immediately in some heat, and asked his lordship, ' if he did not intend to say any thing more to the jury.' Lord Mansfield. ' No, Sir Fletcher, I did not.' Sir Fletcher. ' I pray to be heard then, and I do publicly aver it to be law, that if one man throws wine out of a glass at another in anger, it is an assault and battery; this I declare for law, and I do here pawn my reputation as a lawyer upon it.' Lord

Mansfield. 'Poo, poo, poo! Sir Fletcher, it is a most trifling affair.' Sir Fletcher. 'Poo, poo, poo, my lord! I don't intend to be poo, poo, poo'd out of it neither. I renew my declaration, and affirm it to be law; and if the jury don't hear law from the court, they shall from the bar. I affirm again, that it is an assault and battery.'

"Here Sir Fletcher sat down and spoke so loud as that the whole court, bar, and jury heard him;—'He had as good retract his opinion now, as do it another time.' Meaning on a motion for a new trial, for mis-direction of the judge on a point of law. Lord Mansfield did not think fit to take any notice of all this.——Compare this with some manœuvres of the *little* gods at the north.

"March 10th. Dined with Thomas Smith Esq. with several gentlemen and ladies. Excellent wines and no politics. Spent the evening at the assembly. Bad music, good dancing, and elegantly disposed supper.

"March 11th. Dined with Roger Smith Esq. —good deal of company—elegant table;—one cloth removed, a handsome dessert, good wines, and much festivity. The ladies were called on for toasts.

"In company were two of the late appointed assistant justices from Great Britain. Their behaviour by no means abated my zeal against British appointments. In company dined Thomas Bee Esq., a planter of considerable opulence, a gentleman of good sense, improvement, and politeness. From Mr —— I received assurance of the truth of what I had before heard, that a few years ago, the assistant judges of the Supreme Court of the province, being natives, men of abilities, fortune, and good fame, an act of assembly passed, to settle £300 sterling a year upon them, whenever the king should grant them commissions, *quam diu se bene gesserint.* The act being sent home for concurrence, was disallowed, and the reason assigned was the above clause. I am promised by Mr —— a transcript of the reasons of disallowance, with the Attorney and Solicitor General's opinions relative to the act. Upon this, the assembly passed an act, to establish the like salary, *payable out of any monies that shall be in the treasury* :—not restricting it to any alteration in the tenure of their commission.

" Mark the sequel. No *assistant* judges had ever before been nominated in England. Immediately upon the king's approving this last act, Lord Hillsborough, in his zeal for American good, forthwith sends over one chief justice, an Irishman, and two assistant justices; the one a Scotchman, and the other a Welshman. How long will the simple love their simplicity? and ye, who assume the guileful name, the venerable pretext of friends to government, how long will ye deceive and be deceived? Surely in a political sense, the Americans ' are lighted the way to study wisdom.'

"I have conversed with upwards of one half the members of the general assembly, and many other ranks of men on this matter. They see their error and confess it;—they own it a rash, imprudent, hasty step, and bitterly repent it. A committee of the house have ranked it in their list of grievances. The only *solamen* is, 'It is done, we will take care never to do the like again;'—the only apology is, that the assistant judges of the province were unwilling to have circuit courts, without a fixed salary; the remote parts of the province complained of being obliged to attend all causes at Charleston; they had great reason of complaint. The regulators of this province were up, as well as those of North

Carolina. Such was the influence of some, that upon the disallowance of the first act, no act for creating circuit courts could be got through, till the salaries were fixed. May Heaven forgive, but *the people* never forget them. Think you that they who eyed the fleece, have got it?—No! as in like cases, American fools, thirsting for honours and riches—beat the bush;—British harpies seize the poor bird.

"March 12th. Dined with Thomas Lynch Esq.,* a very sensible, honest man. Spent the evening with the Friday-night club, consisting of the more elderly, substantial gentlemen. About twenty or thirty in company. Conversation on negroes, rice, and the necessity of British regular troops being quartered in Charleston. There were not wanting men of fortune, sense, and attachment to their country, who were zealous for the establishing such troops here. I took some share in the conversation, and cannot but hope I spoke conviction to some sensible minds. At the close of the evening, plans were agitated for making a certain part of *the militia* of the

---

* See an interesting account of this gentleman in the life of his son, Thomas Lynch Jr, in the Biography of the Signers of the Declaration of Independence.

province, taken in rotation, answer instead of foreign aid. I here learned in a side conversation with Mr ————, that two of the late assistant judges (gentlemen now in high and popular repute, men too of great opulence), who were in the general assembly at the time of the act mentioned some pages back, were the very means of getting it passed.

> 'Quid non mortalia pectora cogis,
> Auri sacra fames!'

That they, hoping to enjoy the emoluments of the grant, were hot, zealous, and perpetually persevering, till they got it through. He informed me also of the specious arguments they used, and the advantages, that they took of the popular commotions. Good heavens, how much more noble a part might they have taken!

"March 13th. Spent all the morning transcribing Mr E. Rutledge's MS. law reports;—at eleven set off for the retreat of T. L. Smith Esq.;—dined there, and spent the remainder of the day most agreeably:—a delightful place indeed.

"March 14th. Bad weather. Spent the day at my lodgings; visited by Mr Lynch, Deis, and others.

"March 15th. Dined with Mr Lynch.—Spent the morning and afternoon in transcribing law reports of E. Rutledge Esq.—Spent the evening with the Monday-night club.

"March 16th. Spent the morning, ever since five o'clock, in perusing public records of the province;—have marked many to be copied for me;—am now going to the famous races.

"The races were well performed—but Flimnap beat Little David (who had won the sixteen last races) out and out. The last heat the former distanced the latter. The first four-mile heat was performed in eight minutes and seventeen seconds, being four miles. Two thousand pounds sterling were won and lost at this race, and Flimnap sold at public vendue the same day for 300£ sterling!

"Took a family dinner with Miles Brewton Esq.—had a fine dish of politics,—had farther light from one of the company, a prerogative man, into the arts used to disunite the colonies;—sounded Mr Brewton, when alone, with regard to a general, permanent, continental literary correspondence;—the matter takes mightily.

"At the races I saw a fine collection of excellent, though very high-priced horses, and was let a little into the singular art and mystery of the turf!

"March 17th. Spent all the morning in the copying Mr Rutledge's reports. Dined with the sons of St Patrick. While at dinner six violins, two hautboys, &c. After dinner six French horns in concert:—most surpassing music. Two solos on the French horn, by one who is said to blow the finest horn in the world. He has fifty guineas for the season from the St Cecilia society.

March 18th. Spent in reading farther reports of Mr Rutledge, paying complimentary visits of departure, and in preparation for my journey northward.

"March 19th. Spent all the morning in hearing the debates of the house;—had an opportunity of hearing the best speakers in the province.

The first thing done at the meeting of the house, is to bring the mace, a very superb and elegant one, which cost ninety guineas, and lay it on the table before the speaker. The next thing is for the clerk to read over in a very audible voice, the doings of the preceding day. The speaker is robed in black, and has a very large wig of state, when he goes to attend the chair (with the mace borne before him), on delivery of speeches &c. T. Lynch Esq. spoke like a man of sense, and a patriot; with dignity, fire, and laconism. Mr Gadsden was plain, blunt, hot, and incorrect; though very sensible. In the course of the debate, he used these very singular expressions, for a member of parliament:—' And, Mr Speaker, if the governor and council don't see fit to fall in with us, I say, let the general duty law, and all, go to the devil, sir; and we go about our business.' Parsons, J. Rutledge, and Charles Pinckney Sen. (the three first lawyers in the province), spoke on the occasion;—the two last, very good speakers. The members of the house all sit with their hats on, and uncover when they rise to speak. They are not confined (at least they do not confine themselves) to any one place to speak in. The members conversed, lolled, and chatted, much like a friendly, jovial society, when nothing of importance was before the house;—nay, once or twice, while the speaker and clerk were busy in writing, the members spoke quite loud across the room to one another—a very unparliamentary appearance. The speaker put the question sitting; the members gave their votes by rising from their seats; the dissentients did not rise.

"March 20th. Set out with Mr Lynch for his plantation on Santee river, on my way to the northward. Had a most agreeable ride, and received much information from Mr Lynch of the manœuvres at the Congress in 1765.

"March 21st. Mr Lynch's plantation is very pleasantly situated, and is very valuable. Took leave of Mr Lynch, and had a three hours' tedious passage up Santee river. Crossed Sampit or Georgetown river just at dusk,—lodged in town, and am now held in durance by a very high equinoctial gale, which prevents me from crossing Winyaw Bay, formed by the junction of Waccamaw, Pedee, and Black rivers. It is very fine travelling weather, and requires no small share of philosophy to be contented with my situation.

"March 22d. Spent the night at Mr J. Allston's, a gentleman of immense income, all of his own acquisition. His plantations, negroes, gardens, &c. are in the best order I have seen. He has propagated the Lisbon and Wine Island grapes with great success. I was entertained with true hospitality and benevolence by this family. His good lady filled a wallet with bread, biscuit, wine, fowl, and tongue, and presented it to me next morning. The wine I declined, but gladly received the rest. At 12 o'clock, in a sandy pine desert, I enjoyed a fine repast, and having met with a refreshing spring, I remembered my worthy host, Mr Allston, and his lady, with warmth of affection and hearty benisons. Mr Allston sent his servant as our guide between thirty and forty miles, much to our preservation from many vexatious difficulties.

" March 24th. Lodged the last night at the plantation of Mr Johnston, (who is now absent at Charleston.) A gentleman came with us as our guide, about ten miles. A most barren, dreary road;—nine cows, and oxen, had perished within a week, for want of sustenance;—great difficulty to get food for either man or beast.

" March 25th. This day left the province of South Carolina and entered that of North.

" The constitution of South Carolina is in very many respects defective, and in an equal number extremely bad. The whole body of this people seem averse to the claims and assumptions of the British legislature over the colonies; but you will seldom hear, even in political conversation, any warm or animated expressions against the measures of administration. A general doubt of the firmness and integrity of the northern colonies is prevalent;

they say 'the Massachusetts Bay can talk, vote, and resolve, but their doings are not correspondent.' Sentiments and expressions of this kind are common and fashionable. They arise from various causes, from envy and jealousy in some, and from artifice in others. The very remarkable difference in their manners, religious tenets, and principles, contributes to the same effect. It may well be questioned whether there is, in reality, any third branch in the constitution of this government. It is true they have a house of Assembly, but whom do they represent? The labourer, the mechanic, the tradesman, the farmer, or yeoman? No,—the representatives are almost wholly rich planters. The planting interest is therefore represented, but I conceive nothing else, as it ought to be. Non-residents may be chosen to represent any town, if they have lands in the county, and hence a great majority of the House live in Charleston, where the body of the planters reside during the sickly months. A fatal kind of policy!—At present the house of Assembly are staunch colonists. The council, judges, and other great officers are all appointed by mandamus from Great Britain. Nay, even the clerk of the board, and assembly!—Who are, and have been thus appointed? Persons disconnected with the people and obnoxious to them. I heard several planters say, 'We none of us can expect the honours of the state; they are all given away, to worthless, poor sycophants.

" State and magnificence, the natural attendants on great riches, are conspicuous among this people; the number and subjection of their slaves tend this way. The yeomanry and husbandmen make a very different figure from those of New England.

" There being but one chief place of trade, its increase is amazingly rapid. The stories you are every where told of the rise in the value of lands seem romantic; but I was assured that they were fact. There is a colossal statue of Mr Pitt at Charleston, much praised by many. The drapery was exquisitely well done; but to me, the attitude, air, and expression of the piece was bad. The staple commodities are rice, indigo, hemp, tobacco, &c. &c.; the two first are the capital.

" A few years ago it is allowed that the blacks exceeded the whites, as seventeen to one. There are those who now tell you that the slaves are not more than three to one,—some say not so many. I took great pains, finding such contra-

riety of opinion, to find out the true proportion; the best information I could obtain, fixes it at about seven to one. My own observation leads me to think it much greater. * * * * * *
* * * * * * * * * * * * *
* * * * * These are but a small part of the mischiefs of slavery,—new ones are every day arising;—futurity will produce more and greater.

"Lodged the last night in Brunswick, N. C. at the house of William Hill Esq., a most sensible, polite gentleman, and though a crown officer, a man replete with sentiments of general liberty, and warmly attached to the cause of American freedom.

"March 27th. Breakfasted with Col. Dry, the collector of the customs, and one of the council, who furnished me with the following instructions given Gov. Martin, and as Col. Dry told me, Gov. Martin said, to all the colony governors likewise.

"Copy. } Additional instruction to our trus-
George R. } ty and well beloved Josiah Martin Esq., our captain general and governor in chief, in and over our province of North Carolina, in America. Given at our court at St James' the fourth day of February 1772, in the twelfth of our reign.

"' Whereas laws have been passed in some of our colonies and plantations in America, by which the lands, tenements, goods, chattels, rights, and credits of persons, who have never resided within the colonies where such laws have been passed, have been made liable to be attached for the recovery of debts, in a manner different from that allowed by the laws of England in like cases: and whereas it hath been represented unto us, that such laws may have the consequence to prejudice and obstruct the commerce between this kingdom and our said colonies, and to affect public credit:—It is therefore our will and pleasure, that you do not, on any pretence whatever, give your assent to, or pass any bill or bills in our province under your government, by which the lands, tenements, goods, chattels, rights, and credits of persons who have never resided within our said province, shall be made liable to be attached by the recovery of debts due from such persons, otherwise than is allowed by law in cases of the like nature within our kingdom of Great Britain, until you shall first have transmitted to us, by one of our principal secretaries of state, the drafts of each bill or bills, and shall have received our royal pleasure thereupon, unless you take care in the passing of such bill or bills, that a clause or clauses be inserted therein suspending and deferring the execution thereof, until our royal will and pleasure shall be known thereupon.

'G. R.'

"March 27th. Col. Dry is a friend to the regulators, and seemingly warm against the measures of British and continental administrations. He gave me an entire different account of things from what I had heard from others. I am now left to form my own opinion,—and am preparing for a water tour to Fort Johnston. Yesterday was a most delightful day,—Fort Johnston is as delightful a situation.

"March 28th. I go to church this day at Brunswick—hear W. Hill read prayers,—dine with Col. Dry,—proceed tomorrow to Wilmington, and dine with Dr Cobham, with a select company. Col. Dry's mansion is justly called the house of universal hospitality.

"March 29th. Dined at Dr Thomas Cobham's in company with Harnett, Hooper, Burgwin, Dr Tucker, &c. in Wilmington,—lodged also at Dr Cobham's who has treated me with great politeness, though an utter stranger, and one to whom I had no letters. Spent the evening with the best company of the place.

" March 30th. Dined with about twenty at Mr William Hooper's—find him apparently in the whig interest,—has taken their side in the House—is caressed by the whigs, and is now passing his election through the influence of that party. Spent the night at Mr Harnett's, the Samuel Adams of North Carolina (except in point of fortune.) Robert Howe Esq., Harnett, and myself made the social triumvirate of the evening. The plan of continental correspondence highly relished, much wished for, and resolved upon, as proper to be pursued.

" April 1st. Set out from Mr Harnett's for Newbern.

" April 2d. Reached Newbern about eleven o'clock A. M. Waited upon Judge Howard, and spent about an hour with him. Did not present the rest of my letters, because of the fine weather for travelling, and no court of any kind sitting, or even in being in the province. Judge Howard waited upon me in the evening with recommendatory letters to Col. Palmer of Bath, and Col Buncombe of Tyrrell county.

"April 4th. Reached Bath in the evening—did not deliver my letters, but proceeded next morning to Mr Wingfield's parish, where I spent the Sabbath.

"April 5th. Breakfasted with Col. Buncombe, who waited upon me to Edenton Sound, and gave me letters to his friends there. Spent this and the next day in crossing Albermarle Sound, and in dining and conversing in company with the most celebrated lawyers of Edenton. From them I learned that Dr Samuel Cooper, of Boston, was generally (they said, universally,) esteemed the author of 'Leonidas,' who, together with 'Mucius Scævola,' was burnt in effigy under the gallows by the common hangman. There being no courts of any kind in this province, and no laws in force by which any could be held, I found little inclination or incitement to stay long in Edenton, though a pleasant town. Accordingly, a guide offering his directions about evening, I left the place and proceeded just into the bounds of Virginia, where I lodged the night.

"The soils and climates of the Carolinas differ, but not so much as their inhabitants. The number of negroes and slaves is much less in North than in South Carolina. Their staple commodity is not so valuable, being not in so great demand, as the rice, indigo, &c. of the South. Hence labour becomes more necessary, and he who has an interest of his own to serve, is a labourer in the field. Husbandmen and agriculture increase in number and improvement. Industry is up in the woods, at tar, pitch, and turpentine;—in the fields, ploughing, planting, clearing, or fencing the land. Herds and flocks become more numerous. You see husbandmen, yeomen, and white labourers scattered through the country, instead of herds of negroes and slaves. Healthful countenances and numerous families become more common as you advance north. Property is much more equally diffused in one province than in the other, and this may account for some, if not all the differences of character in the inhabitants. However, in one respect, I find a pretty near resemblance between the two colonies;—I mean the state of religion. It is certainly high time to repeal the laws relative to religion, and the observation of the Sabbath, or to see them better executed. Avowed impunity to all offenders, is one sign at least, that the laws want amendment, or abrogation. Alike as the Carolinas are in this respect, they certainly vary much as to their general sentiments, opinions, and judgments. The staple commodities of North Carolina are all kinds of naval stores, Indian corn, hemp, flax-seed, some tobacco, which they generally send into Virginia, &c. &c. The culture of wheat and rice is making quick progress, as a spirit of agriculture is rising fast. The favourite liquors of the Carolinas are Claret, and Port wines, in preference to Madeira or Lisbon. The commerce of North Carolina is much diffused through the several parts of the province. They in some respects may be said to have no metropolis, though Newbern is called the capital, as there is the seat of government. It is made a question which carries on the most trade, whether Edenton, Newbern, Wilmington, or Brunswick,—it seems to be one of the two first. There is very little intercourse between the northern and southern provinces of Carolina. The present state of North Carolina is really curious;—there are but five provincial laws in force through the colony, and no courts at all in being. No one can recover a debt, except before a single magistrate, where the sums are within his jurisdiction, and offenders escape with impunity. The people are in great consternation about the matter; what will be the consequence is problematical.

"April 6th. Lodged at Suffolk.—April 7th. Dined at Smithfield, two considerable towns in Virginia. As I verge northward, the lands, and the culture of them, have gradually changed for the better. Excellent farms, and large cleared tracts of land, well fenced and tilled, are all around me. Peach trees seem to be of spontaneous growth in these provinces, and I saw them all along in the finest bloom. Whole fields of them looked beautiful. I saw about six acres, all in high bloom, and very regularly planted, every other row being trees of the apple and pear kind, not yet in blossom. An extent of about twelve or fifteen acres of peach-trees regularly set in equidistant rows, intermixed all about with many small pine trees of exquisite verdure, formed a prospect to the eye, most delightful and charming.

"April 9th. I arrived this morning at about ten o'clock at Williamsburg, the capital of Virginia. It is a place of no trade, and its importance depends altogether on its being the seat of government, and the place of the college. I have just been taking a view of the whole town. It is inferior to my expectations. Nothing of the population of the north, or of the splendour and magnificence of the south. The college makes a very agreeable appearance, and the large garden before it, is of ornament and use. There are but two private buildings of note, the Governor's and the Attorney General's. The college is in a very declining state. The statehouse is more commodious inside, than ornamental without. The council chamber is furnished with a large, well chosen, valuable collection of books, chiefly of law. The court of justice is ill contrived. This day I purchased a very handsome edition of the Virginia laws. I was present at their General Court, which is the supreme court of justice, and the court of chancery, of this province. I had only an opportunity of hearing short motions made by their most eminent counsel at the bar; the chancery business being always the employment of the first week, and that of the crown or civil business of the second, and succeeding weeks. The constitution of the courts of justice and equity in this province is amazingly defective, inconvenient, and dangerous, not to say absurd and mischievous. This motley kind of court, called the General Court, is composed of the governor and council, who are appointed and created by mandamus from the crown, and hold *bene placito*. I am told it is no uncommon thing for this court to sit one hour and hear a cause as a court of law, and the next hour, perhaps minute, to sit and audit the same cause as a court of chancery and equity,—and if my information is good, very often give directly contrary decisions.

"It was a matter of speculation with me, how such a constitution and form of judicial administration, could be tolerable. I conversed with many who seemed to have experienced no inconvenience, and of course to apprehend no danger from this quarter; yet they readily gave in to my sentiments upon this subject, when I endeavoured to show the political defects and solecism of this constitution. However, I saw none who gave me any satisfactory account of the true reason, that more mischievous consequences had not flowed from this source. Perhaps it was owing to my misfortune in not having letters to any of the bar, and but one to any gentleman within many miles of Williamsburg, although I had many to persons of distinction expected in town next week. I can only regret many circumstances, which deprive me of the means of remedying this inconvenience.

"April 11th. I spent the evening with two of the council of the province, and our conversation was wholly political. They invited me to dine with the council next day, and offered to introduce me to the governor, the Earl of Dunmore,—but I was unfortunately obliged to wave the invitation.

"April 12th. Upon farther inquiry, I find that the Council of this province, hitherto have been, and now are (one instance excepted) generally appointed from among the most opulent persons and landed men of the province, whose views, connexions, interests, or inclinations, have generally been such, as to keep them from baser betrayments of their trust, and the more atrocious prostitution of their enormous power and authority. This may account in some measure for the matter I just now mentioned,—but surely it is not in these latter times any security or proper safeguard, from future invasions, and oppressions. I am mistaken in my conjecture, if in some approaching day Virginia does not fully see the capital defects of her constitution of government.

"An aristocratical spirit and principle are very prevalent in the laws and policy of this colony; and the law ordaining that entailed estates shall not be barred by common recoveries, is not the only instance thereof.

"April 16th. Crossed the Potomac river, and arrived in Maryland. Through Virginia we find agriculture carried to great perfection, and large fields, from ten to twenty acres in extent, planted with peach trees, which being all in bloom, made my journey vastly agreeable. The purpose of raising these trees, is the making of brandy, a very favourite liquor. The melody of the fields and woods through Virginia is greatly beyond that of the Carolinas. The culture of corn and wheat is supplanting very fast that of tobacco in this province.

" The soils through Virginia and Maryland are mostly of a reddish colour, and sandy substance. Maryland is very hilly, and abounds with oak trees. To the South of Virginia, the public roads are through a level, sandy, pitch-pine barren. When we enter Virginia, and in proportion as we come North, we change the plain, for hills, and pitch-pines for oaks;—and the goodness, value, and improvement of the soil is correspondent to this alteration of appearances. The tobacco of Maryland, as I was uniformly told, both there and in Virginia, bears a preference in all foreign markets, and carries a proportionable advance of price. The Maryland tobacco goes under the name of coloured tobacco, and is of a bright yellow. This colour arises chiefly from the nature of the soil, but in some measure also from the mode of curing it; the Marylander in this respect taking more pains than the Virginian. The culture of tobacco is declining, and that of grain rising fast in this province. St George's county and Elk Ridge tobacco, is deemed here to be of the best quality. Maryland is a fine wheat country. These extensive fields of wheat and other grain afford great pleasure to the lover of mankind and the useful arts; and the exquisite verdure which at this season covers their fields, presents a prospect highly gratifying to the lover of nature.

"April 22d. I spent about three hours in company with the celebrated Daniel Dulany Esq., the Attorney General of the province, and several others of the bar,—and gentlemen of the province. A most bitter and important dispute is subsisting, and has long subsisted in this province touching the fees of the officers of this colony, and the Governor's proclamation relative thereto. At the conference of the two houses, the dispute was conducted with good sense and spirit, but with great acrimony, by Daniel Dulany of the council, and the speaker, Tillingham, of the lower house.

" I attended the Supreme (called the Provincial) Court, two days ; but one cause or motion was argued, and I had therefore no opportunity to judge of the talents of the bar. The commonalty seem in general through this province to be friendly towards strangers, and tolerably industrious ;—but I saw nothing to lead me to suppose that they in any measure surpassed the New Englanders in either of these respects. Baltimore is the largest, most populous and trading town in this province. Annapolis is the metropolis, or seat of government, and the residence of many of the most wealthy citizens.

" April 23d. As soon as we enter Pennsylvania, the regularity, goodness, and the straight, advantageous position of the public roads, are evidences of the good policy and laws of this well regulated province. Pennsylvania is said to be not so fine a wheat country as Maryland, but a better grazing country. Cattle cover the pastures in great abundance. Very fine streams of water are every where dispersed through the land, and as you approach the capital, a prospect of the river Delaware, on which Philadelphia is situated, affords a most delightful scene. My journey for these several days has not only been delightful from the gratification of the eye, but the exquisite scent from blooming orchards gave a rich perfume, while sweetest melody of birds was truly charming to the ear.

" April 24th. Went to public worship at St Peter's church, and heard the celebrated orator, the Rev. Mr Coombs, an Episcopalian. He laboured to speak with propriety, and was therefore not altogether natural :—he was a little affected, but spoke well. This may seem a paradox, but I cannot better convey my idea of him. In prayer, he had the faults of most clergymen who use established forms ; his emphasis, look, accent, and gesture, were not conformable to his subject, station, and language. He made an extempore prayer before sermon, which, in point of sentiment, propriety of expression, and true sublimity, exceeded any thing of the kind I ever heard. This prayer he uttered with singular grace. His sermon was twenty minutes in length, and was an extremely fine, moral, elegant declamation—decorated with all the beauties of style, language, and rhetorical utterance.

"The church is beautifully neat;—there is no Lord's Prayer, Commandments, or Creed, over the communion table.

"April 25. This morning at sunrise took a delightful ride of about fourteen miles into the country,—it is a perfect garden, I had almost said an Eden;—however, I saw it at the highest advantage. On my return, was visited by young Dr Shippen, Mr Thomas Smith, a merchant, and Mr Arodi Thayer. Dined with the Superior Court judges, and all the bar, on turtle, &c. &c. Had much conversation with "The Farmer," J. Dickinson Esq., Mr Galloway, the Speaker of the House, and others, on politics. Introduced by Mr Reed, an eminent lawyer, to whom I had letters from the Hon. Thomas Cushing Esq.

"April 28th. This forenoon John Dickinson Esq., "The Farmer," visited me at my lodgings— spent an hour with me, and engaged me to dine with him on the third of May, at his country seat. Dined with Mr Jonathan Smith, a very worthy and sensible merchant, with several very eminent lawyers.

"April 29th. Dined with Mr Thomas Smith, merchant, in Philadelphia, and a select company— was visited in the morning by the Rev. Mr Ewing, who spent two hours with me, and with whom I dine on the 5th of May. He appears quite the man of sense, breeding, and catholicism, and he gave me much insight into the present state of the college in this place.

"April 30th. Visited this morning for an hour by Chief Justice Allen and his sons. Dined at the house of that very sensible, polite, and excellent lawyer, J. Reed Esq., in company with "The Farmer," Judge Jared Ingersoll, and several other lawyers and merchants. Towards evening Judge Ingersoll and Mr Reed went with me round the town to show me the environs and public buildings.

"May 1st. Took a three hours' ride with J. Reed Esq. round the vicinity of Philadelphia.

"May 3d. The morning of this day spent in reading, and amusements of the itinerary kind. Dined with John Dickinson Esq., the celebrated Pennsylvanian "Farmer," at his country seat about two miles and a half from town. A large company were very elegantly entertained. This worthy and able politician (for such he is, though his views and disposition lead him to refuse the latter appellation) here enjoys "otium cum dignitate" as much as any man.

"May 6th. This afternoon went with a number of gentlemen to see the hospital, and hear a lecture from young Dr Shippen. The curiosities of this hospital are far beyond any thing of the kind in North America. Dr Shippen gave a very learned, intelligible, elegant, and concise discourse, which did him honor as a physician and orator.

"May 9th. This day I was to have dined with Mr Peter Wycoff, merchant, but having met Thomas Oliver Esq of Cambridge, who was returning home, I embraced the opportunity of such agreeable company, and set out for New England ten days earlier than I intended. I was also obliged to decline the invitation of Chief Justice Allen to dine with him, on the same account. Our tour through Pennsylvania, on the borders of the river Delaware, was variegated by those enchanting prospects of navigation, industry, and plenty, which serve to delight the senses and elevate the mind.

The Pennsylvanians, as a body of people, may be justly characterized as industrious, sensible, and wealthy. The Philadelphians, as commercial, keen, and frugal. Their economy and reserve have sometimes been censured as incivility and avarice; but all that we saw in this excellent city, was replete with benevolence, hospitality, sociability, and politeness, joined with that prudence and caution, natural to an understanding people, who are alternately visited by a variety of strangers, differing in rank, fortune, and character. The legislative body of this province is composed of the governor, and the representatives of the people; and the style of their acts is in the name of 'The Governor, by and with the consent and advice of the Freemen of the Province of Pennsylvania.' I attended three several days the sitting of the Superior Court. The bar are a very respectable body. The alms-house, hospital, and statehouse are the public buildings of this city, but are better calculated for use, than elegance or show. All sects of religionists compose this city.

There is a proprietary influence in this province, destructive of a liberal conduct in the legislative branch, and in the executive authority, here. The house of representatives are but thirty-six in number; as a body, held in great and remarkable contempt;—much despised for their acquiescence with the views and measures of the proprietary party, and singularly odious for certain provincial manœuvres, too circumstantial to relate. Their debates are not public, which is said now to be the case of only this house of commons, throughout the continent. Many have been the attempts to procure an alteration in this respect, but all to no purpose. The influence which governs this house is equal if not superior to any thing we hear of, but that which governs the British Parliament; and the proprietor is said to have as dead a set, in a Pennsylvanian assembly, as Lord Bute, or North, in the English house of commons. This province is in great danger from this quarter. * * * * * * * *

Notwithstanding the proprietary influence here spoken of, there is a certain Quaker interest which operates much against the proprietor in land causes, in the courts of common law, where the jury frequently give verdicts against the opinion of the judges. In the house of representatives, the leaders of the Quaker party, are often of the proprietary likewise.

All general questions and points are carried by the Quakers;—that is, by their union they defeat the operations of all other sects, in questions which any way relate to, or may in the end affect religious concerns. But they are very public-spirited in all matters of public edifices, and charitable institutions. There is also throughout the whole province among the husbandmen, a spirit of industry, and of useful improvement. There is no militia in the province, and of course no seeking after petty commissions, &c. &c.

"The advantages and disadvantages of this, is a topic of doubtful disputation;—we shall never all think alike on this head. Many of the Quakers, and all the Moravians, hold defensive war lawful, offensive, otherwise. The streets of Philadelphia intersect each other at right angles; and it is probably the most regular, best laid out city in the world.

"This city and province are in a most flourishing state, and if numbers of buildings, inhabitants, artificers, and trade, are to settle the point, Philadelphia, is the metropolis of this northern region.

"The Philadelphians boast of their market,—it is undoubtedly the best regulated on the continent.

"The political state of Pennsylvania is at this time the calmest of any on the continent.

"May 10th. Owing to the company with which I was now associated, I passed through New Jersey with unusual, and comparatively unprofitable speed. Burlington, which I saw at a small distance, and Trenton, which I passed hastily through, are pleasantly situated and appear flourishing. Princeton, where we staid one night, is a delightful and healthy situation. The college is charmingly situated, and is a commodious and handsome edifice. It is said to be in a flourishing state. The soil and culture of the Jerseys are equal if not superior to any yet settled in America. It is indeed a fine country. Having passed rapidly through this province, and for that reason declined delivering any of my letters, I am quite an incompetent judge of the constitution, laws, policy, and manners of the people. In the evening we reached Powles Hook ferry, and next morning crossed to New York. In the afternoon and evening we traversed the whole city, and spent the night at our lodgings, in company with Major R. Bayard and Mr Hyde.

" May 11th. Breakfasted with Major Bayard, —received a few complimentary visits, and an invitation to dine with Col. Wm Bayard, at his seat in the country. Went to the theatre in the evening,—saw the Gamester and the Padlock performed. The actors make but an indifferent figure in tragedy,—a much better in comedy. Hallam has merit in every character he acts. I was however, upon the whole, much amused; —but as a citizen and friend to the morals and happiness of society, I should strive hard against the admission, and much more the establishment of a theatre, in any state of which I was a member.

"May 12th. Spent the morning in writing and roving, and dined with Col. Wm Bayard at his seat on the North river. Attended a public concert, which was very full,—the music indifferent,—the ladies sprightly and beautiful.

"May 13th. Spent the day in riding and rambling.

"May 14th. Prepared for departure.

"May 15th. By the desire of Col. Oliver and some other gentlemen, I took passage down the Sound to Newport. I was the rather induced to this tour by water than through Connecticut, having before been through that colony, and my horses being so fatigued by their journey, as to render it doubtful whether they could reach home by land. Excepting a storm which occasioned our lying at anchor one day, our passage was pleasant, and we reached Newport safely this day about noon.

"The equestrian statue of his Majesty, near the fort, is a very great ornament to the city of New York. The statue of Mr Pitt has all the defects of that at Charleston. Being now so near the place of my birth and residence, my sentiments and opinions may be presumed to be too much affected by former impressions and influences, to make me an impartial judge or wholly indifferent relator. I therefore wave a detail of my observations and judgments upon the two colonies of New York and Rhode Island.

" Thus *currente calamo*, have I given some idea of the impressions made upon my own mind in this agreeable tour. Opinions and sentiments formed in haste, and (as Lord Bacon says) ' upon the spur of the occasion,' are liable to many exceptions ; and may probably be erroneous. However, they are evidences of one's own judgment, and may serve the valuable purpose of bringing past scenes into present and future view, and be a landmark of our own errors. Some of the most durable pleasures are of the retrospective kind ; some of the best preservatives from present mistakes, are written transcripts of past errors. What I have set down will be chiefly useful to myself. A bird of passage may easily collect, peradventure bear away, food for itself; but can transport on its fleeting tour very little if any thing, of sufficient solidity for the nourishment of others.

"Were I to lament any thing, it would be the prevalent and extended ignorance of one colony, of the concerns of another;—were I to breathe a wish, it would be, that the numerous and surprisingly increasing inhabitants of this extensive and fertile continent, may be thoroughly attentive to, and suitably actuated by the blessings of Providence, the dangers which surround them, and the duties they owe to God, themselves, and posterity."

On the return of Mr Quincy to his native town, he resumed his professional and political labours, with characteristic ardour. The new and intimate intercourse, which during his tour he had laboured to establish, resulted in a correspondence with several of the eminent men of that period, who are mentioned in the preceding journal. The ensuing letter from Jonathan B. Smith Esq. has reference to a question much agitated at that time, and maintained with great firmness by the friends of American freedom, ' that the original purpose of the early emigrants to this country was, to escape, absolutely, from the jurisdiction of the parent state ; and, that this intention was fairly to be deduced from the early *charters.*' In the letter from Mr Clymer will be seen the different degree of ardour which at that time existed among the various colonies, touching the great question of resistance to Great Britain.

Doubts concerning the firmness or patriotism of one or the other of the colonies were common, and were not unfrequently expressed to each other, by those ardent spirits, whose boldness and sagacity would not permit them to follow tracks, which seemed to them timid or timeserving.

The reply of Mr Quincy is a short exposition of the principles and means by which union might be effected among the colonies, and resistance against foreign oppression organized.

The ultimate union and faithfulness of those colonies, whose firmness was at that time questioned, soon dispelled all such patriotic apprehensions. It was to be expected, in the great diversity of interests, habits, knowledge, and connexion with the parent state, which existed in the several colonies, that the impressions made on each by the same acts of the British ministry should be different ; and that the necessity of resistance, and the degree to which it ought to extend, should be in each differently estimated. Hesitation, doubt, and want of concord, under such circumstances, cannot be a matter of surprise. The real cause of wonder is, that a harmony so perfect, and an union, as it respected the end and means of opposition, so general, should have been effected at such an early period. A knowledge of the nature and extent of these fears, existing in the colonies in relation to each other, is, however, necessary, in order to a perfect understanding of the difficulties by which those were surrounded, who saw the necessity of independence, and whose courage permitted them to stop at nothing short of its complete achievement.

TO JOSIAH QUINCY JUN. ESQ., BOSTON.

"*Philadelphia, May* 12, 1773.

"Sir,

" Agreeably to my promise I now enclose you a copy of one of the first American charters. It is made out from an impression of (A. D. 1600) ' Hackluit's Voyages,' which is now out of print, and perhaps the copy, from which it is taken, is the only one in America. Had your Governor Hutchinson a copy within his reach, it might have furnished him with perhaps not the least curious, and it may be important paper in his collection. How far this and the other papers of those early times may discover the intentions of the adventurers to America, and of government, with respect to the unlimited authority of Great Britain over the colonies to be planted, is a question that may admit of a quick decision, especially if the approving act of Parliament, some time after passed, be attended to. As for the enclosed, I think you may depend upon it as exact and correct. I hope this may meet you happy in the enjoyment of your family and friends.

"I am, Sir, very respectfully yours,
"JONATHAN B. SMITH."

TO JOSIAH QUINCY JUN.

"*Philadelphia, July* 29, 1773.
"Dear Sir,

"I returned home a few weeks ago, considerably better for my eastern journey, and have already let too long a time slip, without acknowledging the obligations your many civilities have laid me under. I have thanks to return to many gentlemen of Boston on that score, and could wish my own countrymen were not justly accused of falling so far short of yours, in the great virtue of hospitality. But hospitality was not the only virtue I had reason to admire there—your patriotism is the great support of the common cause, and I trust will in time diffuse itself so universally as to make all attempts against American liberty as vain as they are wicked. At present indeed it seems to have taken but shallow root in some places, particularly at New York, where all political principles are truly as unfixed as the wind. One year sees the New-Yorkers champions for liberty, and the next hugging their chains. Our Pennsylvanians I take to be in the mean betwixt both. I cannot call it the *golden mean*, for surely it is not alone sufficient when our liberties are so greatly threatened, to think justly of the danger, or to have the principles of freemen. These principles should direct the conduct of every individual, and of the public.

"I beg you will make my particular compliments to Mr Hancock and Mr S. Adams. There are no men more worthy of general esteem;—the latter I cannot sufficiently respect for his integrity and abilities. All good Americans should erect a statue to him in their hearts. Our acquaintance has yet been but short, but, believe me, it will leave an impression on me of longer date, and a strong desire with it of cultivating your friendship. I sincerely wish you and yours every possible happiness, and am, dear Sir,

your most obedient servant,
GEORGE CLYMER.

TO GEORGE CLYMER ESQ.

"*Boston, August,* 1773.

" Dear Sir,

" It gives me great pleasure to hear of your safe return to your family. The reflection of having contributed to Mr Clymer's happiness, gives his friends a real satisfaction. I hope your confidence in the universal diffusion of public virtue will not be frustrated. Force is not all we have to fear ; fraud is a more concealed, and therefore a more dangerous enemy. Political artifice is used to divide, while ministerial manœuvres destroy us. Instability is not peculiar to the New-Yorkers ; it is the characteristic of men in all ages and nations. Let us forgive each other's follies, and unite while we may. ' To think justly, is [certainly] not sufficient'— but we must think *alike,* before we shall form a union ;—that truly formed, we are invincible.

They who have the principles of freemen, feel them;—the sensation once felt, it directs 'the band of the undivided and free.' A spark of fire inflames a compact building, a spark of spirit will as soon enkindle a united people. Our hemisphere is calm, but the diviners of our political sky see a cloud at the horizon, though not bigger than a hand. They who have reason to fear a storm, will seek a shelter. The impression of our short acquaintance was most certainly mutual, and a cultivation of future friendship, as cordially embraced as it is offered. A mutual exchange of sentiments will give us, as men, a knowledge of each other; that knowledge naturally creates esteem, and that esteem will, in the end, cement us as colonists. As men, and as brethren then, in one common cause, let us think, converse, and act. When the guilty combine, let the virtuous unite; else individuals and communities will fall a sacrifice, one by one, in an inglorious, despicable struggle. Present me, in terms expressive of great affection and respect, to Mr Dickinson and Mr Reed, and believe me with sincere regard, and warm wishes, your most humble, obedient servant,

"JOSIAH QUINCY JUN."

The controversy between the colonies and the parent state, now became daily more alarming and critical. Lieutenant Governor Hutchinson had succeeded to the chair of state in Massachusetts, on the embarkation of Governor Bernard for England in the autumn of 1769. His convocation of the General Assembly at Cambridge instead of Boston, in 1770 ;—his acquiescence in the dismissal of the troops at Castle Island, which had formerly been in the pay of the province, and suffering that fortress to be placed in the hands of a regular British force ;—his refusal to approve a bill which had passed both branches of the legislature for the more frequent inspection and discipline of the militia ;—the duplicity with which he had acted on that occasion ;—the misrepresentations which he had made to the British ministry, both as to the conduct of the council, and that of the metropolis ;—his accepting a salary from the crown in April 1771 ;—objecting to the general tax-bill, unless the officers of the crown were exempted ;—refusing his assent to the resolve of the legislature for the payment of their agent in England ;—openly advocating the doctrine that the liberties of the province depended on the grant of the crown, and that the colonies were bound to obey all laws of the parent state;—his refusal to answer the inhabitants of Boston, when they inquired by a committee, ' whether the salaries of the judges were also to be paid by the crown,' and negativing their application for a convocation of the General Assembly, for the purpose of adopting measures to prevent so great an evil;—had formed an aggregate of offensive acts, the effect of which, on his character and influence, no talents could uphold, no popularity support, no artifice either palliate or evade.

From being a man of the greatest influence and popularity, he became the most obnoxious of all the tools of the British ministry. No man had obeyed their mandate with more boldness. No man had advocated their principles with more effrontery. He had not merely acted on the defensive, he had sought opportunities to show his zeal and forwardness in the cause of his employers. At this time, June 1773, the letters of Bernard, Hutchinson, and several commissioners of the revenue, were discovered and transmitted from England by Franklin, and communicated by Samuel Adams to the House of Representatives in Massachusetts.

Their effect was convulsive. The legislative hall and the press teemed with resolves and reproaches. Among others, Mr Quincy recommenced a series of essays under the title of "Marchmont Nedham," in a tone of bold invective against those whom he considered as the authors and instigators of the oppressive measures of the British ministry. The spirit of the writer will appear from a single paragraph. "If to appear for my country is treason, and to arm for her defence is rebellion,—like my fathers, I will glory in the name of rebel and traitor,—as they did in that of puritan and enthusiast."

In May 1774, he published his chief political work, entitled "Observations on the act of Parliament, commonly called 'The Boston Port Bill,' with Thoughts on Civil Society and Standing Armies." After this work was advertised as being in the press, he received the following anonymous letter, from the British coffee-house.

TO JOSIAH QUINCY JUN.

"Sir,

"I am compelled by the common principles of humanity to warn you of the imminent hazard which I consider you to be in, of the loss of life, and confiscation of your estate. It is now become very apparent that the supreme power of Great Britain, viz. King, Lords, and Commons, which you some time since, as I am informed, were pleased to term, ' *a transmarine power, to which we were not amenable,*' hath taken a resolution to assert its sovereignty over this his Majesty's colony of Massachusetts Bay, a sovereignty, which has never been disputed by any of the other colonies, except in the article of taxation, and not by this but a very short time since. Every measure necessary to carry this resolution into execution, hath been taken. A force is employed for this purpose, to oppose which in our weak, forlorn condition, it would be madness to attempt. This being the case, it cannot be supposed, that if there should be a continuance of these insults and indignities, which for some years past have been put upon the government, and the servants of it, that the leading promoters of such insults and indignities will escape with impunity. Those actions and words, which by the laws of Great Britain are there determined to be treasonable and rebellious, will be considered as such here; and the authors of them suffer the pains and penalties, which are inflicted on traitors and rebels in Great Britain or any other part of the realm. Of all this you seem to me to be altogether insensible, at which I cannot but express the greatest surprise, as I consider you to be a person of quick discernment, to be well versed in the knowledge of government, law in general, and more particularly of the laws and constitution of the parent state. Your political enthusiasm and popular attachment must certainly have totally blinded the eyes of your understanding; otherwise, I cannot conceive it to be possible that a man of your good sense, instead of promoting such measures at our late town meeting, which in our most calamitous condition might have a tendency to soften the resentment of government, and to induce his Majesty and his privy council to remove those evils, which are justly brought upon us for our past crimes, should endeavour by inflammatory harangues to keep up the phrenzy of the poor, deluded people of this town; to persuade them, that they have resources sufficient within themselves, if they were united and firm, to extricate themselves out of these difficulties, and to obtain a complete conquest over Great Britain, even without the assistance of the neighbouring towns of this province, and of the sister colonies; but if they should join us, that our victory would be beyond a doubt ; that some Cromwell would soon rise, and trample under his feet our enemies, viz. King, Lords, and Commons of Great Britain, for you could mean no other, they being the only enemies you were speaking of. You did indeed, in express terms, charge them with ignorance and effrontery (in another word, with impudence), for passing the late act, which will shut up our port. Not content with these bold speeches, you were the principal mover of sundry votes, passed at this meeting, which can be considered in no other light by Great Britain, than as an hostile attack upon her ; as by those votes, the neighbouring towns of this province, and all the colonies from the Floridas to Newfoundland, are to be stimulated by committees of correspondence to put a force upon her trade.

" Reflect a moment upon this conduct ; consider the present strength of administration, who have carried their measures against you without the least opposition ; consider the power they have at present in their hands (however weak they may be, when your formidable Cromwell steps forth,) to bring to condign punishment all offenders against the state ; and I am sure you will think with me, that your situation is truly alarming. You will very probably get into the hands of a power, from which no power you can look to will be able to deliver you. You have gone such lengths that I am fearful nothing can save you. I know but of one expedient left you, which is that of acknowledging on Wednesday next to this distressed people, that you have been in an error,—that you have deceived yourself,—that you have deceived them. Employ, for God's sake, those rare talents with which he has blessed you, in convincing them that they have nothing to do, but to submit, and make their peace with that government, which they have, under the influence of you and other factious demagogues, so long offended. You may by these means probably make your own peace, and ward off the punishment that hangs over your head.

"It is barely possible that government may still continue its great lenity, and overlook your offences. If this should be the case, permit me to observe, there is another danger to which you are exposed.

"The inhabitants of this wretched town would, if proper measures were taken, be saved from total destruction;—but if, by the mad pursuits of you and others, their ruin should be completed,—

if thousands of the poor, who depend upon their daily labour for their daily bread, should be in a starving condition,—if those who can now calculate upon such incomes from their real estates, as to be able to live in affluence, should find their estates to yield them not sufficient to subsist them, they will begin to look round for the real authors of their ruin, and wreak their vengeance upon them. They will no longer consider Bernard, Hutchinson, Oliver, commissioners of the customs, &c. &c. as their enemies; they will put the saddle on the right horse. We shall see an Adams, a Young, a Cooper, a Warren, a Quincy, with certain learned doctors of divinity, either destroyed by, or fleeing in their turn from their rage, and applying to that power, which they have so long insulted, for protection.

"I have conversed with many of the thinking part of this community, and find very few who do not condemn your proceedings. Nothing has prevented a public protest appearing against you, but the fear of that most formidable tyranny which the ruling part of this town have so long, by having the command of an heated populace, exercised over it. Upon the appearance of any power that will be sufficient to emancipate them from this terrible hydra, you will find that spirit which now vents itself in secret curses, break out into open violence. I can hear you in almost all company I go into, styled villains, scoundrels, rascals; and many wish that the vengeance of government had been pointed at the authors of all our misery,—meaning your particular junto, where, it is said, it ought to have fallen,—and not upon the whole community, a large portion of whom are innocent.

"Let me conjure you to weigh well what I have offered to your consideration, and believe me to be

"Your Wellwisher."

The reply of Mr Quincy to the preceding anonymous letter was published in the Massachusetts Gazette, No. 3685.

"*Boston, May*, 1774.

"Mr Draper,

"Having this day received from the British coffee-house an anonymous letter, in which the author 'warns me of the imminent hazard which he considers me to be in, of the loss of life, and confiscation of my estate,' I desire, through the medium of your paper, to acknowledge the receipt of it, and, in turn, communicate my own sentiments to the author.

" The good or ill design of the writer being problematical, I suspend my censure, and he surely will not expect my thanks. Had he, instead of concealing himself beyond the power of discovery, desired a conversation with me in person, his frankness would have been an evidence of his sincerity, and my cordiality on the occasion should have testified my gratitude.

" The danger and the wrongs of my country are to me equally apparent. In all my public exertions, I feel a sense of right and duty, that not only satisfies my conscience, but inspires my zeal. While I have this sentiment, I shall persevere, till my understanding is convinced of its error ; a conviction that will not be wrought by the arm of power, or the hand of an assassin.

" Threats of impending danger, communicated by persons who conceal their name and character, ought never to deter from the path of duty ; but exciting contempt rather than fear, they will determine a man of spirit to proceed with new vigour and energy, in his public conduct.

"My place of abode is well known, and I am easily found. The author of the letter referred to, if he will favour me with a visit, shall receive the best civilities of my house ; and if he will appoint a meeting, I will give him my presence, either alone, or in company ; till which time he surely will not expect that I shall endeavour to point out his mistakes, or flatter himself that anonymous papers will answer the end he professes to have in view.

"JOSIAH QUINCY JUN."

Notwithstanding these threats, the pamphlet was immediately published. Although temporary in its nature, yet its connexion with the character of the times and that of the writer, as well as with one of the most important periods in the history of the metropolis of Massachusetts, gives it a permanent interest. It is therefore republished in this volume. It is impossible for any citizen of the United States, now in the enjoyment of all the blessings, which have been consequent on the struggle and the excitement of that period, to read the eloquent anticipations with which that pamphlet closes, and not exclaim, in the language of the writer,—" What was then prophecy, is now history!" To him, indeed, the great men whom the scenes of our revolution were so soon to develop, were without a name or reputation. The fame of Washington himself was heard only among the broken and uncertain rumours of a distant Indian warfare. That noble band of heroes and of statesmen, whose deeds now cast a glorious light upon our age and country, were hidden in that impenetrable cloud, which rests, as it respects man, on every thing future. Yet the brightness of the coming day was apparent to his intellectual vision. Providence permitted him to see in prospect, what it did not permit him to witness in person, and to utter the suggestions of his foresight with a glow of language, which reality itself scarcely exceeded.

"—————— Spirits and genii like these rose in Rome, and have since adorned Britain. Such, also, will one day make glorious this more western world. America hath in store her Bruti and Cassii,—her Hampdens and Sydneys;—patriots and heroes, who will form a *band of brothers*: —men, who will have memories and feelings, courage and swords;—courage, that shall inflame their ardent bosoms, till their hands cleave to their swords,—and their swords to their enemies' hearts."

The following letter from Samuel Quincy, to his brother, on receiving a copy of his "Observations on the Boston Port Bill," shows that, notwithstanding they were opposed in political sentiments, their affection for each other remained unaltered. Such evidences of the mutual attachment of these brothers will be read with interest, when it is remembered, that by a singular and hard destiny, the one sacrificed his health and prematurely terminated his existence by his efforts in a cause, the success of which exiled the other for life, from his home and his country.

TO JOSIAH QUINCY JUN.
"*Boston, June* 1, 1774.

" Dear Brother,

"The pamphlet you presented me yesterday was doubly acceptable, as the billet that accompanied it assures me of your desire to live in amity with an only brother. Such a testimony of your respect I cannot fail of remembering with pleasure. The convulsions of the times are in nothing more to be lamented, than in the interruption of domestic harmony. We have hitherto, I trust, happily seconded the friendship of blood, by the friendship of the heart and affections; and though our intercourse is not so free, or frequent, as it could be wished, yet the caution we have preserved when together, in conversing on the subject of politics, will continue to prevent a clashing of the fiercer passions.

" Our natural frame and constitution, are not in all respects alike, nor is a difference in the turn of mind among branches of the same family an uncommon appearance. A love of ease and retirement, though not idle, nor unemployed in the valuable purposes of life, may be the predominant passion in one; while another, carried out by the zeal and fervour of imagination, strength of genius, and love of glory, shall snatch at the wreaths of fame, through the turmoils of public action.

" Both of these, nevertheless, may be actuated by the purest principles of virtue and integrity; nay more, may be equally serviceable in that community wherein Providence has assigned them a being. A state of inaction, among philosophers the 'Vis inertiæ,' is in some degree a state of criminality: but innocence ought never to be condemned, whether the gem lies uncultivated, or is found polished in the courts of princes. Ignominy cannot sully virtue, which is the same in all conditions, and must ever challenge respect. A consciousness, therefore, of having done his duty, will support every man against the attacks of obloquy, and reproach, even though he should meet with the frowns and contempt of the world, at a time when he ought to inhabit its praise and admiration.

"Our notions, both of government and religion, may be variant,—but perhaps are not altogether discordant. The complexion of our external conduct, as men and citizens, may have its cast from such variance; but I hope cannot be fairly imputed to either of us, as a defect of conscience, or uprightness of intention. Want of communication often produces a contrariety of opinion, and is sometimes a source of disquietude and division. Should we at any time disagree upon matters that require an explanation, it will be my study to obviate the effect of such an infelicity.

"God preserve you in health and longevity, the friend and patron, and at length the father of your country, and the eclat of your own times record you with honour to the memory of the latest ages, and especially, the prayer nearest my heart, may you continue, and have reason to continue, the friend and companion of your most cordially affectionate brother.

"SAMUEL QUINCY."

The following letters indicate, not only the general jealousies and fears which existed at the period in which they were written, but also, the particular apprehensions prevalent in some of the other colonies, in relation to the conduct of the inhabitants of Boston, under the oppressions, to which they were subjected. Among the adherents of the British ministry, the indignant sense entertained and exhibited by the people of Massachusetts, and particularly by the inhabitants of Boston, of their sufferings and wrongs, was denominated " impatience of good order and just authority," and was censured, as " irregularities and extravagancies" not to be countenanced or justified. The best friends of American freedom were also not without very natural fears, lest Massachusetts should be quickened into measures of open resistance, before the public opinion of the other colonies would justify them in uniting their fate with hers.

In all the colonies, however, prescient and noble spirits, like those of Clymer and Dickinson, were found, who could appreciate both the nature of the wrongs, and the just spirit, which characterized the leaders of opposition in Boston and its vicinity ; and who were chiefly anxious that the course of measures in Massachusetts, should so be regulated as most surely and easily to bring all the colonies into one indissoluble phalanx for effectual resistance. The ensuing letters of Mr Clymer and Mr Dickinson are full upon this point. The reply of Mr Quincy to the latter gentleman, shows how little he could brook that the patriotism of the metropolis of Massachusetts should be questioned, in a matter of prudence, any more than of duty; and how deeply he deprecated "timid or lukewarm counsels," in the crisis which then impended over the colonies.

These, as well as all letters published in this work, are from originals, found among Mr Quincy's papers. His replies also are taken from copies he was in the practice of preserving.

TO JOSIAH QUINCY JUN.

"*Philadelphia, June* 13, 1774.

"Dear Sir,

"The business I have been engaged in, almost ever since I had the pleasure of seeing you, has in a great measure prevented me from improving a friendship and a correspondence, in which I expected the greatest satisfaction.

" Knowing how much you have at heart the welfare of your country,—the character you sustain, and your circle of connexions, any information from you respecting the true springs and motives of action in your people on many late occasions, would have been extremely agreeable to me; feeling myself much interested in every thing that can affect them.

" I have ever been an advocate for the political conduct of the people of Boston, wherever it has been made the subject of conversation; but manners dissimilar to those of many of the more southern colonies, and perhaps some other causes, have most undoubtedly contributed to fix prejudices, which nothing but a clear knowledge of circumstances can possibly remove.

" I sincerely believe, that fair representations of things would always have freed them from any suspicions of an impatience of good order, and of just authority. Those among us of the most enlarged sentiments and who have elevated ideas of liberty, are unwilling to censure any irregularities, or even extravagancies, which a zeal for her cause may have produced; but narrow minds can scarcely, in any case, be brought to approve, where domestic economy and good order seem to be disturbed. I would willingly hope that the number of such shortsighted censurers is diminished, and that the distress now so unjustly inflicted upon the town of Boston, has fixed their attention more upon the danger which so fatal a precedent has made common to all the Americans. At present, I believe this to be the case, and that almost every one amongst us sees the necessity of checking the progress that arbitrary power is making.

"Would to God your relief could be speedily effected by the means pointed out by the vote of your town; but the minds of men, at least in two of the principal colonies, cannot yet be brought to combat with the most powerful principle in human nature; I mean *self-interest*, which must be so generally renounced during a suspension of trade. Many indeed, who are not swayed by selfishness are for offering the olive branch to the mother country, unaccompanied by the threats and menaces implied in that measure; and proposing through a general congress such terms of accommodation, as will leave us the essential rights of Englishmen, and suffering her at the same time, to reap those advantages in trade, which some suppose she had in contemplation in first settling these colonies,—notwithstanding the opinion which old charters in many early transactions justify, that the absolute independence of the colonies was intended. If these two ideas are not to be fairly reconciled in theory, they think, perhaps, a temporary compromise, which should leave any determinate principles out of the question, may be effected. Our people seem bent upon first trying this experiment; the necessity of harmony and perfect unanimity, which all seem sensible of, has reconciled very different interests among us, and by yielding to each other, the Quakers and Presbyterians and other contending sects have met in this point.

"A measure of this kind seems calculated rather as a general barrier against the encroaching power of Parliament, than to give immediate relief to people in your situation. We all wish, however, that your firmness should remain unshaken, until the remedy, to be applied, shall have had its operation; but this seems hardly possible. Patriotism, assailed by poverty and want, has seldom stood its ground. The general subscription to be opened here, which I hope will be followed in other places, will show that your neighbours have not *absolutely* forsaken you in the day of distress; it will in some measure alleviate the wretchedness of the poor, and stifle their clamours for bread. Would to heaven this proposed charity may be in the least adequate to the occasion, that the hard necessity of complying with dangerous and disgraceful terms, might be utterly taken away.

"It is said there is a crisis in political, as well as in natural disorders; this may be, when the apprehensions of any great evils shall have made such progress as to incline men to make the strongest and most decisive efforts to avoid them. I believe we are not yet ripe for these efforts,— the two bills before Parliament for taking away the peculiar privileges of your province, and making the soldiery masters of your lives, will probably quicken and mature our resentments, and give us a greater certainty of approaching tyranny.

"But I have to ask your pardon for this tedious letter. I expect in a few weeks to see you at Boston with a brother of Mr Dickinson's. * *

"I am, dear Sir,
"Your most obedient servant,
"GEORGE CLYMER."

TO JOSIAH QUINCY JUN.

"*Fairhill, June* 20, 1774.

" Dear Sir,

" I sincerely thank you for your kind letter, and the present attending it. This, without flattery, I think highly valuable, and it gives me inexpressible pleasure to find myself addressed in so friendly a manner, by a gentleman I so heartily wish to call a friend.

" As far as I have been able to collect the sense of the colonies, they are very unanimous in the measure you mention of a congress. You and your worthy fellow-sufferers would receive a glimpse of joy, amid your distresses, to know with what sympathy the inhabitants of this province consider your case. What never happened before, has happened now. The country-people have so exact a knowledge of facts, and of the consequences attending a surrender of the points now in question, that they are, if possible, more zealous than the citizens, who lie in the direct line of information. Doubt not that every thing bears a most favourable aspect. Nothing can throw us into a pernicious confusion but one colony's breaking the line of opposition, by advancing too hastily before the rest. The one which dares to betray the common cause, by rushing forward, contrary to the maxims of discipline established by common sense, and the experience of ages, will inevitably and utterly perish.

" May God Almighty bless you, and my beloved brethren of Boston and Massachusetts Bay. My heart is full; the time will come, I hope, when I may congratulate them on a more stable security of their liberty than they ever yet have enjoyed.

"I am, Sir, with truth,
   " your very affectionate
      " and very humble servant,
         " JOHN DICKINSON.

" Our country-people appear to me to be very firm. They look to the last extremity with spirit. It is right they should, if they will submit their resentment to the guidance of reason."

TO JOHN DICKINSON ESQ.

" *Boston, August* 20, **1774**.
" Much respected and dear Sir,
   " Your cordial approbation of my poor work communicates a happiness, surpassed only by your kind invitation of me into the circle of

your friends. Believe me, sir, that I recollect no feeling which would give me more solid, heartfelt satisfaction, than being considered by you as an honest friend, unless I except a consciousness of deserving that rank and confidence.

"Your sentiments relative to that 'colony which shall advance too hastily before the rest, contrary to the maxims of discipline,' &c. are no doubt just. Yet permit me, sir, to use a freedom, which your partiality seems to invite, and observe, that those maxims of discipline are not universally known in this early period of continental warfare; and are with great difficulty practised, by a people under the scourge of public oppression. When time shall have taught wisdom, and past experience have fixed boundaries to the movements of a single colony, its intemperate and over-hasty strides will be more unpardonable. But if we should unfortunately see one colony under a treble pressure of public oppression, rendered impatient by the refinements, delays, and experiments of the Philadelphians; of their less oppressed, and therefore more deliberate brethren; —I say, if a colony thus insulted, galled from without, and vexed within, should seem to advance, and 'break the line of opposition,' ought it to incur the heavy censure of 'betraying the common cause?' Though not to be justified, may not its fault be considered venial? Believe me, dear sir, you know not all our patriotic trials in this province. Corruption (which delay gives time to operate) is the destroying angel we have most to fear. Our enemies wish for nothing so much, as our tampering with the fatal disease. I fear much that timid or lukewarm counsels will be considered by our congress as prudent and politic. Such counsels will inevitably enslave us;—we subjugated,—how rapid and certain the fall of the rest. Excuse my freedom of telling what I dread, though seeming to differ from those I honor and revere. We are at this time calm and temperate; and, partiality to my countrymen aside, I question whether any ancient or modern state can give an instance of a whole people suffering so severely, with such dignity, fortitude, and true spirit. Our very enemies are dismayed, and though they affect to sneer at our enthusiasm, yet they so far catch the noble infirmity, as to give an involuntary applause.

"I see no reason to apprehend our advancing before our brethren, unless the plans they should adopt should very evidently be too languid and spiritless to give any rational hopes of safety to us in our adherence to them. *Sobrius esto* is our present motto. At the urgent solicitation of a great number of warm friends to my country and myself, I have agreed to relinquish business, and embark for London, and shall sail in eighteen days certainly. I am flattered by those who perhaps place too great confidence in me, that I may do some good the ensuing winter, at the court of Great Britain. Hence I have taken this unexpected resolution. My design is to be kept as long secret as possible,—I hope till I get to Europe. Should it transpire that I was going home, our public enemies here would be as indefatigable and persevering to my injury, as they have been to the cause in which I am engaged, heart and hand; perhaps more so, as personal pique would be added to public malevolence.

"I would solicit, earnestly, intelligence from you, sir, while in London. I shall endeavour to procure the earliest information from all parts of the continent. As I propose dedicating myself wholly to the service of my country, I shall stand in need of the aid of every friend of America; and believe me, when I say, that I esteem none more capable of affording me that aid, than those who inhabit the fertile banks of the Delaware.

" If you can lead me into any channel of doing real service to the common cause, I flatter myself you are not disinclined, and though it should never be in my power to cancel the obligation, it will ever be my study to remember it.

"I am your most humble,
"obedient servant,
"Josiah Quincy Jun."

TO JOSIAH QUINCY JUN.

"*Charleston, July* 12, 1774.

" Dear Sir,

" I this day received your polite favour of the 29th of May, and can only say I wish it had been in my power to show more civility to a gentleman I so much esteem as I do Mr Quincy. You have my best thanks for your pamphlet. Too many cannot step forth at this alarming crisis, in defence of the much injured rights of America; and those that do, should, and no doubt have, the united thanks of the friends of America. * * *

" Your situation at this time is truly hazardous and alarming, but you will not fall for want of friends, because all British America are your friends. For God's sake be firm and discreet, at this time. The good people of this colony have sent for your port one sloop-load of rice, and we shall send more soon.

"The 6th, 7th, and 8th instant, we had the greatest assembly of the inhabitants of this colony I ever saw. After much debate it was determined, that Henry Middleton, John Rutledge, Thomas Lynch, Christopher Gadsden, and Edward Rutledge, should, on the 1st of September, meet the General Congress at Philadelphia. Their powers are unlimited, and I hope the other colonies will do the same, and place entire confidence in their deputies;—they can do nothing effectual without such powers. I should suppose the first step taken by Congress would be to remonstrate, and petition King, Lords, and Commons. Our grievances should be all stated in the way of a Bill of Rights, and some of the deputies should go to England with the petition. If redress does not come, then all to enter into a non-import and non-export agreement. I think this seems to be the sense of almost all the colonies. * * * * * Our fears are only about you, that you may despond and give up; for I am sorry to see you have so many adders in your own bosom, who may sting you to death. We have our share also of internal foes. Pity it was that Hutchinson should have gone home with so many names to petitions; it will do you no good, but much harm, I fear. * * * * * * * * * * *

"I beg to hear as often from you as business permits. It is not trifling to write or speak upon public affairs at this time of imminent danger. Politics should be the theme of the day; and our dreams at night should be of the hapless situation of our country. However, bad as it is, if Boston does but persevere, and be prudent, her sisters and neighbours will work out her salvation, without taking the musket. Unanimity must be our leading star.

"I am, with great regard,
"Your most obedient and obliged servant,
"MILES BREWTON."

It will be seen by Mr Quincy's letter to Mr Dickinson, that in August 1774, at the urgent solicitation of his political friends, he had determined to relinquish business and embark for England. The circumstances of the times, and the singular boldness of his political course, rendered it necessary that his intention should be kept secret, lest the enemies of the patriotic cause should take measures to counteract the effect of his presence and representations in England. It was accordingly concealed from all but his nearest relations, and those political friends, who had proposed the measure.

The ensuing letters, from three of the most distinguished patriots of that period, will show the concurrence of their opinions upon the subject of his voyage, and in favour of its probable utility.

TO DR AMORY, IN LONDON.

"*Boston, September* 13, 1774.

" Rev. Sir,

" The bearer of this, Mr Josiah Quincy, is a gentleman of good powers, a fine genius, and thorough acquaintance with the constitution of the American colonies; nor has any one a more perfect knowledge of what has happened in this part of the world, both previous to, and in consequence of the late acts of the British Parliament respecting Boston, and the Massachusetts province, of which it is the metropolis. You may from him, if you desire it, be let into a clear and full idea of the true situation of our political affairs. He goes to England, strongly disposed to serve his country wherein he may be able, and he will be the better able to do this, if he may, by the help of gentlemen of character at home, have opportunity of conversing with those, either in or out of administration, who may have been led into wrong sentiments of the people of Boston and the Massachusetts province in these troublesome times.

"The favour I would ask of you is only this, that you would take so much notice of him, as to introduce him either yourself, or by one or another of your friends, into the company of those who may have it in their power to be serviceable to the colonies in general, and this province in particular, which is the first in the intention of the administration to be reduced to a state of slavery.

"We groan under the oppressive burdens that lie heavy on us. I could easily enlarge on them, and the expedients in contemplation in order to a deliverance from them,—but I purposely avoid it, as you may have it done much better *vivâ voce* by Mr Quincy.

"Be pleased to accept the enclosed pamphlets; one of which was written by Mr Quincy, and will give you an idea of him as a truly sensible man, as well as a fast friend to the cause of liberty.

" I am, dear Sir, your assured friend,

"Charles Chauncy."

TO JOSIAH QUINCY JUN.

"*Philadelphia, Sept.* 18, 1774.

" Dear Sir,

" I am to acknowledge the receipt of your kind letter, and to thank you for it, and then seal my letter.

" Business, ceremony, visits, and a thousand *et-ceteras*, take up my time so entirely that I can scarce find half enough for sleep. I have spoken to several gentlemen concerning you, and shall to more.

" I wish you a prosperous voyage, and much of the exalted pleasure of serving your country. You are surrounded with active scenes in our province at present. We are not idle here; but how long it will be before the world will know our meditations, I cannot say.

" Our country is in the post of honour and danger, and she behaves in character. The congress is sensible of it, and will act in character too, I hope and believe.

"Adieu.

"JOHN ADAMS."

TO DR CHARLES CHAUNCY.

"*Philadelphia, Sept.* 19, 1774.

"Rev. Sir,

"I have had the pleasure of receiving a letter from you since my arrival in this city. Our friend, Mr Quincy, informed me before I left Boston, of his intention to take a passage for England. I am persuaded he may do great service to our country there. Agreeably to his and your requests I have desired gentlemen here, to make him known to their friends and correspondents.

"Last Friday, Mr Revere, brought us the spirited and patriotic resolves of our county of Suffolk. We laid them before the congress. They were read with great applause, and the enclosed resolutions were unanimously passed, which give you a faint idea of the spirit of the congress. I think I may assure you, that America will make a point of supporting Boston to the utmost. I have not time to enlarge, and must therefore conclude with assuring you, that

" I am, with great regard,
" Your affectionate and humble servant,
SAMUEL ADAMS.

Mr Quincy embarked privately at Salem on the 28th of September, 1774. The motives of this voyage, and the sensation occasioned by his sudden and secret departure, when it was publicly avowed, may be farther gathered from the following letters, which are published in the order of their dates, that his English journal and letters may be afterwards presented in an unbroken series. They all eminently characterize the state and spirit of the times, and the patriotic ardour of the respective writers.

The letter from Dr (afterwards Major General) Joseph Warren, is peculiarly interesting, because few similar records of his mind remain, and as it evidences, that the life he sacrificed on Bunker's Hill was offered, not under the excitement of the moment, but with a fixed and deliberate purpose. No language can be more decisive of the spirit, which predominated in his bosom. "It is the united voice of America to preserve their freedom or lose their lives in defence of it."

TO JOSIAH QUINCY JUN.

"*Braintree, October,* 1774.

" My dear Son,

" It is now four weeks since you sailed, and if my prayers are heard and the petition of them granted, your health is restored, your voyage comfortable, and your arrival safe. News, that would be almost as joyful and reviving to your aged father, as to hear that, through your mediation, peace and harmony were restored between the parent state and her injured and oppressed children upon this continent. I have not, nor shall forget to inform you of facts as they have taken, or may take place, since you left us; but my retired situation will not permit my gratifying you so much as I should otherwise be glad to do.

" All the tories and some of the whigs, resent your clandestine departure. Many of the former say, that as soon as your arrival is known, you will be apprehended and secured. Some say you are gone to Holland, and from thence to the south of France. Others say, the general congress have appointed and commissioned you their agent at the court of Great Britain, and that you had your credentials and instructions from them, before you went away. Your friends say, your principal motive is the recovery of your health, which if Providence should please to restore, they rest assured of your best endeavours to procure a redress of the grievances, and a speedy removal of the intolerable burdens, with which your native country is and has been long oppressed.

"God Almighty grant, if your life and health are spared, that you may succeed in every respect.

"When in town I found two political productions,—'An Essay on the Constitutional Power of Great Britain over the Colonies in America;'—and 'A Letter from Lord Lyttleton to Lord Chatham, on the Quebec Bill.' They are each of them esteemed masterly productions by their respective partizans. Before this reaches you, I doubt not you will have received the former from its author. I regret his allowing Great Britain a revenue from the colonies, whilst she persists in her claim of an exclusive trade with them, which appears to me to be an overbalance for all the protection she has, or can afford them, especially when it is considered that all the profits resulting from the immense extent of territory ceded to her at the treaty of Paris, remains solely to her. At the same time, we are restrained from the profitable whale and cod fisheries in the bay of St Lawrence, and the straits of Belle Isle, which we formerly enjoyed without interruption. If I am not greatly mistaken, there is not a single argument in Lord Lyttleton's letter, whereby he endeavours to prove the justice, wisdom, benevolence, and policy of Parliament in indulging the Canadians with the French laws, which will not much more forcibly conclude in behalf of the colonies, that their respective constitutions and laws should remain inviolate, and the rights and privileges secured by them, upon no pretence whatever to be abridged. Where then is the wisdom, benevolence, and justice of Parliament? What besides low cunning and left-handed policy, could induce them to their past and present violent measures, which must ultimately be as injurious to them as they are, or can be, to us. But his lordship in the close of his letter tells us, 'It is necessary to conciliate the affections of the Canadians, and thereby induce them to assist administration in coercing America!' Read this passage, attend to the meaning of it, and then, if you can, suppress your indignation. What! have we Americans spent so much of our blood and treasure in aiding Britain to conquer Canada, that Britons and Canadians may now subjugate us? Forbid it, Heaven!

"Is this the 'policy,' which he recommends as 'best calculated to unite natural-born, and adopted subjects, in one common bond of interest, affection, and duty?' But I must quit the subject. * * * * * * * * * * *

"I have filled my paper, and have only room to add the affectionate regards of your family, joined to those of

"Your unalterably fond parent,
"JOSIAH QUINCY."

TO J. QUINCY JUN.

"*Boston, October* 28, 1774.
"My dear Sir,
"You will see by the papers that immediately after you sailed, a proclamation was issued, to discharge the members from attendance upon that general court, for which precepts, you know, had been given out. They judiciously slighted this, sticking to charter-rule; and upon finding

Mr Gage did not attend to his proper duty, they resolved themselves into a provincial congress, to meet at Concord tomorrow. They will be strenuous, I expect, in pressing the General to desist from his fortifications. Yet what can he do? He cannot declare in plain English, that he is only striving to make the minds of his officers and men easy; and yet I believe that to be the truth, and the whole truth.

" I told you at parting, that if I was deceived in my countrymen, and found they turned out poltrons, I would not inform you of it, though such was your request. Let not that speech detract from my credit, when I tell you they rise every day in character. It is become a downright task for the warmest patriots of our town and county, to confine the spirit of the other counties to an attention to the causes, rather than to the executors, of our wrongs. I am really pained at finding that the wickedness of ministerial conduct has brought the province so generally to make the idea of an engagement between fellow subjects so familiar to their minds. How would such a thought have shocked us all, a few years ago! But the insolent appearance of the works on the neck has roused the inclinations of the vigorous country youth to play over again the Niagara game of filling trenches with round bundles of hay, under which they advanced securely. The folly and weakness of the works may easily be proved to be fully equal to the insolence. Our besiegers, sensible how much nature is against them, talk of employing constantly great numbers of their soldiery to break the ice of the two bays, little knowing, however, what mighty reparation will be made in only one of our freezing nights; and little considering also, the non-importance of its being broken in bays, which are a dead *flat* upon every ebb. I wish again and again, that the temptations to chastise the insult were not so glaring; as the provincial congress, with all their efforts to confine the inland spirits solely to the defensive, will surely fail upon notice of ministerial determination to continue hostile. Nothing, I think, but a speedy knowledge of a change of measures in England, can prevent a capital winter stroke. They press us to leave the town in the strongest manner. Many are for doing it, and others for sending off their most valuable articles, to be in readiness.

Our friend, Molineux, overplied in the good cause, was last evening laid to rest, where the incomparable Mayhew, and the brother patriots, Dana and Thatcher, await the morning of a glorious resurrection! and where you and I had nearly gone to rest before him. May it not prove unimportant to ourselves, and to the public, that a gracious Providence has been pleased to mark down for us some later date.

" I am informed that a letter was yesterday read in provincial congress from Mr S. Adams, purporting that things went in the continental congress, without any motion of our members, as perfectly to his liking, as if he were sole director, and that in a very few days he doubted not his friends here would receive the most satisfactory intelligence. Though the 'Kingfisher' has orders to sail, yet, the weather being bad, I had thoughts of risking the chance, that I may gain some further light concerning this matter, but finding a general suspicion of the insecurity of conveyance by a king's ship, I am led to think most of your friends will wait other opportunity. I therefore close for the present, that you may not think yourself neglected, in consequence of what, I think, an ill grounded suspicion. We have London news so late as Sept. 2d. If the people of England, our fellow subjects, will cease obstinately to shut their eyes to the justice of our cause, we ask no more. Conviction must be the consequence of a bare admission of the light. God preserve you, my friend.

" I remain your friend,
" and obliged, humble servant,
" JAMES LOVELL."

JOSEPH REED ESQ. TO JOSIAH QUINCY JUN.

" *Philadelphia, October* 25, 1774.
" Dear Sir,

" I hope this will find you safely arrived in Great Britain, a country, wherein I have spent many happy hours, before she began to play the tyrant over America. The cloud which hung over the colonies, at the time of your departure, begins to disperse. Instead of divided counsels, and feeble measures, which at one time there was too much reason to apprehend, all now is union and firmness, and, I trust, we shall exhibit such a proof of public virtue and enlightened zeal, in the most glorious of all causes, as will hand down the present age, with the most illustrious characters of antiquity. I have with great difficulty procured you the proceedings of the general congress, which is now rising, but your delegates, from whom I received it, beg you will not make any public use of it, as the copy is incorrect. Your friend, Mr John Adams, has written something to this effect, in the first page. As the proceedings of this great assembly are so important and interesting, I could not think of this vessel's going, without carrying them to you. Another ship will sail in a few days, by which I shall send you what remains, being the list of grievances, and claim of rights. The congress would not adjourn, but have recommended another to be held, the tenth of May, at this place. They part with each other on terms of the utmost friendship: it will have the most happy effect in cementing the union of the colonies, not only by the ties of public interest, but of private friendship.

This ship will carry you the account of the destruction by fire, of both ship and cargo, which arrived at Annapolis. The owners of both, to avoid a more dreadful punishment for their presumption and folly, offered to set fire with their own hands, which they did. These proofs of the spirit of the people will, I trust, be of some service to Boston. The people of England must see that opposition to parliamentary tyranny, is not local or partial. It will also have a happy effect on the non-importation agreement resolved by the congress, as the owners of ships will not choose to hazard them with forbidden wares.

I congratulate you, my dear sir, upon the rising glory of America: our operations have been almost too slow for the accumulated sufferings of Boston, but I trust they will prove effectual for their relief. Should this bloodless war fail of its effect, an infinite majority of all the colonies will make the last appeal, before they resign their liberties into the hands of any ministerial tyrant.

I shall be always happy in hearing from you, by every opportunity; and you may rely on my sending you a faithful and speedy account of every transaction here. I have written to an old correspondent of mine, Mr Hugh Baillie, a true friend to liberty, and the cause of America, that if he will call and see you, you will show him the proceedings of the congress, which I failed in procuring for him. I salute you with much esteem, and wishing you health and happiness,

"I am, dear Sir,
"Your most obedient, humble servant,
"J. R."

"P. S. I only put the initials of my name, as I believe you remember the handwriting; if not, you will recollect to whom you wrote in this place, just before you embarked.

"*October* 27, 1774.

"When I wrote you yesterday, the captain of the vessel, which carries this, had resolved to sail immediately, but having been induced to wait, in order to carry the address of the congress to the king, gives me an opportunity of sending you the addition, which we have since had from the press, of their proceedings.

I congratulate you, my dear sir, on the spirit, and firmness, and unanimity of this great assembly, the most respectable ever known in this country, and am, with real regard,

"Your affectionate, humble servant.

"J. R."

TO JOSIAH QUINCY JUN.

"*Fairhill, October* 28, 1774.

"My dear Sir,

I should have answered your last letter before you left Boston, if I had not imagined from what you said in it, that you must have sailed, before it could have reached that place.

" I now congratulate you on the hearty union of all America, from Nova Scotia, to Georgia, in the common cause. The particulars, you are no doubt acquainted with. The congress broke up, the day before yesterday ; and if it be possible, the return of the members into the several colonies will make the people still more firm. The most peaceable provinces, are now animated; and a civil war is unavoidable, unless there be a quick change of British measures. The usual events, no question, will take place, if that happens ;— victories and defeats. But what will be the final consequence ? If she fails, immediate distress, if not ruin. If she conquers, destruction at last. But from the best judgment I can form, she will not wait long for her fate. Several European powers, it is probable, will fall on, as soon as she is entangled with us. If they should not, what can she effect, at three thousand miles' distance, against at least four hundred thousand Freemen fighting ' pro aris et focis ?'

"I cannot but pity a brave and generous nation, thus plunged in misfortune by a few worthless persons. But it may be said, how can she retract with dignity in the present position of affairs? I answer, her dignity is not at all concerned, unless it be to punish those, who have abused and betrayed her into measures inconsistent with her welfare. Is a nation bound in honour to support every mad, or villanous, step of a ministry? It is mean to persist in errors because we have committed them: but what is to be said of those, who talk of asserting their own dignity, by vindicating the errors of others?

The present cause is that of Bute, Mansfield, North, Bernard, Hutchinson, &c., not of Great Britain. Let her renounce their detestable projects, which point at her, as their ultimate object; and reconcile herself to her children, while their minds are capable of reconciliation.

" ' Oh! for a warning voice,' to rouse them to conviction of this important truth, that the reconciliation depends upon the passing moment, and that the opportunity will, in a short time, be irrecoverably past, as the days beyond the flood.

Every thing may yet be attributed to the misrepresentations and mistakes of ministers, and universal peace be established throughout the British world, only by a general acknowledgment of this truth, that half a dozen men are fools, or knaves. If their character for ability and integrity is to be maintained by wrecking the whole empire, Monsieur Voltaire may write an addition to the chapter on the subject of 'little things producing great events.'

"As to your complaint against an expression of mine in a late letter, know, dear sir, I wrote in agonies of mind for my brethren in Boston. I trembled lest something might have happened which I could not only forgive, but applaud, but which might have been eagerly and basely seized by others, as a pretence for deserting them. This was the sense of men in Philadelphia, the most devoted to them, and under this apprehension we agreed to make use of the strongest expressions.

"May the Father of mercies bestow every blessing upon you, is the fervent prayer, of

"My dear Sir,

"Your faithful and affectionate friend,

"JOHN DICKINSON."

TO JOSIAH QUINCY JUN.

"*Boston, November* 3, 1774.

" Dear Sir,

"The enclosed letter I wrote with a view to its going by the first vessel that went from us since you embarked for London, but the vessel unhappily sailed before it got to Marblehead. The special reason of my writing was, that you might see a few resolves of our continental congress; as I supposed this would give you the first sight of them.

"The fortifications at the neck are nearly finished; the troops sent for from Philadelphia, New York, and Canada, are mostly, if not wholly, arrived. The grand congress, it is supposed, are broke up either by dissolution or adjournment. Our delegates are expected in town next week. Our provincial congress is likewise adjourned, to the thirteenth of this month,—November. You will see what has been done by both the congresses, so far as what they have done is known by the newspapers. Poor Molineux is dead, and died suddenly. Our sufferings in the town increase as the winter comes on; and our situation becomes more distressingly difficult, as we are guarded, both by sea and land, that we may be restrained from going out of town, and may lie at the mercy of those, who are sent on purpose to distress us.

"Would our circumstances permit it, the town would be immediately evacuated of its proper inhabitants, and this will certainly be the case, should administration determine to proceed in an hostile manner against us. It may be depended upon, that the colonies are marvellously united, and determined to act as one in the defence of this town and province, which they esteem the same thing with defending themselves. We are impatient to hear what is likely to be the resolution of administration; upon their knowing, as they do by this time, the union of the colonies in their resolution to defend their rights and liberties even to the utmost. The spirit in the colonies, especially the four New England ones, instead of being lowered since you went from us, is raised to a still greater height; insomuch that there may be danger of rashness and precipitancy in their conduct. I hope all prudent care will be taken to govern its operations by the rules of wisdom. It is the wish of every sober, understanding man amongst us, that harmony, love, and peace may be restored between Great Britain, and the colonies. They dread nothing more, slavery only excepted, than a bloody conflict for the security of their liberties; and yet this, so far as I am able to judge, they will readily and universally go into, rather than submit to such cruelly hard and tyrannical measures as are imposed on them. I hope you are by this time in London. The weather has been uncommonly clear and mild, since your departure.

" Wishing you prosperity in all your affairs, especially in your endeavours to serve your country,

" I am your assured friend,
" and humble servant,
" CHARLES CHAUNCY."

JOSEPH REED ESQ. TO JOSIAH QUINCY JUN.

"*Philadephia, Nov. 6, 1774.*

" Dear Sir,

" I wrote you the latter end of last month, expecting it would be the first advice you would receive of the proceedings of the American congress; but by a delay of the vessel, and her being obliged to put into New York in distress, it is probable that my well intended efforts will fail. The congress broke up soon after, and your Boston brethren returned in high spirits at the happy and harmonious issue of this important business. Since that time, there has been a stagnation of public intelligence and advices.

"On Saturday next, agreeably to the directions of the congress, a great committee is to be chosen in this city to carry the association of the congress into execution. The Quakers, who you know form a considerable part of this city, act their usual part. They have directed their members not to serve on the committee, and mean to continue the same undecisive, neutral conduct, until they see how the scale is like to preponderate; then I doubt not they will contribute to the relief of Boston, and appear forward in their cause. But American liberty, mean time, must take her chance for them. However, there is no danger of the enemy being let in through this city;—there is a band of staunch, chosen sons of liberty among some of our best families, who are backed by the body of the people in such a manner, that no discontented spirit dares oppose the measures necessary for the public safety. I am more afraid of New York,—there has been a strange delinquency and backwardness during the whole summer. If you have any correspondence there, I wish you would endeavour to animate them. While they are attending to the little paltry disputes, which their own parties have produced, the great cause is suffering in their hands.

" There is too much reason to fear the powerful rhetoric of corruption, in which the present administration is too well versed, has not been used in vain. Their public papers are the vilest collection of invectives upon the cause, and every private character that appears in support of it, and are so replete with falsehoods, invented to mislead, and deceive, that we have little doubt they are bought by some agent of administration, and applied to promote their infamous purposes. You must therefore hear and read from these, with some caution. You see by the example I set you of writing by every vessel, that you cannot oblige me more than by letting me hear often from you. I heartily wish you health, and as much happiness as the situation of your suffering country will allow you to take, and am with much esteem,

"Dear Sir, your very obedient
"and affectionate, humble servant,
"J. R.

"The villanous tricks of the post office, against which we are cautioned from your side the water, induce me only to put the initials of my name; but I trust you will be at no loss to determine who this letter is from."

TO JOSIAH QUINCY JUN.

"*Boston, Nov.* 15, 1774.

" Sir,

"When I parted from you, I fully intended to have written you before this time; be assured I have not been unmindful of you, but public and private business has entirely engrossed my time.

"Your leaving this country so privately has been matter of general speculation. Some say you went away through fear; others that you went to make your peace; others that you went charged with important papers from the continental congress; many conjectured you were gone to Holland; upon the whole it was a nine days' wonder. Since you left us, there has been a provincial congress, which consisted of about two hundred and fifty members, in which matters of the greatest importance were debated. All their proceedings, which I have liberty to communicate, you will see in the prints.

"The town continues to meet from time to time, without molestation. There have been frequent affrays between the inhabitants and soldiers, which have generally ended to the mortification of the latter. The selectmen and town committees have frequent interviews with the General; he declares he has no expectations that this people will ever submit to the late acts; he converses more freely with the inhabitants than Hutchinson did, on matters of a public nature, though we are not off our guard, knowing that it is the part of a General to deceive. The inhabitants persisted in refusing to build barracks for the soldiers, but have in some measure assisted them in refitting old houses and stores. The autumn has been remarkably moderate, so that the soldiers are but now entering their winter quarters. The main guard is kept at George Erving's warehouse, in King street. Almost the whole soldiery in America are now collected in this town. The new erected fortifications on the Neck are laughed at by our old Louisburgh soldiers, as mud-walls, in comparison with what they have subdued,—and were it necessary, they would regard them no more than a beaver-dam.

" The spirit of the inhabitants both in town and country is as firm as ever ; determined to defend their rights to the utmost. The continental congress broke up the 26th ult. and our members all returned safe last Wednesday evening. The bells rang the whole evening. An extract of their proceedings you will doubtless have, before this reaches you. It is the universal voice of this people, that they will sacredly observe the injunctions and recommendations of the grand congress. The provincial congress meet by adjournment the 28th inst. The neighbouring towns and colonies continue to send in their generous donations to the poor of this town. We have our woollen manufactory in good forwardness, having completed a considerable quantity of baizes; and should it be necessary, we see that we could easily carry on any branch of woollen or linen manufacture.

" We have great expectations from your abilities and attachment to the rights and liberties of your country. We are sure you will not be an idle spectator, but will, with your usual spirit, be an active advocate for truth and justice, which is all we wish to take place in our present unhappy disputes with Great Britain.

" It is said the ministry cannot recede, now they have gone so far. I wish they would consult the good bishop of St Asaph, who I am sure could put them into an honorable way.

" Mr Molineux died after a short illness, about three weeks past. All friends that I recollect are well. I presume you will receive several letters from your friends by this opportunity, which will doubtless be more entertaining than I can be. Depending upon a line from you as soon as your leisure will permit, I conclude at present.

" With great respect,
" Your sincere friend,
" and humble servant,
" NATHANIEL APPLETON."

TO JOSIAH QUINCY JUN.

" *Boston, November* 21, 1774.

" Dear Sir,

" As nothing interesting, which I am at liberty to communicate, has taken place since your

FAC SIMILE.

Boston November 21.st 1774

It is the united voice of America to preserve their freedom; or loose their lives in defence of it. Their resolutions are not the effects of precipitate Rashness, but the Serious result of sober enquiry and deliberation. I am convinced that the true spirit of Liberty was never so universally diffused through all ranks and orders of People, in any Country on the face of the earth as it now is through all North America.

I am dearest your most obedient

Josiah Quincy Jr of Massachusetts

departure from home, except such matters as you could not fail of being informed of by the public papers, I have deferred writing to you, knowing that upon your first arrival in London, you would be greatly engaged in forming your connexions with the friends of this country, to whom you have been recommended. Our friends who have been at the continental congress, are in high spirits on account of the union which prevails throughout the colonies. It is the united voice of America, to preserve their freedom, or lose their lives in defence of it. Their resolutions are not the effect of inconsiderate rashness, but the sound result of sober enquiry and deliberation. I am convinced that the true spirit of liberty was never so universally diffused through all ranks and orders of people, in any country on the face of the earth, as it now is through all North America. The provincial congress met at Concord at the time appointed. About two hundred and sixty members were present. You would have thought yourself in an assembly of Spartans, or ancient Romans, had you been a witness to the ardour which inspired those who spoke upon the important business they were transacting. An injunction of secrecy prevents my giving any particulars of their transactions, except such as by their express order were published in the papers; but in general you may be assured that they approved themselves the true representatives of a wise and brave people, determined at all events to be free. I know I might be indulged in giving you an account of our transactions, were I sure this would get safe to you, but I dare not, as the times are, risk so important intelligence.

"Next Wednesday, the 23d instant, we shall meet again according to adjournment. All that I can safely communicate to you shall be speedily transmitted. I am of opinion that the dissolution of the British Parliament, which we were acquainted with last week, together with some favourable letters received from England, will induce us to bear the inconvenience of living without government until we have some farther intelligence of what may be expected from England. It will require, however, a very masterly policy to keep the province, for any considerable time longer, in its present state. The town of Boston is by far the most moderate part of the province; they are silent and inflexible. They hope for relief, but they have found from experience that they can bear to suffer more than their oppressors or themselves thought possible. They feel the injuries they receive,—they are the frequent subject of conversation; but they take an honest pride in being singled out by a tyrannical administration, as the most determined enemies to arbitrary power. They know that their merits, not their crimes, have made them the objects of ministerial vengeance. We endeavour to live as peaceably as possible with the soldiery, but disputes and quarrels often arise between the troops and the inhabitants.

" General Gage has made very few new manœuvres since you left us. He has indeed rendered the entrenchments at the entrance of the town as formidable as he possibly could. I have frequently been sent to him on committees, and have several times had private conversations with him. I have thought him a man of honest, upright principles, and one desirous of accommodating the difference between Great Britain and her colonies in a just and honourable way. He did not appear to be desirous of continuing the quarrel in order to make himself necessary, which is too often the case with persons employed in public affairs,—but a copy of a letter via Philadelphia, said to be written from him to Lord

North, gives a very different cast to his character. His answer to the provincial congress, which was certainly ill judged, I suppose was the work of some of that malicious group of harpies, whose disappointments make them desirous to urge the governor to drive every thing to extremes; but in this letter (if it be genuine) he seems to court the office of a destroyer of the liberties and murderer of the people of this province. But you have doubtless read the paper, and thought with indignation on its contents.

"I wish to know of you how affairs stand in Great Britain, and what was the principal motive of the dissolution of Parliament. If the late acts of Parliament are not to be repealed, the wisest step for both countries is fairly to separate, and not spend their blood and treasure in destroying each other. It is barely possible that Britain may depopulate North America, but I trust in God, she never can conquer the inhabitants;—and if the cruel experiment is made, I am sure, whatever fortunes may attend America, that Britain will curse the wretch, who, to stop the mouths of his ravenous pack of dependants, bartered away the wealth and glory of her empire.

" I have not time to say more at present than to assure you that from this time you may expect to hear from me, news or no news, by every vessel, and that my earnest wish is that your abilities and integrity may be of eminent service to your country.

"I am, dear Sir,
"Your most obedient servant,
"JOSEPH WARREN."

TO JOSIAH QUINCY JUN.

"*Boston, December* 30, 1774.

" Dear Sir,

While at Philadelphia, I received your favours of the twentieth and twenty-fifth of August last, and agreeably to your request I spoke to divers gentlemen to favour you with letters and with intelligence. I should have written you from Philadelphia, but I was so engaged that I had not a moment's time; and as Mr John Adams and Mr Reed told me they should write you by the same conveyance that I wrote Dr Franklin, I knew you would by them be favoured with the proceedings of the congress, and the necessary intelligence, and therefore that my writing would at that time be needless. Since I have returned home, I have had nothing of importance to communicate.

" The proceedings of the continental congress are universally approved, and will be sacredly adhered to. The inhabitants of Canada are much dissatisfied with the late acts relative to that province, and instead of aiding administration in carrying the late acts relative to this province into execution, they will unite with the continent in measures to obtain their repeal. When you left the province, it was in a convulsed state ; they had a complication of difficulties and distresses to encounter. Under these circumstances it was necessary to have a provincial congress to consult upon measures to save themselves from impending ruin, and to preserve their inestimable liberty. They met in October last. If in any of their proceedings they have gone beyond the true line marked out by the constitution, certainly people of candour and consideration will excuse it, and make all due allowance for a people in such an alarming, perplexed, and critical situation, and under the dreadful apprehension of having their dearest rights and liberties torn from them by the hand of violence. You are fully acquainted with our distressed situation,—you doubtless have been furnished with the proceedings of the provincial congress in October last, and as you are capable, so, I doubt not, you will be disposed to make the most favourable representation of our conduct during this time of perplexity.

The provincial congress adjourned from October 29th to November 23d, when they met at Cambridge, and dissolved on the 10th inst. Their proceedings, or most of them, you have in the public papers. The late order of the king in council, prohibiting the exportation of powder, or any sort of arms or ammunition, from Great Britain, unless by special license, has alarmed the people in America; it forebodes the most vigorous exertions of martial force. They are therefore adopting the most effectual methods to defend themselves against any hostile invasion of the enemies to America. The people of Rhode-Island have used the precaution to remove the powder, cannon, and other military stores from the fort at Newport, into the country. The people at Portsmouth, in New Hampshire, have done the like by their cannon and other military stores at the fort at New Castle, at the entrance of their harbour.

"I remain, with strict truth,
"Your friend and humble servant,
"Thomas Cushing.

"Pray let me hear from you how it is like to fare with my dear country."

TO JOSIAH QUINCY JUN.

"*Braintree, January* 3, 1775.

"Dear Son,

"I have written two long letters to you, since your departure, the last of which, for want of a safe conveyance, is, I suppose, now in Boston.

"Yesterday presented me with the most valuable, the most welcome New Year's gift I ever received,—the doubly joyful news of your safe arrival in England, and your health restored. May that all-perfect Being, who has bestowed such inestimable blessings upon us, impress our minds with a correspondent grateful sense of them, manifested by a constant exertion of our rational powers in pursuit of their proper objects. * * *

"No sooner were the results of the continental and provincial congress published to the world, than the presses, from north to south, have been delivered of innumerable productions in opposition to, and defence of them, all which will doubtless be transmitted to you in newspapers and single pamphlets. However, I cannot deny myself the pleasure of noticing one, said to be written by your friend G——l L——, which has afforded great relief to the minds of those who entertained most fearful apprehensions of an open rupture with the parent state. * * * * * * *

"I should have told you before, that we were no sooner relieved from our anxiety about your safe arrival, and the recovery of your health, than our concern commenced, or rather revived, to know whether you were safe arrived in London, and what reception you met with from the court and city;—whether your enemies are to be gratified by ministerial persecution, or your friends by the esteem and honour with which they hope to hear you are received and entertained, not only by those friends to whom you have been recommended, but all those friends to liberty, and the rights of mankind, who may honour you with their acquaintance and friendship.

"You will readily believe me when I tell you we are all, whether whigs or tories, quite solicitous to hear how the new parliament opens;—what the king's sentiments are relative to American affairs;—how many new members have obtained seats in the house of commons, because they are esteemed enemies to despotism, and friends to liberty;—whether they are likely to gain a majority by being above corruption;—or whether, for want of a sufficient number of inflexible patriots, the public affairs of the nation are, as has been often foretold, running headlong to ruin, and the enemies of the British constitution in its purity, are likely to succeed in their endeavours for its subversion. * * * * * * * *

"You must excuse my rambling from one thing to another. Mr W—— brings intelligence from Boston, that the seamen on board the fleet are grown mutinous;—that one of the navy officers, meeting with a land officer at K——x's shop, told him that on board all the ships their men were grown so uneasy and tumultuous, that it was with great difficulty they could govern them. Upon which the land officer observed, that the uneasiness among the soldiers was full as great, if not greater, than among the seamen.

* * * * * * * * * * *

"If it was certainly known that a rupture was to take place in the spring, there could not be more diligence, or greater application in studying the science of war, than there is at present throughout New England, and I believe through the continent; which surely must convince the ministry that not only an immense treasure, but rivers of blood must be expended before the spirits of freeborn Americans can be made to submit to parliamentary legislation, and submissively bow their necks to the yoke of bondage, their fellow subjects in power have prepared for them.

"Pray make my affectionate and friendly regards acceptable to good Dr Franklin, and any other friends who are kind enough to remember and ask after me.

"I cannot express how near your interest, your health, and your happiness lie to my heart, nor how ardently I wish my longing eyes may be blessed with the sight of you before they are closed in everlasting darkness, and the dear relation is annihilated between you and

"Your unalterably affectionate parent,
"JOSIAH QUINCY."

The Journal and letters of Mr Quincy, during his voyage and short residence in England, will present all that is known of this last period of his life. Much of the information they contain respecting the men and transactions of that time, are to be derived from no other source.

This Journal cannot be read without leaving a deep impression on the mind, of the exclusive and entire devotion of the writer's soul to the great purpose of his voyage,—the service of his country. Possessed of an exquisite sensibility to the beauties of nature and art, in a land, which constantly presented to him, on every side, objects calculated to excite and detain his imagination, and gratify his taste, his notices of them are of the most cursory kind. A single word, indicating either his satisfaction, or his surprise, occasionally escapes from his pen. Even this is often immediately followed by an expression of regret and self-reproach, at permitting *any thing* to occupy his mind, except thoughts concerning his country.

As the best mode of preserving the continuity of events, and impressions, the letters of Mr Quincy from England will be published according to their dates, in connexion with those parts of the journal, in which they are noticed as having been written.

JOURNAL OF A VOYAGE TO ENGLAND, &c.

"September 28, 1774. Wednesday morning ten o'clock, embarked on board the ship Boston Packet, Nathaniel Byfield Lyde, master, and sailed for London. With us went passengers Messrs W. Hyslop and son, Dr Paine, and Rufus Chandler Esq. of Worcester, Mr Higginson of Salem, and Mr Sylvester Oliver, son of the late Lieutenant Governor. Some of us might say, 'Nos dulcia linquimus arva,' while others were obliged to mourn, 'Nos patriam fugimus.'

"Though in low health when I entered on ship-board, the salutary effects of the sea air soon contributed to relieve my complaints, and in less than twenty days, gave me confirmed health.

"November 5th. Latitude 49° 45', wrote a letter to Mrs Quincy.

At sea, Nov. 5, 1774, two in the morning. Lat. 49° 45' N.

"We generally estimate the value of our possessions by their loss, and the worth of our friends is seldom better realized, than in their absence. * Believe me, you cannot think with how much tender solicitude I look towards you and my children. My country, my friends, and my family, occupy my whole thoughts, and while I see myself blessed with a promising prospect of doing some little service to the one, and of being returned in safety to the other, it inspires me with sensations I must leave you to realize. Why should I detain you with reflections, while to a friend who is absent, nothing can be more grateful than to tell you how I have been, and where I am. After an agreeable and very refreshing ride to Salem, we sailed from thence at ten in the morning, and were clear of the land about two in the afternoon. Though the weather was fine, yet in less than an hour I was confined to my cabin, but was happy in finding my sickness neither so violent nor unremitting as in my former voyage. Five and twenty days rolled away with much of the uninteresting vacuity and sameness of a sea life. I had, however, the pleasure of perceiving a gradual daily advantage from my voyage, and my retired moments were grateful in reflecting upon the many prayers and benisons which were breathed towards me by my American friends.

"Such was the unremitted favour of the winds during the whole of the preceding period, as that we never failed of being able to lay our course, which was a circumstance no one on board had ever known for so long a time, except in the latitude of the trade winds. But this felicity was in a great measure destroyed by the poor improvement we were able to make of it; our ship was deep laden, and as bad a sailer as was ever navigated by a Dutch commander; not a sail on the ocean but what passed by us as if we had been at anchor. Had we been only in a tolerably going ship, we should in all probability have been at Land's End in one or two and twenty days; instead of which, at the end of about eight and twenty, the winds set in strong at the southeast, where they have continued ever since, and seem at this time as likely to continue as ever. These circumstances, at sea, are a little more vexatious than those on land easily imagine. But as for myself, I had less reason than any one on board to be uneasy. Every day has surprisingly added to my health; the benefit from the sea is far beyond any thing experienced in my voyage to South Carolina. Ever since the day I left land, I have never had one symptom of my former complaints; they did not leave me by degrees, but entirely and at once; so that while writing this, no one on board appears freer from disorder, and none most certainly in better spirits. Indeed, if it were not for my concern about America, and my friends there, I should not feel one uneasy sensation.

"Tell my American friends, that I see more reason than ever, that they should write me minute statements of facts. Tell them the period to false representations of American affairs is not yet come. I shall probably enlarge on this head in another letter, and if I should write under a new signature, you must not be surprised. I know not by what opportunity I shall send this. The season is so far advanced, and the winds have of late been so favourable for the departure of American bound ships, it is probable I shall have no very speedy conveyance. However, as there is a possibility of meeting some vessel bound to one of the colonies, either in the Channel, or Downs, I write at this time, so as to be able to embrace the opportunity on the shortest notice.
* * * * * * * * * * * * * *

"November 8, 1774. Ten o'clock in the morning. Just stepping aboard a pilot-boat, and going up to Falmouth. In very great haste,
"Yours,
"JOSIAH QUINCY JUN."

JOURNAL CONTINUED.

"November 8, 1774. Tuesday morning, (six weeks, wanting a day, since leaving Salem,) landed at Falmouth.

"Having reached the famous island of Great Britain, I am prone to contemplate the glorious deeds that have made it immortal,—but alas! my affections, and my duty, call me to consider the state of my native country.

"I found considerable advantage by attending to my companions, and often collected much information of men and things, that from the political jealousies and cautions prevalent in America, I could not there so readily attain. One of the first convictions I received, was touching the source of many American injuries, and one of my first emotions was indignation against public conspirators. I find that there was very great doubt whether I was going to embark for Europe; but certain Americans were very sure I should never dare to go up to London.

"November 8th. Wrote another letter to Mrs Quincy.

Falmouth, Great Britain, Nov. 8, 1774.
"My dear Friend,

"I have already written to you this day; I shall therefore write nothing very material at this time. I am now on shore, every thing around me happy and agreeable as to myself. The people crowd round me, eager to hear about American affairs,—I gratify them. This place is in situation delightful; the country and cultivation surpass description. I long to paint the scenes around me. All things are heightened by my uncommon health and spirits. I am almost afraid I shall meet with a damper, but I was never better prepared to conflict with adversity.

"Since writing the above, I have been regaled with the profusions of Great Britain to—*those who have money.* I have read also about twenty of the late London papers. I would have sent them, but could not procure them. They contain the resolves of the congress relative to the late Suffolk proceedings. They also seem to breathe a spirit favourable to America. I am in some pain on finding that six men-of-war sailed for Boston, on the twenty-sixth of October. I have conversed with several sensible people here. I have not yet met one, but what wishes well to the Americans. And one or two expressed great veneration for *the brave Bostonians*.

" We have a report that the congress have agreed upon a non-importation agreement; and also upon a non-exportation agreement, to commence the first of August next. I have also been informed that Lord North had desired leave of his Majesty to resign; to which the King replied, —' Your Lordship's policy hath made an American snarl, and your Lordship's dexterity must untie it, or it must *be cut*; and when Englishmen once begin that work, they will probably go much further.'

" I have no room for more, except that to-morrow I proceed towards Plymouth by land.

" Adieu.

" JOSIAH QUINCY JUN."

JOURNAL CONTINUED.

" November 8th. Took a two hours' walk over the town of Falmouth. A delightful situation. * * * * In my view of Pendennis Castle, and indeed of every thing about me, I am struck with the great appearance of antiquity.

"November 9th. Proceeded from Falmouth to Bodmyn, twenty-two miles. Passed through the town of Pendryn, and several small villages. The roads hilly and good, affording agreeable riding, and delightful land prospects. The cultivation of the land can scarcely be realized by a mere American; it is to a wonderful perfection. The first reflection upon the immense labour that must be bestowed on these fields was, where the men lived, who did the work. Extensive fields, highly tilled, without a house. This was an object, which occurred almost every hour. The villages in which the labourers and peasantry chiefly reside, are built of small stones and clay, generally miserable accommodations for honest labour. The lower orders of people are servile in their obeisance, and despondent in their appearance.

"I could not help remarking, that if the little liberty diffused through Britain, could give such a beautiful face to nature, what would be the appearance, if there was as much general liberty, as was consistent with that fundamental principle of social policy, 'the greatest happiness, of the greatest number.' * * * *

"The Briton says, 'See France, Spain, and Italy,—the calamities of slavery!' The liberal-minded, who use a larger scale, will think it not needful to go so far. Nothing is more common than to hear in America, both north and south Britons declaim against the hypocritical duplicity and fraud of New-Englandmen; but certain it is, that Great Britain, in variety and abundance of frauds and deceits, far surpasses any part of North America.

"November 10th. From Bodmyn, a very considerable manufacturing town, I rode through several villages to Plymouth Docks, about thirty-three miles. Saw the elegant seat of Lord Edgecombe, a most delightful situation.

"November 11th. Though a very cold and stormy day, I viewed Plymouth Docks, and went on board and all over the Royal George, a first-rate, pierced for two hundred and ten, and carrying two hundred guns. The rope-walks, buildings, armory, arsenal, naval and warlike stores, exceed the power of the human mind to conceive, that doth not actually behold.

"I will not attempt to describe what I could scarcely realize to be true, while I was actually viewing. My ideas of the riches and powers of this great nation are increased to a degree I should not have believed, if it had been predicted to me.

"I also saw many 64, 74, 80, and 100 gun ships; and went on board a loaded Indiaman just arrived; but this, being after viewing the preceding magnificence, did not much move me. The various materials, and the several degrees of building, from the laying of the keel, to the finishing an hundred gun ship, which were very carefully viewed by me, in several instances, excited an astonishment I never before experienced.

"November 12th. Proceeded farther to view Plymouth and its environs; saw the beautiful assembly room at Bath, and the baths for the nobility and gentry;—elegance and splendour. Proceeded to Plymouth, viewed the town and castle of Plymouth;—incredible strength, natural and artificial. The statue of George the First is very elegant and beautiful.

"November 13th. Having arrived at the great and ancient city of Exeter, I viewed the city, cathedral, and bishop's palace. The cathedral surprisingly grand and antique;—amazing work of superstition! Went to church and saw the procession of the Mayor and Aldermen, the parade of the bishops, archdeacons, deans, &c.

* * * * * * * * * * * *

"The North walk in this city is beyond expression beautiful.

"November 14th. Went from Exminister, to the city of Salisbury.

"November 15th. Viewed the famous Druid Temple at Stonehenge, which the learned and the virtuosi call one of the greatest wonders of the island. It is a wonderful piece of antiquity.

"Went to the seat of the Earl of Pembroke. His statuary and paintings are said to surpass those of any nobleman in the kingdom. There is no such thing as describing what authors have written whole volumes upon.

"Viewed the cathedral, which is called (and perhaps justly) one of the finest in the kingdom.

"November 16th. Proceeded, and lodged at Staines, on the Thames. The number of delightful seats &c. increases very much; among others that of the Earl of Portsmouth, very superb.

"November 17th. Proceeded to London, where I arrived about eleven o'clock, A. M. The extent, numbers, opulence, &c. of this great city, far surpass all I had imagined. I was visited by Messrs Thomas Bromfield, C. Dilly, and

J. Williams, from all of whom I received many civilities. Waited upon Dr Franklin, and drank tea with him. He appears in good health and spirits, and seems warm in our cause, and confident in our ultimate success. I find many friends to liberty and America, rejoiced on notice of my arrival.

"I find among a certain set of Americans it was a matter of great wonder at the New England coffee-house, what brought me to London. My 'Observations' have been reprinted here, I understand. Wrote a long letter to Mrs Quincy.

"*London, November* 17, 1774.
"My dear Friend,
"About ten hours ago, I arrived in this great city, and am now at my lodgings, near the Haymarket. With you, and my friends, the first object and inquiry will be about my health and spirits. In one word (for just now I am a man of too much business to use many) they are both surprisingly fine,—rather bordering upon extravagance, than under par. Indeed, how could they be otherwise? From sea, I landed in fine health, and have now finished a most delightful journey of

three hundred miles. The scenes of Plymouth Docks, Stonehenge, Wilton House (containing the statues and paintings of the Earl of Pembroke), exceed all description : nay, I will venture to say, that the imagination stretched to its utmost limits, cannot form any idea of their grandeur, without a view. The same may be said of Exeter and Salisbury cathedrals.—But why do I waste time upon any other subject, than my country ?

"I have spent about two hours to-day with Dr Franklin. He appears the stanch friend of America, and confident of the ultimate success of its friends. He has promised me his patronage, and I have reason to believe him sincere. He inquired particularly after 'his old friend,' my father.

"Mr Jonathan Williams Jun. has waited upon me and treated me with great civility and politeness. He lives with Dr Franklin, and he told me, that upon his waiting on him with intelligence of my arrival, he asked, if it was the author of the 'Observations' &c., and being answered in the affirmative, he replied,—'I am very glad of it.'

"Mr Bromfield has shown me every mark of respect. He told me that when it was known to-day at the New England coffee-house that I had arrived, certain Americans made a great wonder—'what I had come for.' One of the friends of liberty in this city came to him also, and told him that a certain gentleman in the coffee-room, said,—'Yes, Quincy has been blowing up the seeds of sedition in America, and has now come to do the same here.' I returned my compliments, and sent word, that, 'if I had done nothing but blow up seeds, they would probably be very harmless, as they would never take root; but if I should have the good fortune to sow any here, and they should afterwards ripen, he, or the ministry might blow them about at their leisure.'

"I am well informed that the friends of America increase here every day. In the west of England, a very considerable manufacturer told me, " If the Americans stand out, we must come to their terms.' I find our friends here dread nothing so much as lest the congress should petition. Should they adopt that mode, it will be injurious to our cause. The ministry have carried their men at a late election, but the people seem to be rousing. You see I have been a short time in London. I can as yet communicate but little intelligence. A large field is opening to me. I am preparing for the course with feelings, which render me careless, whether I shall be pursuing, or pursued. Tell my political friends, I shall soon write to them, and that when I informed Dr Franklin of the pains I had taken to establish an extensive correspondence, he rejoiced at it much. Let their intelligence be as frequent, and as minute as possible. Let them all direct to Mr Bromfield, or Mr Dilly. This is my third letter to you. Not a line yet from America. Salute all my friends with due respect.

* * * *

JOURNAL CONTINUED.

" November 18th. This morning, J. Williams Esq , inspector of the customs in the Massachusetts Bay, waited upon me, and we had more than an hour's private conversation together. He informed me, that Governor Hutchinson had repeatedly assured the ministry that a union of the colonies was utterly impracticable; that the people were greatly divided among themselves, in every colony; and that there could be no doubt, that all America would submit, and that they must, and moreover would, soon. It is now not five minutes, since Mr Williams left me, and these I think were his very words; he added, also, that Governor Hutchinson had not only repeatedly told the ministry so, as several Lords had informed him, but that Governor Hutchinson had more than once said the same to persons in the ministry, in his presence. Mr Williams desired to wait on me to see Lord North and Lord Dartmouth,—but as it was not at their Lordships' desire he made the request, I declined going for the present. Mr Williams also presented the compliments of Corbin Morris Esq. (one of the commissioners of the customs, and a gentleman high in the sentiments of administration) with a request, that I would come and dine with him to-day; but being engaged to dine out this, and several succeeding days, I was obliged to decline the invitation.

"Dined with Dr Franklin, in company with Dr Bancroft and Mr Williams. Dr Franklin confirmed the account given by Mr Williams relative to Governor Hutchinson, so far as that several of the nobility, and ministry, had assured him of the same facts.

"Went this evening to Covent Garden Theatre; saw the 'Beggar's Opera,' with the farce of 'Cross Purposes.' Shuter acted well the part of Peacham, and the actresses in several striking elegancies of gesture, voice, and action, convinced me that women equal men in the powers of eloquence. I am still further satisfied in my opinion, that the stage is the nursery of vice, and disseminates the seeds of it far and wide, with an amazing and baneful success.

"November 19th. Early this morning J. Williams Esq. waited upon me with the compliments of Lord North, and his request to see me this morning. I went about half past nine o'clock, and found Sir George Savil (as Mr Williams informed me) in the levee room. After a short time his lordship sent for Mr Williams and myself into his apartment. His reception was polite, and with a cheerful affability his Lordship soon inquired into the state, in which I had left American affairs. I gave him my sentiments upon them, together with what I took to be the causes of most of our political evils;—gross misrepresentation and falsehood. His lordship replied, he did not doubt there had been much, but added, that very honest men frequently gave a wrong statement of matters through mistake, prejudice, prepossessions, and biases, of one kind or other. I conceded the possibility of this, but further added, that it would be happy, if none of those who had given accounts relative to America had varied from known truth, from worse motives.

"We entered largely into the propriety and policy of the Boston Port Bill. In the conversation upon this subject I received much pleasure. His lordship several times smiled, and once seemed touched. We spoke considerably upon the sentiments of Americans, of the right claimed by Parliament to tax,—of the destruction of the tea,—and the justice of payment for it. His lordship went largely and repeatedly into an exculpation of the ministry. He said they were obliged to do what they did; that it was the most lenient measure that was proposed; that if administration had not adopted it, they would have been called to an account; that the nation were highly incensed, &c.

"Upon this topic I made many remarks with much freedom and explicitness, and should have said more, had not his lordship's propensity to converse been incompatible with my own loquacity. His lordship more than thrice spoke of the power of Great Britain, of their determination to exert it to the utmost, in order to effect the submission of the Colonies. He said repeatedly, 'We must try what we can do to support the authority we have claimed over America. If we are defective in power, we must sit down contented, and make the best terms we can, and nobody then can blame us, after we have done our utmost; but till we have tried what we can do, we can never be justified in receding. We ought, and we shall be very careful not to judge a thing impossible, because it may be difficult; nay, we ought to try what we can effect, before we determine upon its impracticability.' This last sentiment, and very nearly in the same words, was often repeated, —I thought I knew for what purpose.

" His lordship spoke also upon the destruction of the Gaspee, and in direct terms twice said, that the commissioners were appointed to try that matter, and had transmitted accounts that they could obtain no evidence. This declaration being in flat contradiction to what I had several times heard Chief Justice Oliver declare to be the case from the bench, when giving his charges to the grand jury, was particularly noticed by me. His Honor ever most solemnly declared, in public and private, that the commission was to inquire whether any such event had happened, in order to send word to England, that so a trial might, or might not be ordered, as the evidence might be ; and in the most express terms declared the commissioners had no power to try.

" In the course of near two hours' conversation, many things more passed between us. As many letters and messages were delivered to his lordship while I was present, I several times rose to depart, telling his lordship I was afraid I should trespass on his patience, or the concerns of others ; but being requested to stay, I remained about two hours and then rose to go, but his lordship kept standing, while he continued his conversation with his usual spirit. Upon my departure he asked me when I should leave England. I told him it was uncertain,—but imagined not this twelvemonth. He hoped the air of the island would contribute to my health, and said he thought the most unhealthy months were past ; and then saying, ' I am much obliged to you for calling on me,' we left each other to our meditations.

" Mr Williams the same morning presented the compliments of Mr Commissioner Morris, before mentioned, and requested my dining with him on Tuesday next.

" Traversed St James' Park, and then went to Islington to dine with Mr Bromfield, where I met three or four high, sensible whigs, whose conversation and politeness enlivened and gratified me. Mr Welsh, one of the company with whom I dined, desired me to be upon my guard against the temptations and bribery of administration. 'If you are corruptible, sir,' added he, 'the ministry will corrupt you.' This sentiment was confirmed by all present. They further informed me, that as all the morning papers mentioned me by name, as the author of the 'Observations,' and as having arrived in town;—several at the coffee-houses wondered how 'I dared to come.'

" I am often told, that many rejoice that I am come over; and have many evidences hourly given me, to induce me to think I have some, and reason to hope that in time I shall have more, friends.

" It is whispered that orders are gone to America to apprehend General Lee. But I do not believe it.

" November 20th. Went to hear divine service at Westminster Abbey;—cursorily viewed that astonishing work, which I intend shortly to give more attention to.

"Dined with Messrs Dilly in company with Dr Franklin, Mr Sheriff Lee, Dr Davis, and others; with whom I spent the afternoon and evening. Mr Lee said he had long thought of, and would soon set on foot, a subscription for the Americans. I find every day more reason to think that multitudes of fervent friends to America reside in this island.

"November 21st. Went to Westminster Hall, and attended the Court of Chancery, King's Bench, and Common Pleas.

"Waited on Governor Pownall, and had two hours' conversation with him. Dined with Sheriff Lee with several friends of liberty.

"November 22d. Dined with Corbin Morris Esq., one of the commissioners of the customs (supposed framer of the annual ministerial budget, being a choice friend of the ministry), in company with one of the officers of the treasury, and J. Williams Esq. Mr Morris was sensible, intelligent, and very conversable. The whole conversation was on American affairs. He entered largely into the claims, the rights, and the duty of Parliament. He spoke as might be expected.

I observed a remarkable conformity of sentiment between him and Lord North; and an equally observable similarity of language. Mr Morris expatiated largely upon the infinite resources of commerce, wealth, and power of the English nation. I heard him.

" The following address to me was not a little singular.

" ' Mr Quincy, you are a man' &c. (flummery.) ' You have seen some of the ministry, and have heard more of the dispositions of administration. You find that they have no inclination to injure, much less to oppress the colonies. They have no wish but that of seeing the Americans free and happy. You must be sensible of the right of Parliament to legislate for the colonies, and of the power of the nation to enforce their laws. No power in Europe ever provoked the resentment, or bade defiance to the power of this island, but they were made to repent of it. You must know your countrymen must fail in a contest with this great and powerful people. Now as you find how inclined administration are to lenity and mildness, you should, you ought, to write to your friends this intelligence, and endeavour to influence them to their duty. I do not doubt your influence would be very great with them, and you would by this means be doing a lasting service to your country.'

"November 23d. Dined with Messrs Dilly, and a few friends of liberty, and spent the residue of the day in delivering letters. At night Mr Inspector Williams waited on me, with the compliments of Lord Dartmouth, and requested my waiting on him tomorrow at ten o'clock. Mr Williams gave me a curious account of a conversation with his lordship relative to my 'Observations.' Received the compliments of Governor Pownall to breakfast with him.

"November 24th. Waited upon Lord Dartmouth, and had about an hour and a half conversation with him. I was convinced that the American and British controversy would be much sooner, and much more equitably settled, if it were not for the malevolent influence of a certain Northern personage now in Great Britain.

"Lord Dartmouth being called out for a few minutes to attend the physicians of his lady, made his apology, and taking up a pamphlet that lay on his table said, 'I would entertain you with a pamphlet ("Observations on the Port Bill"), during my absence, but I fancy you have seen *this*.

I think you know the author of it.' His lordship bowed with a smile, which I returned, and he retired for a few minutes. * * * * * * *

"Was introduced by Dr Franklin and Dr Price, and spent part of the afternoon and evening with the Royal Society. Spent the residue of the evening with a club of friends of liberty at the London coffee-house. Was there introduced, by Dr Franklin and Dr Price, to Mr Alderman Oliver, Mr Vaughan, eight or nine dissenting clergymen, and several other gentlemen.

"I find the most sanguine hopes of good from the spirit of the Americans, and the most ardent wishes for their success. Dr Franklin acknowledged to me, that he was the author of 'The Way to make a great Empire a little one;'—and 'The Edicts of the king of Prussia.'

"November 25th. Received complimentary visits from Governor Pownall, Mr Wentworth, and others. Went and viewed the inside of St Paul's.

"November 26th. Breakfasted with Governor Pownall, and spent three hours with him in conversation upon American affairs. Governor Pownall said to me, 'Mr Quincy, I do assure you, all the measures against America were planned and pushed on by Bernard and Hutchinson. They were incessant in their application to administration, and gave the most positive assurances of success; and I do assure you, America has not a more determined, insidious, and inveterate enemy than Governor Hutchinson. He is now doing, and will continue to do, all he can against you.'

"Dined with Mr Rogers (a banker), at Newington Green, in company with many of the friends of liberty.

"November 27th. Dined with Dr Franklin, and spent the evening with him and his friends.

"Wrote a letter to Mrs. Quincy, and another to Josiah Quincy Esq. by the December packet.

TO MRS. QUINCY.

London, November 24, 1774.

"My very dear Friend,

"Having written you many letters since my arrival in this island, as my bosom friend, I now address you as my political confidant. Finding it impossible to write to all my political friends, they must consider my letters to you as intended for them.

"Ever since my arrival here, I have been an object of much more attention and respect than I had any right to claim. However, these circumstances have not flattered my vanity, because I know that it was not my merits that procured this distinction.

"The principle I laid down to regulate my conduct, was to make no appearance in any noted coffee-houses, and no very conspicuous figure in any public place. The next rule I observed was, to wait upon no public characters, though ever so much solicited, till the compliment of a request to see me was first paid.

"Lord North was the first who desired my attendance, Mr Commissioner Morris next requested my dining with him, and Lord Dartmouth, as soon as he arrived in town, appointed an hour for my attending him. With neither of these gentlemen had I less than two hours' conversation.

"I long to communicate the substance of these interviews, but I have not time to transcribe it from my Journal. Indeed I have not an hour's time to myself:—the friends of liberty, and the friends of the ministry, engross my whole time. I am in a delicate situation. I have a very difficult task. Each party makes great professions of friendship; with what views or sincerity you may conjecture. Governor Pownall has detained me several hours in conversation on American affairs, and is now writing on that subject. Dr Franklin and Mr Sheriff Lee, with very many others, appear my stanch friends. With these I spend, and shall spend, almost every day, considerable portions of time.

"Critical as my situation is, yet (save the concern I feel for my country) I have high pleasure. My health is good beyond example, and my spirits are truly American. In all companies I have endeavoured to give a true state of the affairs of the continent, and the genuine sentiments of its inhabitants. I find many things I advance are said to be new,—but I have openly and repeatedly declared (even to the characters before mentioned) my willingness to meet, and controvert, face to face, any who dispute the justice of my opinions, or the truth of what I relate. Whether it be a good or ill omen, my friends may judge; but certain it is, that all (even the highest) with whom I have conversed, declare, they have no doubt but that my coming over will be of great service to both countries. To a great officer of state who expressed this sentiment, my reply was

' There is a certain *influence* which will counteract all I can possibly do.' I was understood *not* to mean a *British* influence, and the reply was,— ' Perhaps not.'

" America hath none to fear so much as her own children. Some of these are inveterate and persevering beyond example or conception. Seeing I have not time to give you a regular detail of all I have heard and seen, you will probably inquire—What is the substance of what you collect? What is your own private opinion? To gratify my friends on these heads was the cause of my snatching this hasty moment, and transmitting my opinion.

" The minds of people are strangely altered in this island :—the many are now as prone to justify and applaud the Americans, as, but a little while ago, they were ready to condemn and punish. I have conversed with almost all ranks of people for these fifteen days past, and having been in very large circles of the sensible part of the community during that time, my opportunity for information was the more fortunate. I came among a people, I was told, that breathed nothing but punishment and destruction against Boston, and all America. I found a people, many of whom revere, love, and heartily wish well to us. Now is it strange that it should be so? for abstracted from the pleasure that a good mind takes in seeing truth and justice prevail—it is the interest, the highest *private interest* of this whole nation, to be our fast friends:—and strange as it may seem when you consider the conduct of the nation as represented in Parliament, the *people* know it. The following language has been reiterated to me in various companies, with approbation and warmth.

" ' We are afraid of nothing but your division, and your want of perseverance. Unite and persevere. You must prevail,—you must triumph.'

" This and similar language hath been held to me with a zeal that bespoke it came from the heart,—with a frequency that proved such sentiments dwelt upon the mind. I could name you the first characters for understanding, integrity, and spirit, who have held such language ;—but it would be improper to name those who might perhaps be discovered through the indiscretion of American friends, or the prying villany of public conspirators. Bowdoin, Winthrop, Chauncy, Cooper, Warren, &c., can recollect whom they introduced me to, and thence conjecture a few of those, whose British hearts are thus in America.

"Great is the anxiety here, lest the congress should petition or remonstrate. In the arts of negotiation, your adversaries are infinitely your superiors. If that mode of proceeding is adopted by the congress, many, very many friends will sink,—they will desert your cause from despondency. At present (as I am assured and as I verily believe), could the voices of this nation be collected by any fair method, twenty to one would be in favour of the Americans. You wonder and say, 'Then whence is it that they do not exert themselves?' One American phrase will give you the true reason. The people are 'cowed' by oppression. It is amazing,—it is incredible how much this is the case. Corruption, baseness, fraud, exorbitant oppression never so abounded as in this island. And will you believe me when I say, that Englishmen,—that boasted race of freemen,—are sunk in abject submission.

"From Parliament, therefore, expect no favour, but what proceeds from fear,—from the people here, expect no aid. It is yourselves, it is yourselves must save you; *and you are equal to the task.* Your friends know this, and your very enemies acknowledge it. But they believe you are as corrupt and as corruptible as themselves; and as destitute of union, spirit, and perseverance, as the friends of freedom are in this country. For your country's sake, depend not upon commercial plans alone for your safety. The manufacturers begin to feel,—they know, they acknowledge, they must feel severely; and if you persevere, they must be ruined. But what are these men,—what are the body of this people? *The servants of their masters.* How easy it is for the ministry to frown or flatter them into silence. How easy to take the spoils of the nation, and, for a season, fill the mouths of the clamorous. It is true, your perseverance will occasion, in time, that hunger which will break through stone walls. But how difficult is it, how impracticable is it, for *mere commercial virtue* (if indeed it have any existence) to persevere. I repeat, therefore,—depend not upon this scheme for your deliverance. I do not say renounce it,—I say continue it; but look towards it in vast subordination to those noble, generous, and glorious exertions which *alone* can save you. Before I came among this people, the friends of liberty desponded; because they believed the Americans would give up.

They saw the irretrievable ruin of the whole cause, lost in that fatal yielding. I feel no despondence myself,—I am sanguine my country must prevail. I feel the ardour of an American; —I have lighted up the countenances of many; —I am speaking conviction every day to more. In short, I am infected with an enthusiasm which I know to be contagious. Whether I have caught or spread the infection here, is no matter needful to determine.

"*November* 27*th*.

"Since writing the above I have spent three hours in private conversation with Governor Pownall. He confirmed me that the people of Boston are not mistaken in the man whom they have most reason to curse of all others. I have his very words down in my journal, but they are too many here to transcribe.

"Tomorrow I am to see Lord Chatham. In the afternoon I am to dine with Lady Huntingdon. On Tuesday I am to go to the House of Lords, at the opening of Parliament, and on the same day shall converse with Sir George Saville. My whole time is dedicated to the common cause. My heart and soul are engaged in it.

"Be careful what parts of this letter you publish; without absolute necessity, do not publish any. Dr Franklin and others complain much of their letters being made public. It is a fear of that, that prevents him and many more from writing to you.

"Dr Franklin is an American in heart and soul. You may trust him;—his ideas are not contracted within the narrow limits of exemption from taxes, but are extended upon the broad scale of total emancipation. He is explicit and bold upon the subject, and his hopes are as sanguine as my own, of the triumph of liberty in America. It would entertain you, if I could spare time to relate all that is said of me and my designs; but I have no leisure for amusements of this kind.

Not a line yet from America;—judge of my impatience to hear of your welfare. Collect all the intelligence possible, and transmit accounts by every conveyance. This is my sixth letter. My last went enclosed to Mr Mason;—this I shall convey to Mr Benjamin Clarke, but without signature. Don't forget to pay the postage to him. I have not time to correct or peruse this letter. Adieu! The support and blessing of heaven be with you, and

"Your assured friend.

"P. S. You are desired to let no part of this letter be printed, but what Mr Phillips shall advise to. You may communicate a sight of it to all candid friends, and if it should fortunately happen that a whole circle should be present, desire them to let one of the company sit down, and in their presence give me their joint sentiments and counsels.

"I yesterday heard two eminent bankers and three very wealthy merchants say,—that as soon as America shall free herself from the tyranny of this country, they would take their all and remove to New England; and they affirmed that they knew many more resolved to do the same.

"In the last ships there sailed for Pennsylvania, under the auspices of the great Dr Franklin, two very wealthy farmers, from the county of Norfolk, with their families to settle. If these should succeed, hundreds will follow from that fertile county, which contains the best husbandmen on the island."

JOURNAL CONTINUED.

"November 28, 1774. Went to Westminster Hall and heard Lord Chief Justice Mansfield deliver the opinion of the court, in Campbell's case of the $4\frac{1}{2}$ per cent. duty. He was perspicuous and eloquent. Dined with Mr Keen, and spent the afternoon and evening with Lady Huntingdon.

"November 29th. Went to the House of Peers, saw the grand procession of the king, his reception of the new house of commons, in his robes and diadem, surrounded with his nobles and great officers. I was not awe-struck by the pomp. 'The trappings of a monarchy will set up a commonwealth,' (John Milton, Robert Howard.)

"Went to Drury Lane Theatre; saw Garrick in the 'Beaux' Stratagem.' He is a most surprising actor.

"November 30th. Went to the House of Peers; got to the foot of the throne, and saw the formality of presenting a new speaker by the Commons. Heard the king deliver his speech from the throne. Heard the Bishop of Litchfield and Coventry read prayers, as most bishops do—* * * Spent the afternoon and evening with Mr Pearson and his friends.

"December 1st. Dined with Mr Rogers of the treasury, in company with a commissioner of the treasury, two members of Parliament, and others. Went at six o'clock with Dr Franklin to the seat of Samuel Vaughan Esq. at Wanstead, where we spent our time very happily till Saturday night.

"December 4th. Dined with Sheriff Lee, and Mr Arthur Lee.

"December 5th. Breakfasted with Sir George Saville, in company with Mr Hartley, a member of Parliament, and had two hours' conversation on American affairs. Dined with Colonel Boyd at the Edinburgh coffee-house.

"The exertion of my lungs for a number of days past has brought on my raising of blood again.

"December 6th. About 10 this morning Mr Commissioner Morris waited on me, and staid an hour and a half. His conversation was much on the propriety of my laying down some line of conduct to which the colonies would accede, and by which the present controversy might be amicably adjusted. He urged much my waiting *again* upon Lord North and Lord Dartmouth, and insisted upon the propriety and expediency of this step. I thought I could discern the origin and drift of this curious discourse. He also in the course of conversation said, ' Mr Quincy, you can have no idea of the taxes of this kingdom, and the distress of our poor. I do not mean our manufacturers, but our hedgers, ditchers, and threshers. They have not now their twelve pence, ten pence, or eight pence a day, but they are glad to get six pence a day for their labour, and may be once a week they may have a little kind of something given them by way of charity, for dinner. They are extremely poor, and wretched indeed; every thing here is taxed to the utmost. The colonies must relieve us. They must ease us of our taxes,' &c. &c. He also affirmed to me that Governors Hutchinson and Bernard were principally attended to, in the late measures against the colonies. But he added, that government had found that many things had turned out different from Mr Hutchinson's representation, and that things had not been at all conformable to what he foretold.

" December 7th. Mr Inspector Williams called on me this morning, and again renewed to me his assurances that Governor Hutchinson was the sole cause and presser-on of the measures against Boston and all America. ' It is his advice that dictated the steps of administration, and it is his present opinion and assurances that keep up the spirits and measures of the ministry,' were his very words.

"Wrote a long political letter to Mrs Quincy."

"*London, December* 7, 1774.
"My very dear Friend,
"There never was a time in which I wished more ' to speak without a tongue,' and ' to be heard without ears:' then, as Shakspeare expresses it, ' in despite of broad-eyed, watchful day,' ' I would into thy bosom pour my thoughts.' This kingdom never saw a time in which the minds of all ranks were more upon the rack with expectation; and when I tell you that yesterday in the coffee-room adjoining the House of Commons, one of the ministerial members offered to lay a wager of seventy-five guineas to twenty-five, THAT BOSTON WAS NOW IN ASHES,—you will not think my own bosom free from anxiety! It is now more than two months since any advices have been received from America, of the state of things in your province. The subalterns of the ministry give out that the most peremptory orders went to General Gage last October, to proceed to extremities, with vigour; they therefore vapour with

much vaunting upon the expectation of hearing, in a few days, that you are all subdued, and in deep humiliation. Should the reverse of this prove true, as God grant it may! your enemies will sink, and sink forever. Let me here tell you a great truth. The people of this country have too generally got an idea that Americans are all cowards and poltrons. This sentiment is propagated and diffused with great industry and success.

"Now it is agreed on all hands, that your courage—your courage, I repeat it—will be brought to the test. Should it prove answerable to your ostentations,—worthy your ancestors, your friends will amazingly increase. Your hearty friends will be in raptures, and your very enemies will applaud you. I could easily explain to you the reason of all this, but I must leave you to consider of that yourselves. Read the paragraph again, and make your own reflections.

"Will you believe me, when I tell you, that your letting a certain character escape from your justice is imputed to you on all hands as a fault. Your enemies impute it to your cowardice; your friends to your want of political sagacity. Certain it is, that from one man,—from one man, I say, and he neither a Bute, a Mansfield, a North, or a Bernard, are all your miseries supposed to flow. This supposition is not made by those alone who are sanguine in your common cause; it is the general sentiment of all parties, and were I to show you my journal, in which I enter the sentiments and expressions of those with whom from time to time I converse, you would find unexpected characters, intimating, or speaking out, the same idea. ' It was his advice that dictated the steps of administration, and it is his present opinion and assurances, that keep up the spirits and measures of the ministry,'—were the very words uttered to me, not twenty minutes ago, by a gentleman in office in the customs. I should take a satisfaction in naming to you those who are my informants; but a fear lest your indiscretion in publishing what I write, should discover the author of your intelligence, denies me that indulgence. Remember, in whatever you publish, to beware you do not print any thing that may betray the writer. Not that I am conscious of any wrong, but I am here surrounded by great villains, who have will and power to injure, but want a pretext.

" Apropos,—this leads me to speak of your friend, Mr Quincy, who lately arrived in this city.

In the House of Lords, last week, when the address to the king was in debate, Lord Hillsborough said, that 'there were then *men* walking in the streets of London, who ought to be in Newgate, or at Tyburn.' Upon which the Duke of Richmond rose and said, that 'he was surprised that his Lordship should cast such a heavy reflection on his Majesty's ministers, by suggesting a matter, which, if true, proved they were guilty of a gross neglect of duty,' and called upon his Lordship for an explanation of whom, and what, he meant. Upon which Lord Hillsborough rose, and pointed out, though not by name, yet so as every body knew whom he meant,—Dr Franklin and Mr Quincy. The latter gentleman he mentioned as *author* of a late publication, called 'Observations on the Boston Port Bill and Standing Armies.'

"The character of your Mr Samuel Adams runs very high here. I find many who consider him the first politician in the world. I have found more reason every day to convince me that he has been right, when others supposed him wrong.

"But why should we spend time in looking back. *Look forward!* God grant you penetration that you may see the great duties which lie before you. May you have fortitude to suffer,—courage to encounter,—activity and perseverance to press forward.

"Prepare, prepare, I say, *for the worst.* I fear your delays have been your ruin. I know that your energies may already, or in future, bring upon you many and great calamities; but I am, from my own observation, and the judgment of very many others, most sure, that your forbearance, your delays, your indecision,—in short, what your enemies call your 'arrant cowardice' —hath brought or will bring upon you many more, and greater evils.

"These are important truths. Weigh, commune, consider, and act, as becomes your former professions, and your highest duty.

"You see my heart gets the better of my head; my feelings rise paramount to my discretion. Thus it will always be with those who are warm in the cause of their country,—their zeal banishes caution;—you see however I still retain some discretion, but even that I had rather lose than be 'unpregnant of my cause, or lack gall to make oppression bitter.' God knows whether this letter will ever reach you; were I sure it would, I should write a volume.

"I have lately written largely to you on political matters. Tell me what my enemies write of me from this side the water; write me what my friends think of me on your side the ocean.

"My whole time is taken up in my *duty*. I never was more busy. I never was more talkative. I wrote you fully relative to my health in former letters;—I have as yet had no symptom of taking cold since I have been in London, but incessant application,—incessant talking with several members of Parliament, and others, these four days past, has brought on a little fever, and some raising of blood. But otherwise I was never better in my life,—certainly I never was in better spirits. Do not be concerned about this circumstance. I would not have mentioned it but in fidelity to one, from whom I cannot conceal any thing which concerns my welfare.

"I am urged by Dr Franklin to go down with him and spend Christmas with the Bishop of St Asaph. I have not yet given my answer. On Friday I expect to see Lord Shelburne, and have very lately conversed several hours with Sir George Saville.

"You must know that many of your friends here in both houses will not take a decisive part, till they see how you act in America. For should they take a determined part now, in favour of that country, and in a short time America should give back, their hopes of rise into power and office (which is the hope of all British statesmen) would be forever at an end. Therefore, till the colonists discover that union and spirit, which all parties here agree must force success, you are not to expect any great exertions in your favour. But when once there is a conviction that the Americans are in earnest,—that they are resolved to endure all hazards with a spirit worthy the prize for which they contend, then, and not till then, will you have many firm, active, persevering, and powerful friends, in both houses of Parliament. For, let me again tell you, that strange as it may seem, there is great doubt here among many, whether you are *really in earnest*, in the full force and extent of those words. I am called out. Peace be with you. Salute my friends, and remember, in ancient love,

" Your most affectionate and fast friend.*

---

* This letter, in which Mr Quincy speaks of himself, as of another person, like many others written to his wife

"*London, December* 7, 1774.

" My dear Wife,

"You will form a poor idea of my feelings for you, and for my country, if you do not consider that I have had no tidings of you since I sailed. Not only my breast, but the breasts of ministers and kings,—nations and empires, are big with expectations of American events. That ' tide' —— but I forbear.

" I this day wrote you very largely, and prior to that again very full. These letters were signed with a new political signature. The chief design of my now writing is to let you know this, by sending the present letter by some other ship. I would have transcribed my letters, but have not time to write duplicates, and I have yet found nobody whom I dare trust to copy for me.

" My whole heart is with you ; my whole time is employed in endeavouring to serve my country. It is now three weeks since I came to this city ; yet I have never dedicated but two evenings to the entertainments of the town; and although

---

from England, was with an assumed signature; in consequence of the danger, to which correspondence with Boston was at that period exposed.

Garrick has acted four nights, I have seen him but once. You will wonder how I spend my nights and days in serving my country; but in one word I find every body eager to hear, most people willing to be set aright, and almost all grossly ignorant of the American world. I have been taught to believe that I have spoken conviction to many sensible minds. My friends are many, my spirits excellent, and my health as I mentioned in my last. Make it your business to inquire out the December packet, and do not rest till you get the letters I sent by it.

"Believe me, I know not when to leave writing, and were I sure of a safe conveyance, I should write a volume. My heart feels for you all very exquisitely when I think of you, which is eighteen hours out of the twenty-four.

"Adieu, my best friend.

"Give me the earliest intelligence of the dates of those letters which you receive."

JOURNAL CONTINUED.

"December 8th. Spent the day and night at Mr Thornton's elegant seat at Clapham.

" December 9th. Returned from Mr Thornton's, dined at home, and spent the afternoon and evening with Dr Franklin alone.

" December 10th. Dined with Mr Allyne, an eminent counsellor at law, and spent the evening with him, Dr Franklin, Messrs Lees, Galloway (a member of Parliament), and others.

" December 11th. Spent the day and evening at books.

" December 12th. At the desire of Lord Shelburne (transmitted by Dr Price) I waited on his Lordship, and spent two hours in conversation on American affairs. His Lordship appeared a very warm friend to the Americans, approved much of their conduct and spirit, and said if they continued united they must have all they ask. He said the ministry would not be able to carry on a civil war against America; that they began to hesitate and would be obliged to give way.

" His Lordship confirmed my former intelligence of Governor Hutchinson's assiduity, assurance, and influence, but in the end observed that the eyes of the nation and ministry must soon be opened. He particularly said that Lord Mansfield, last session, assured the House of Lords, that the plan they had laid would go down in America, *sine clade;* and affirmed that he had the best intelligence what might be carried through there. Lord Shelburne intimated that he had no doubt Lord Mansfield's opinion was grounded on Governor Hutchinson's information. I had before had a very similar account of Lord Mansfield's declarations in the House, from Mr Counsellor Allyne and Mr Arthur Lee.

" Went to Drury Lane theatre, and saw Garrick in Hamlet. He is certainly the prince of players; but also, most certainly, not without his faults as an orator. Received letters from W. Phillips Esq., and Mrs Quincy.

" December 13th. Dined with Mr Hollis, brother to the late benefactor of Harvard College, with a large circle of friends to liberty, and spent the evening with Dr Franklin.

" 14th. Wrote to Mrs Quincy.

" *London, December* 14, 1774.
" My dear Friend,
" I have lately written to you, by the packet, two very long letters, and, by some other ships, three or four more, upon politics. I therefore shall

not now resume the subject, any farther than to say,—*Be true to yourselves.*

"There is not a sensible man of either party here, but acknowledges your ability to save your country, if you have but union, courage, and perseverance. But your enemies pretend to be sanguine, that your avarice of commercial riches will dissolve your union and mutual confidence, that your boasted courage is but vapour, and that your perseverance will be as the morning cloud.

"Let me tell you one very serious truth, in which we are all agreed, *your countrymen must seal their cause with their blood.* You know how often, and how long ago I said this. I see every day more and more reason to confirm my opinion. I every day find characters dignified by science, rank, and station, of the same sentiment. Lord —————— said to me yesterday,—'It is idle, it is idle, Mr ——————; this country will never carry on a civil war against America, we cannot, but the ministry hope to carry all by a single stroke.' I should be glad to name the Lord, but think it not best. Surely my countrymen will recollect the words I held to them this time twelvemonth. 'It is not, Mr Moderator, the spirit that vapours within these walls that must stand us in stead. The exertions of this day will call forth events which will make a very different spirit necessary for our salvation. Look to the end. Whoever supposes that shouts and hosannas will terminate the trials of the day, entertains a childish fancy. We must be grossly ignorant of the importance and value of the prize for which we contend;—we must be equally ignorant of the powers of those who have combined against us;—we must be blind to that malice, inveteracy, and insatiable revenge, which actuate our enemies, public and private, abroad and in our bosom, to hope we shall end this controversy without the sharpest—the sharpest conflicts; to flatter ourselves that popular resolves, popular harangues, popular acclamations, and popular vapour, will vanquish our foes. Let us consider the issue. Let us look to the end. Let us weigh and consider, before we advance to those measures which must bring on the most trying and terrible struggle, this country ever saw.'

" Hundreds, I believe, will call these words, and many more of the same import, to remembrance. Hundreds, who heretofore doubted, are long ere this convinced I was right. The popular sentiments of the day prevailed; they advanced with ' resolutions ' to hazard and abide the consequences. They must now stand the issue,—they must preserve a consistency of character,—THEY MUST NOT DELAY,—they must ———————— or be trodden into the vilest vassalage, the scorn, the spurn of their enemies, a by-word of infamy among all men.

"In the sight of God, and all just men, the cause is good;—we have the wishes of the wise and humane, we have the prayers of the pious, and the universal benison of all who seek to God for direction, aid, and blessing. I own I feel for the miseries of my country; I own I feel much desire for the happiness of my brethren in trouble; but why should I disguise, I feel, ineffably, for the honour,—the honour, I repeat it,—the honour of my country. Need I explain myself farther? When you shall act agreeably to your past ostentations, when you have shown that you are, what Englishmen once were,—whether successful or not, your foes will diminish, your friends amazingly increase, and you will be happy in the peaceful enjoyment of your inheritance; or at least, your enemies will, in some measure, stay their intemperate fury from a reverence of your virtue, and a fear of reanimating your courage. But if in the trial, you prove, as your enemies say, arrant poltrons and cowards, how ineffably contemptible will you appear; how wantonly and superlatively will you be abused and insulted by your triumphing oppressors!

"Will you believe it? I took up my pen with a design only of saying that the mail for the December packet was staid from Wednesday to Saturday, for no apparent reason, because Parliament had not the affairs of America under consideration; therefore it is generally believed that it was to inspect all letters. If so, two of mine are in the hands of the ministry. I have received your letter of the 17th of October, and your father's of the same date. Lord North has, I hear, given out that I have my price. Tell my father that Dr Franklin is my great friend and daily companion.

"Adieu."

JOURNAL CONTINUED.

"December 14th. Spent the evening with Mr Sayre, in company with Dr Franklin and others. In the course of conversation Dr Franklin said, that more than sixteen years ago, long before any dispute with America, the present Lord Camden, then Mr Pratt, said to him, 'For all what you Americans say of your loyalty, and all that, I know you will one day throw off your dependence on this country; and notwithstanding your boasted affection for it, you will set up for independence.' Dr Franklin said, that he assured him no such idea was entertained by the Americans, nor will any such ever enter their heads, unless you grossly abuse them. 'Very true,' replied Mr Pratt, 'that is one of the main causes I see will happen, and will produce the event.'

"December 15th. Breakfasted with Sir George Saville, and spent three hours with him, and two other members of Parliament.

"Dined with Mr Towgood, with a large circle of warm friends to America.

"December 16th. Attended the House of Commons, and heard a debate on American affairs. Heard Lord North explain what he meant, when he said, 'he would have America at his feet.' Heard also Lord Clare, Governor Johnson, Mr Rigby, Charles Fox, Mr Hartley, Mr Cruger (his first essay), and others, in the course of the debate.

"Supped, at the request of Alderman Oliver, with Mr Rose Fuller,* and several members of

---

* Mr Rose Fuller.—See Burke's speech on "Conciliation with America," page 3.

Parliament, at the King's Arms tavern, where I spent the evening in conversation on political subjects, affecting the colonies.

" N. B. Mr Rose Fuller told me his late election cost him ten thousand pounds sterling, and more!

" Wrote a letter to Mrs Quincy.

"*London, December* 16, 1774.
" My very dear Friend,
" Permit me to congratulate my countrymen on the integrity and wisdom with which the congress have conducted. Their policy, spirit, and union have confounded their foes, and inspired their friends. All parties agree in giving them a tribute of honor and applause. I have this moment attended a desultory, despicable, because trifling, debate, in the House of Commons, relative to America. My Lord North apologized for, and endeavoured to explain away, his expression, ' I will have America at my feet.' The important questions relative to America will not be agitated till after the holidays are over. There is great talk, and much hope and fear about you, and your friends seem to intend pressing a suspension for

three years, of all acts made since 1764 relative to the colonies. Your stanch friends say, ' If they are unjust, repeal them; we then shall treat with you as friends. At all hazards recall your troops, for we will not treat with the sword at our breast.'

" Be the event as it may, continue true to yourselves, and the day is your own. If they only suspend—do not, for heaven's sake, think of relaxing your agreements, while you are treating. Beware of the arts of negotiation ; the ministry are adepts in them ; at least they are skilled in the science of corruption. By the way, there is no doubt but the ministry sent large sums to New York, in order to bribe the continental delegates. It was openly avowed and vindicated, and great boast was made of ministerial success. It was said that they had effected a disunion which would be fatal to the cause of all America. You cannot well imagine the chagrin with which the ministry received the result of that glorious body. They are viewed as the northern constellation of glorious worthies, illuminating and warming the new world. I feel a pride in being an American. Neither my affection nor zeal, in any degree, abates in the cause of my injured country. I have just supped, and spent the evening with a circle of about a dozen influential members of the House of Commons. But whether I see them in the house, or out of it, they appear * * * * * * not fit to represent the inhabitants of North America.

" I should be glad to be informed, whether, in case a suspension of the acts takes place, my friends would choose my continuance on this side the water. If they choose me to be with them, I will repair to my standard, when they shall command.

" The watchmen remind me that it is morning.
* * * * * * * * *
" Yours.

" Dr Price desires his very warm thanks to Dr Winthrop for his letter, which has been read in Parliament, and did much good. Dr Winthrop's name was concealed. Dr Price says, Dr Chauncy is in his debt. Few, if any, are better men than Dr Price."

JOURNAL CONTINUED.

"December 17th. Wrote to Mr McDougall at New York. Inclosed to him my two last letters. Received Mr Reed's letter from Philadelphia.

Spent the morning and afternoon in writing: and the evening with Dr Franklin, Arthur Lee, and Dr Bancroft. Wrote a very long letter to Joseph Reed Esq.

"December 18th. Spent the Sabbath at Islington, with Mr Bromfield.

"December 19th. Wrote a letter to Mrs Quincy and enclosed the rough draft of my letter to Joseph Reed Esq. of Philadelphia.

TO JOSPEH REED ESQ. PHILADELPHIA.

"*London, December* 17, 1774.

" Respected and dear Sir,

" Your favour of the 4th of November came to hand this moment, and to show my sense of the obligation without any delay, I transmit an answer with my thanks.

" The importance of a great cause, and the rising events of every day, demand a mutual and unremitting intercourse of intelligence, sentiments, and counsels, among the friends of America and mankind. Believe me, sir, there is a very culpable negligence in this regard on both sides the water; and I know of no excuse but what betrays a want of zeal, and a timidity, unworthy of men engaged in so glorious a contest.

"The information you give relative to the New York deputies was the least we expected. The ministry, it is confidently said, and universally believed, had beenlavish of monies in that quarter to foment discord. Nay, their setters and tools have made great vaunts of unexampled success with the great men of that city. Our coffee-houses were lately filled with scoffs at American virtue, and they boasted of success in creating a fatal disunion in our great sanhedrim, with a confidence that gained much credit. Did you but know the chagrin that took place on the arrival of the result of the congress, it would gratify your keenest sensations. Be assured that august body have done a lasting service to their country, and that they are paid the well earned tribute of honour and applause, even by their rankest enemies. They are considered as a constellation of the first worthies of our hemisphere: their influence is not confined to the circle of an American world, but they burn with a splendour, that illuminates and warms the continent of Europe. God grant, that many such glorious luminaries may shine in everlasting splendour, the honour and blessing of their country, and of mankind!

"Did the inhabitants of New York, and especially their delegates, know of what easy virtue they have been represented in this city, they would become patriots from indignation, if not from virtue.

"What greater blast could be thrown on the reputation, than to suggest that a little gold had made Americans sacrifice their country to the worst men, in the worst of times? But when you hear this suggestion extended to the elevated character of men appointed guardians of the people,—good God! how hateful the idea!

"Did our worthy brethren of New York know all that is daily said of them in this great world, and the confidence with which the tale is told, they would be singularly touched; they would be careful to have all party spirit cease, and let their conduct give the lie to their defamers. Sure I am, that the ministry have no where such sanguine hopes of a defection as from that quarter;—their influence is no where so forcibly extended, and it is certain they will be astonishingly disappointed if they do not find a sensibility to their touch. Our brethren of New York have an opportunity to display more virtue, and do more real service to the great cause of liberty, than perhaps any Americans, on that side of New England. But New England in my opinion is the great field for the first and most heroic virtues. Should administration be disappointed in exciting discord and defection in New York, they will sink with shame and despondency.

"There was last Friday, a little play in the House upon American subjects. I attended to see the actors, and was confirmed in nothing more, than that English players are no representatives of American heroes. However, this might be only the rehearsal, and at the exhibition soon after the holy-days, the actors may display their talents to more advantage. But brilliant as imagination can figure the splendid actors on this august theatre, I shall not substantially alter my opinion of the heroes of the drama.

"The ministry had never so difficult a task before,—they are plunged. The emotions of chagrin and resentment most conspicuously mark their countenance and conduct. The nation are viewing the present crisis, with equal anxiety as the Americans. All Europe have their eyes fixed on the important conflict.

"How elevated then must be the feelings of an American, who sees his counttymen distinguish themselves as wise and virtuous, calm and brave; rising in the estimation of all mankind, as the illustrious remnant of the sons of freedom. You see, my worthy friend, that the glitter of a court hath not yet fascinated me with its splendour,—nor the corruption of Britain made me an apostate from the cause of my country.

"The pageantry I see here makes me every day more attached to the simplicity of my native soil; and while I hourly survey the extended miseries of enormous wealth and power, I warm with more enthusiastic fervour in the cause of freedom and my country;—and in what cause ought the pulse of man to beat with a more full and genial current? If intemperance is at any time a venial fault, it must be when mighty oppressors, shielded with the forms of law, and defended by the arm of power, spread misery over a happy land, with wantonness and insult. But I desist from the contemplation of this hateful subject, lest the contagion of intemperance prove infectious to my friend.

"Lord North, on Friday last, had hard work to apologize for, and explain away, his vapouring expression,—'I will have America at my feet.' Lord Camden, in the House of Lords, on the day before, said, 'Were I an American, I would resist to the last drop of my blood.'"

"Let me tell you a great truth, which ought at this, and every future day, to have much weight and influence in America. Few men are more ill-disposed towards that continent, than those who are under the greatest obligations to it. Thus the commercial world, like the political, gives us striking instances of favourites of America, who have among them the most sanguine conspirators against her public happiness. Nay, some who ought to have America inscribed on their furniture and equipages, and gratitude to that country written on their hearts, have uttered the bitterest things against it, with licensed freedom and insidious industry. It is true they now are about calling a meeting to petition Parliament in favour of the colonies; but is an ideot at a loss to discern the motive? The manufacturers also are on the move. If Americans continue firm to themselves, they will not only have the honour and reward of emancipating themselves; but even a whole kingdom, roused by their example,— brought to feel, by American economy, and fired by a thousand wrongs, may, peradventure, be brought once more to think a little of those great subjects, national justice, freedom, and happiness.

"But by no means entertain an idea that commercial plans, founded on commercial principles, are to be engines of your freedom, or the security of your felicity. Far different are the weapons with which oppression is repelled; far more noble the sentiments and actions, which secure liberty and happiness to man.

"The friends of America in the House of Commons are now concerting a plan for carrying a suspension of all acts made since the year 1764 relative to America, for three years, in which time, it is said, both sides may cool, and they may then think seriously of negotiation and compromise. I think it was Hannibal who said, 'We treat with *arms* in our hands.' Now whether the weapons of our warfare be commercial, or martial, methinks we should not suddenly lay them down, lest we not only lose the use of them, but become so broken for want of daily discipline, as that we shall not easily embody again, in so united and formidable a band. Besides, the arts of negotiation are much better understood in Europe than America, and great statesmen sometimes pretend to negotiate, when they only mean to corrupt. The economy or religion of British ministers will not restrain them from an essay upon those

FAC SIMILE.

London Dec: 24th 1774

I look to my countrymen, with the feelings of one who verily believes they must yet seal their faith from Fanny to their liberties with blood. This is a distressing witness indeed! But hath not this ever been the lot of humanity?

Adieu my friend! My heart is with you whenever my countrymen commanded my person shall be else.

Jos. Quincy Jun.

To Joseph Reed Esq. Philadelphia.

colony virtues, which, should they prove of easy impression, might hazard mighty blessings.

"Let our countrymen therefore well consider how much a British ministry, as well as themselves, have at stake. No arms, no arts, no plots, or conspiracies will be thought unlawful weapons. Let them look all around them, and be on their guard at every point. The blessings of the wise, and the prayers of the pious, universally attend you; even throughout this nation.

"My dear sir, before I close, I cannot forbear telling you that I look to my countrymen with the feelings of one, who verily believes they must yet seal their faith and constancy to their liberties, with blood. This is a distressing witness indeed! But hath not this ever been the lot of humanity? Hath not blood and treasure in all ages been the price of civil liberty? Can Americans hope a reversal of the laws of our nature, and that the best of blessings will be obtained and secured without the sharpest trials?

"Adieu, my friend,—my heart is with you, and whenever my countrymen command, my person shall be also.

"Tell your worthy friend, Mr Dickinson, I flattered myself with hopes of his counsels while, in this world of trial. Tell that good man, George Clymer, if I did not love him too much, I should call him an apostate from his professions and promises. Believe me with great truth and equal esteem your affectionate friend.

" JOSIAH QUINCY JUN."

TO MRS QUINCY.

London, December 19, 1774.
" My very dear Friend,

" I have so much to do, that instead of writing to you, or any of my friends, I transmit the rough draft of my letter to Mr Reed. It contains all I wish to say to you at this time on political subjects.

" Gratitude, love, and affection fill my heart towards my country, and so many of my personal friends, that I must transmit my whole soul to them, before I can do justice to myself. Therefore, in one word, to all my friends say,—that I love, honour, and revere them as much as ever, that I am the same man as when I abode with them beyond the great waters.

" As to you, my dear friend, I trust that nothing will ever be more acceptable to you than to be assured that I am still the same. * * * * * * * * * * J. Q.

JOURNAL CONTINUED.

" December 19, 1774. Wrote a letter to Alexander McDougall of New York, enclosing to him my six last letters. Dined with colonel Boyd, in company with three members of Parliament, two or three of the bar, and several other gentlemen.

" Spent the evening with Dr Franklin. This evening received a letter from John Dickinson Esq. of Philadelphia.*

" December 20th. Wrote an answer to Mr Dickinson and sent it to Mr McDougall by the same conveyance.

" Dined with Mr Dilly, in a large circle of friends.

" December 21st. Spent the morning at home, —visited by Mr Hartley, member of Parliament. Dined at the Cecil coffee-house.

---

* See page 192.

"Spent the evening at Covent Garden theatre, where was presented 'Jane Shore,' and Milton's 'Masque of Comus.' Mr and Mrs Barry performed well;—Mrs Hartley better. 'Comus' was altered much for the worse, and no part was performed well, but the part by Miss Catley.

"December 22d. Breakfasted with Mr Hartley above named,—spent about two hours in conversation on American affairs, and afterwards a like space of time with Rose Fuller Esq., another member of the House. Spent the residue of the day and evening at the London coffee-house, with the Wednesday-night club of 'Friends to Liberty and Science.' A question was debated, by assignment, 'Whether capital punishments are, in any case, warrantable or right.'

"Mr Inspector Williams called on me, and assured me that Governor Hutchinson was a most inveterate and indefatigable enemy against me, with the ministry; and very broadly intimated that Lord Dartmouth and Lord North had both told him so.

"Received two letters of the 25th and 27th of October last, from my good friend Joseph Reed Esq. of Philadelphia.* Wrote to Mrs Quincy."

---

* See page 189.

"*London, December* 22, 1774.

"My very dear Friend,

"I have lately written to you so many letters, that there is less need of my now resuming the pen. But the ship by which I have written several letters being unexpectedly delayed, I embrace the opportunity of saying a few words more. I this day have spent six hours with four very influential members of the House of Commons. I have as yet heard or seen nothing to alter my sentiments of the duty of my countrymen, since I so fully wrote my opinion of the part they ought to act. But the facts which the before mentioned gentlemen assured me of, were, the infinite perplexities of the ministry, and the general commotion now beginning to take place among the merchants and manufacturers. Indeed if it was not for the treachery and base designs of certain merchants trading to the colonies, the manufacturers would long ago have been clamorous in your favour. I was shown two letters to two of the first manufacturing towns, written by their member now in Parliament, which I have his promise to give me a copy of in a few days. As soon as I receive these copies, I shall transmit them, and they will give you great insight into the commotions now beginning to take place. Only be men of common integrity and common sense, and you will do wonders. People here have no idea that any body of men can be virtuous,—but surely you have common sense, and if you have, pride will keep you from any infraction of your agreements.

"You see I write in so much haste, that I can only *hint* a sentiment; and must leave you to collect the full import of what, if I had time and leisure, I should be glad to say. But I should be glad that my friends would be deliberating, and corresponding upon what part to take, in case Parliament suspend all the acts enumerated by the Congress, or repeal the Tea Act and the three acts relative to the Massachusetts Bay and Boston.

"Your Parliamentary friends say, 'Snatch the opportunity for peace and reconciliation.' Your sanguine and warm partizans say, you 'are united and inspired *now;* circumstances that may never happen again.' Seize the glorious, happy opportunity, for establishing the freedom and social felicity of all America! 'There is a tide in the affairs of men.' God direct you!

* * * * *

JOURNAL CONTINUED.

"December 23d. Passed the evening with Dr Franklin.

"December 24th. Dined with Mr Vaughan, and went to Wanstead and kept Christmas.

"December 27th. Returned from Mr Vaughan's, and dined in company with a circle of friends at Mr Dilly's. This evening went to Cox's museum, which exhibits the most superb piece of mechanism in the world.

"December 28th. Visited by Governor Pownall, Mr Thornton, &c. &c. Spent the afternoon and evening in preparing for a tour to Bath, with Mr Arthur Lee and Mr Williams.

"December 29th. Set off with Mr Williams and Mr Arthur Lee for Bath.

"December 30th. Visited Dr Priestley at Calne, and was received very politely. Visited Lord Shelburne at his superb seat at Bow-wood. I was very much urged to spend the day and night by his Lordship, but declined the invitation, and proceeded to Bath, where I arrived at five o'clock, and then went to a grand ball at the lower rooms.

"December 31st. Visited the celebrated Mrs Macaulay;—delivered my letters to her, and was favoured with a conversation of about an hour and a half, in which I was much pleased with her good sense and liberal turn of mind.

" Was attended by Hon. J. Temple to see the Circus, the Crescent, and other places of public resort at Bath. Then I took a walk of about two hours, round at a distance from the town; where, on the hills encircling this splendid city, I had a most enchanting prospect.

" January 1, 1775. Had half an hour's conversation, at the pump-room, with the celebrated Col. Barré, on American affairs. Went to hear divine service performed at the Abbey church in this city. Went also to the several coffee-houses of public resort, where I had an opportunity of seeing much of the manners of people at Bath. Dined with Mr Temple, and spent the evening with him. Received a very polite billet from Mrs Macaulay to spend a few hours with her on the morrow, or Wednesday.

" January 2d. Was visited by the Hon. Mr Temple, who spent an hour with me. Went again over Bath, in order to review the buildings. Spent the afternoon with Mrs Macaulay, and went in the evening to a ball at the new rooms, which was full and very splendid. The rooms are very elegant, and the paintings which cover the windows, taken from the draughts of the figures found at the ruins of Herculaneum, have a fine effect. This evening I had two hours' conversation with Colonel Barré, and from him I learned that he was once the friend of Mr Hutchinson in opposition to Governor Pownall, but that he had for a long time, and especially since his last arrival in England, wholly deserted him. Col. Barré, while we were viewing the pictures taken from ruins found at Herculaneum, said, ' I hope you have not the books containing the draughts of those ruins with you.' I replied, there was one set, I believed, in the public library at our college. ' Keep them there,' said he, ' and they may be of some service as a matter of curiosity for the speculative, but let them get abroad, and you are ruined. They will infuse a taste for buildings and sculpture, and when a people get a taste for the fine arts, they are ruined. 'T is taste that ruins whole kingdoms ;—'t is taste that depopulates whole nations. I could not help weeping when I surveyed the ruins of Rome. All the remains of Roman grandeur are of works, which were finished when Rome and the spirit of Romans were no more,—unless I except the ruins of the Emilian baths. Mr Quincy, let your countrymen beware of taste in their buildings, equipage, and dress, as a deadly poison.'

" Col. Barré also added in the course of conversation, 'About fifteen years ago, I was through a considerable part of your country;—for in the expedition against Canada, my business called me to pass by land through Pennsylvania, New Jersey, New York, and Albany. When I returned again to this country, I was often speaking of America, and could not help speaking well of its climate, soil, and inhabitants; for you must know, sir, America was always a favourite with me; but will you believe it, sir, yet I assure you it is true, more than two thirds of this island at that time thought the Americans were all negroes!'

" I replied I did not in the least doubt it, for that if I was to judge by the late acts of Parliament, I should suppose that a majority of the people of Great Britain still thought so;—for I found that their representatives still treated them as such. He smiled, and the discourse dropped.—Col. Barré was among those who voted for the Boston Port Bill.

" January 3d. Agreeably to the polite invitation of Lord Shelburne, I took a post-chaise, and went from Bath to his lordship's magnificent seat at Bow-wood.

"I met Lord Shelburne walking alone, at a considerable distance from his mansion-house, and alighted to walk with him over his grounds. His lordship politely walked into the fields to show me several newly invented ploughs, and other like curiosities. He next called his shepherd, and we viewed his flock of a thousand sheep; and then proceeded to a place where were found many remains of Roman art; such as paved ways, gold and copper coins, medals, ruins of their baths, &c. &c. We then viewed the artificial lake, &c. &c. When we arrived at the house, we were regaled with a very sumptuous table and very fine wines. His lordship's two only children are very promising sons, the one about eleven, the other seven years of age. They are educated in the best manner, and seem very sprightly-geniuses. They took leave of the company, on departing for bed, with much grace and propriety. With his lordship I went over his splendid buildings, gardens, &c. &c. Every thing is great and truly noble; surpassing any idea that I can convey by my description.

" Lord Shelburne repeatedly assured me, he should take the tour of America with his two sons as soon as they were a little older. He seemed to be very much in earnest about the matter.

" January 4th. Although much pressed by Lord Shelburne to spend another night with him, I set off for Bath, after having taken a review of his lordship's fine paintings, library, &c. Lord Shelburne's politeness and hospitality deserve my gratitude and applause.

" Arrived at Bath towards evening, went to see Mr Temple, and afterwards concluded the evening by attending the lecture of the celebrated George Alexander Stevens.

" January 5th. Set off from Bath, and arrived at Bristol, about twelve o'clock. Went to view the exchange and other public edifices; after which I drank tea and spent the evening with Mr Joseph Waldo, who received me with much cordial hospitality.

" January 6th. Went over to Clifton, and viewed the celebrated grotto and water-works of Mr Goldney. The view from Clifton Hill is one of the finest I ever saw. Went to the Hot Wells, and drank the waters, and then returned through the Park to Bristol. Dined with Mr Waldo, and spent the evening in company with Mr Cruger, and Colonel Gorham, at the American coffee-house.

"January 7th. Went to view the several glass manufactories, and also a shalloon manufactory, in Bristol. Viewed also Radcliffe church, built by the Knights Templars, and its three famous paintings. After which I took another tour round this second commercial city in the kingdom. Wrote to John Dickinson Esq. Wrote to Mrs Quincy by Captain Caldwell, who engages to deliver my letter with his own hand.

TO MRS QUINCY.

"*Bristol, January* 7, 1775.

"My very dear Friend,

"The holy-days have been improved by me in visiting Bath, Bristol, and some manufacturing towns in the vicinity. Did Americans realize their commercial powers, spirit and obstinacy would characterize their future measures. Had the non-exportation agreement been appointed to commence on the first of March, Britain would ere this have been in popular convulsions. This is the sentiment even of adversaries.

" The manufacturing towns are now in motion, and petitions to Parliament to repeal the late acts on commercial principles, will flow from all quarters. London is setting the example, which this city and other manufacturing towns are preparing to follow.

" The commonalty of this kingdom are grossly ignorant; the tools of the ministry, for their reward, are incessantly retailing the same stale falsehoods, and the same weak reasonings every day. The consequences are easily conceived. The people of this country must be made to feel the importance of their American brethren. If the colonies have one spark of virtue, in less than a twelvemonth Britain must feel at every nerve. Believe me, the commonalty of America are statesmen, philosophers, and heroes, compared with the 'many' of Great Britain. With the former you may reason,—the latter you must drive. I have endeavoured to study the character of both countries; this sentiment is the result of my observations.

" I have lately read various letters from several inland manufacturers to their mercantile correspondents, and I find that the 'address' to the people of this country, hath wrought, and is still working wonders.

"Oh! my dear friend! my heart beats high in the cause of my country. Their safety, their honour, their *all* is at stake! I see America placed in that great 'tide in the affairs of men, which, taken at the flood, leads on to fortune.' Oh! snatch the glorious opportunity. Oh! for a 'warning voice,'—or our lives are bound in vassalage and misery.

"The ministry, I am well satisfied, are quite undetermined as to the course they must take with regard to America. They will put off the final resolutions to the last moment. I know not, and, any further than mere humanity dictates, *I care not*, what part they take. If my own countrymen deserve to be free—*they will be free.* If, born free, they are contented to be slaves, e'en let them bear their burdens.

"You must know that I am a perfect infidel, in matters of mercantile virtue. It will not therefore be sufficient, when we find a commercial apostate, to mouth 'perdition catch the villain.' The patience, the lenity, the humanity of Americans towards public conspirators and public traitors, hath been the source of infinite mischief. From this circumstance our friends have become despondent, and our foes have taken courage. I have a thousand things to say, which I would wish to 'speak without a tongue, and to be heard without ears.' For this reason therefore, if the three acts relative to the Massachusetts Bay are not repealed, I intend to be in Philadelphia, in May next.

"I am sure, if you knew all that I could tell you, it would strengthen your hands, and inspire your hearts. I have this day written very similar sentiments to my friend, Mr Dickinson, at Philadelphia. You will perceive part of this letter copied by my friend Williams, from mine, to that great and good man. We are both now writing in the midst of a coffee-house, surrounded by the intolerable racket of dice boxes, and the noise of party cabal. If therefore you make public any part of this letter, print that which relates to the cause of my transcribing part of my letter to Mr Dickinson, which will carry an apology to that gentleman, who may otherwise be displeased at seeing the same sentiments to different persons.

"Last Tuesday and Wednesday I spent with Lord Shelburne at his magnificent seat at Bowwood. His politeness would have prevailed with me to stay a few days longer, if my other engagements had permitted that indulgence.

" Once, since I arrived, I raised a small quantity of blood; owing to some exertions of my lungs that brought on that old disorder. Since that time I have had no symptom of it, and at this time, and indeed ever since I have been in Britain, I never enjoyed greater health and spirits. This climate undoubtedly agrees with me much better than my own. Neither colds nor fevers have molested me, since sojourning in this land of my fathers.

" Captain Caldwell, who engages to deliver this with his own hand, calls on me to finish.

" Adieu! The blessings of my heart rest upon you.

"J. Q.

" Let our friend, Samuel Adams, be among the first to whom you show my letters."

TO MRS QUINCY.

London, January 11, 1775.

" My very dear Friend,

" Last night I returned from Bath and Bristol, where I have been to spend a few of the holy-days. From the last of these places I wrote to my friend Mr Dickinson, and yourself. The letter to you, together with several others, the captain engaged to deliver with his own hand. Last evening I was regaled with yours of the 3d and 14th of November;—James Lovell's of the 10th, 25th, and 28th of October;—Dr Chauncy's of the 21st of October, and 3d of November, and Oliver Wendell's of the 15th of November. To all these, my remembering friends, present my acknowledgments and thanks. Inform them I shall write answers, if the time limited for the sailing of this vessel is extended.

" Since writing the above, I have received another letter from Dr Chauncy of the 4th of November, but have not yet received the two pamphlets. Let him be the first to whom you transmit this letter. I have also received a very useful letter from my friend, Nathaniel Appleton; let him be the next.

" If the many letters I have sent, come safe to your hands, my friends will see that I am neither less idle nor less earnest in the cause, than when I sojourned with them beyond Jordan. My avocations are so many and incessant, that I find but little time which I cannot employ more to the service of my country by attending to men and things here, than by writing my sentiments to those on the other side of the water. That little time, whenever it does occur, is sacredly dedicated to my correspondence with my brethren in America, which is a substantial pleasure of my life.

" But let my friends in Boston and Massachusetts be reminded, that my literary connexions are extended through the southern colonies, and that therefore, when they think themselves forgotten or neglected, my time has been so wholly employed with occurrences here, or in transmitting advices to our southern friends, that I have been denied any opportunity of paying that tribute of gratitude, respect, and applause, that my Massachusetts friends may justly claim.

" As I have written to you very constantly and largely, upon the subject of our great concerns, I must entreat that those confidential friends to whom you may show my letters, would consider them as information sent the brotherhood in general; and in consequence, by way of return, favour me with their advice and counsels, for which, as I shall ever stand much in need, so I shall be accordingly grateful.

"The cause of the colonies every day grows more popular; that of the ministry, more desperate. The merchants are alarmed, the manufacturers are in motion, the artificers and handicraftsmen are in amaze, and the lower ranks of the community are suffering. Petitions are framing in all parts of the kingdom in favour of their own dear selves, and if America reap any advantage by this movement, be assured her tribute of gratitude is not due either to merchants or manufacturers. America might sink in bondage, and long drag the load of misery and shame, before either of these orders, as a body of men, would feel one generous sentiment, or make one feeble effort, unless their own immediate and obvious interest prompted the exertion. I say, *immediate* and *obvious*, for all know that if the distance is beyond their own nostrils, or clouded by any thing deeper than a cobweb shade, they will neither see nor understand. I speak here of the governing majority; individuals are among them who have knowledge, sentiment, and spirit; but Heaven knows, how little, how incredibly little, these noble qualities have influence here.

"There can be no doubt that the peaceful, spiritless, and self-denying warfare, in which the colonies are now engaged, would yield an ample victory; to be sure, not the most glorious or splendid of any on record, but the tinsel of splendour and the parade of glory may be dispensed with, if we can obtain the object of our wishes by attacks which are truly mock heroic, and weapons which are most certainly not spiritual.

" My great doubt is, whether frugal virtue is a quality deeply ingrafted in the human mind, and whether it contains a spirit sharp and active enough to cement and animate any large popular body, for any length of time.

" However, if my countrymen, after deliberating, are convinced, that they can sacredly keep the pure faith of economy; that they can follow the simplicity of their fathers, and what is more, can compel and keep to the ordinances of self-denial, their whole household, I will venture to assure them, that they shall obtain a bloodless victory, and be crowned with success.

" I am so certain of the truth of what I now say, and that my words are indeed the words of soberness, that I would put my life and my all on the hazard of the trial. These are not the hasty opinions of a moment; they are sentiments founded upon inquiry and reflection, and I am convinced of no one truth more strongly, and I have no one judgment in my own opinion better founded, than what is above transmitted.

"I am thus explicit, because you very well know that I not only wish the safety, but the glory of my country. I have heard its *valour* questioned, I have seen its *honour* touched; of that valour, I have an elevated idea; of that honour, I am jealous. As I wish therefore the peace, the welfare, and the bloodless deliverance of my native land, I hope to see my countrymen prudent, frugal, saving economists; but when I shall wish to see them great and glorious,

'I sure must view them in a *nobler* field!'

Permanent slavery, or a full deliverance from their present burdens, is the alternative now before America. No other country hath ever yet had any choice but that of the sword for their emancipation from bondage. America, favoured above the nations of antiquity, hath an alternative. If her children can withstand the blandishments of luxury, and the delusions of false pride, they may purchase liberty without its price; but if attachment to commercial leeks and onions, an idolatry equally degrading, and in the present case almost as impious as that of Egypt, have debauched the appetite and blinded all sense, they must soon make their election of the load of slavery, or the sword of blood.

"The ministry are evidently plunged. Every thing bears the mark of distraction. Bute and Mansfield are not less your enemies, and Hutchinson is still the same man. Lord Dartmouth is ———; but America can at this day want no information as to his character; when hypocrisy throws away her mask, credulity must renounce her faith. No measures are yet determined upon in the cabinet. Every thing will be done at the meeting of Parliament on the spur of the occasion.

"In the nation you have many friends and hearty well-wishers to your cause. The lords and commons are — *what they are;* but ANOTHER CHARACTER, is in principle your adversary, and will never be reconciled to your deliverance till he sees, what, peradventure, he will not wait long for, a spirit going forth, which compels rulers to their duty. I shall take care to keep you constantly informed of events as they rise. Very important ones must occur in a short time. The stanch friends of our country are here in high spirits. I should flatter your national vanity if I told you all that is said and thought of Americans at this day; but the sentiments of this people are as fluctuating, and sometimes as boisterous as the ocean.

"I find I shall have no time to write to the friends I mentioned above. Send them therefore this letter to peruse by way of apology. My best wishes attend you. Present me to my friends and relatives in the bonds of respect and love. In the same bonds continue to hold

"Yours, &c."

TO MRS QUINCY.

London, January 12, 1775.

"My very dear Friend,

"Yesterday I finished a long letter to you, which will accompany the present; by a considertion of both, my friends will see how difficult the task would be to write severally to them all. I have just come from spending three hours in private conversation with Governor Pownall; and without a moment's delay sit down to transmit some parts of what passed between us.

"After having given him some general account of my intelligence from America, he said, 'Now, sir, I will give you some news also. A king's ship has arrived from Boston with despatches from General Gage; she sailed the 16th of December from that place. She brings certain accounts that notwithstanding the non-importation agreement was to take place the first of December, yet since that day, by connivance, a considerable quantity of pimento, and other articles forbidden by that agreement, have been imported and stored in the city of New York.' I replied, 'I don't believe that what you have heard is true.' 'You may depend upon it, sir; I am satisfied of it, perfectly, myself,' was his answer.

"This matter ought to be inquired into. Do not entertain ill-grounded jealousies of each other, yet watch over one another for good.*

"'I will tell you more, Sir,' added Governor Pownall; 'the provincial congress have chosen

---

* The following letter from Alexander McDougall Esq. (afterwards General McDougall) will explain the state of things, which then existed in New York. The friends of liberty in that city had difficulties of a very peculiar character to encounter; which they met with a corresponding spirit and vigilance; as this letter evidences. In none of the other colonies had the patriots of the revolution so many and so powerful internal enemies to contend with as in this. Their situation, in this respect, exposed them to suspicions and mis-

their general officers; two of them are Colonel Preble and Colonel Pomeroy; I have forgot the third. They have also chosen a committee to

---

representations, which their subsequent sacrifices and exertions in the cause proved to be unfounded and unjust.

TO JOSIAH QUINCY JUN.

"*New York, April* 6, 1775.

" Dear Sir,

" Your favours of the 17th and 19th of December last, enclosing letters for the friends of the common cause in Boston and Philadelphia, arrived here the 10th ultimo, but they were not handed to me before the 25th, owing to their being in a package belonging to a gentleman who was absent when they arrived. Your directions respecting them were strictly observed, and they were forwarded the 27th by safe conveyances. I shall take great pleasure in transmitting your future communications to your friends.

"I wrote you by the March packet under cover to Mr Thomas Bromfield, in which I informed you of the progress then made by our House of Assembly on American grievances. The assurances I gave you, that what remained of the 'Report of the Committee of Grievances,' not then considered by the 'Committee of the House,' would rather be more in favour of liberty than the 'Report,' has since been confirmed; the particulars of which you have in the enclosed printed proceedings of the House. After the 'Statement of Griev-

manage the office of Governor, and another that of the Supreme Court of justice of the province.'

" I shall suspend a comment on this matter.

---

ances was agreed to, and approved of by the House, several of the members who were warm friends to the cause of liberty, having attended the Assembly two months, and their families being very remote from the capitol, and urgent business demanding their return, and considering the most important transactions of the sessions finished, went home. This gave an opportunity to the wicked and designing members of the House, contrary to all order, to *depart* from the spirit of the 'List of Grievances,' in a 'Petition to the King,' 'Memorial to the Lords,' and 'Remonstrance to the Commons.' But the 'Statement of Grievances' agreed to by the fullest House during the sessions must be considered as the basis of all their proceedings on the American controversy. If any regard is to be paid to the sense of the Legal Representatives, that sense is, the 'Statement of Grievances' agreed to in a *full House;* and therefore, whatever difference appears in the 'Petition,' &c., from that 'Statement of Grievances,' is a mere nullity. If the ministry make any dependence on the ' Petition,' &c., as declarative of the sense of this colony, they will find themselves most egregiously mistaken. This city will publicly disavow the vile, slavish sentiments, contained in the 'Petition,' &c., the moment they make their appearance. So far as they are now known, they are condemned, and the patrons of them despised. And if the Provincial Convention, who are to meet here on the 20th instant to elect Delegates for the continental congress, do not disavow the 'Petition,' &c.

"After a long conversation with him on the subjects which grew naturally out of our conversation, I asked him (he being now a member of

which I have reason to conclude they will, they will certainly join with the continental Congress in doing it.

"During the ship ——'s stay in our bay she was continually watched by a sub-committee, and did not enter. But while she lay at the Hook waiting for a fair wind, the night before she departed threatened a storm; and as the boat, on board of which the sub-committee attended, was not so well provided with ground tackling as the ship, the boat was obliged to go into a cove of safety, at some distance from the ship. The owners, who had some goods on board, having previously meditated a plan to land them, availed themselves of this opportunity, and effected it in the night. Of this they were suspected, and our sub-committee of observation, and the committee of Elizabeth Town, having got a clue to a discovery, the owners confessed the matter upon oath. Our citizens were so enraged at them for the horrid deed, that it was with great difficulty they were prevailed upon not to banish them. The fearful apprehensions of these persons and the terms on which they are suffered to abide here, are fully expressed in the printed papers which you have herewith. This is the only violation of the Association we have had since it took place. The punishment they now, and will endure, is sufficient to deter any man, however base, from another breach.

"The friends of the Association, and the great cause, are daily increasing; so that you have no reason to fear a defection of this colony. Time will not permit me to be more particular. I shall continue to enclose you all the printed

Parliament) what he thought the ministry would do at the approaching sessions.

"He answered, 'They will not repeal the Boston Port Bill, because it executes itself. They will not repeal the acts altering your form of government, because these late advices show that you have taken that matter out of their hands. They will not repeal the Quebec Bill, because it is the sense of all parties here, that that is a matter with which no other colony but Quebec hath any thing to do. If they do not complain, the other colonies have no right to intermeddle.'

"I replied to Governor Pownall, I wished I could be satisfied that what he now said would be true; 'It will ease my mind,' added I, ' and would determine my conduct, to sail to America in four-and-twenty hours. I should then be in

---

papers which I may judge of importance to you, regardless of the postage until you direct me to the contrary.

"I am, dear Sir, in great haste,
"But with great respect,
"Your humble servant,
"ALEXANDER MCDOUGALL.

"P. S. As my political character may tempt the tools of government to open letters to me, please to cover your favours to me to Samuel Broome & Co. merchants in New York."

no doubt what the colonies ought to do, and' (with a little elevation of voice) 'I am sure I should not hesitate what part to take myself.'

"'I tell you, Mr Quincy,' continued Governor Pownall, 'what I now say I do not deliver as what I am informed of by the ministry, but as what I have not the least doubt of; it is my solid judgment founded upon facts on which I have reflected, and laid together again and again.' My answer was, 'I have lately been in the western parts of this kingdom. I have conversed ever since I have been here, with all ranks of people who think or converse at all upon these subjects. I am a stranger in this country, I do not pretend to be thoroughly acquainted with their genius, temper, or character; but this I will venture to say, that if the actions of this country are as correspondent with the sense, words, and declarations of its inhabitants, as the words and doings of my American countrymen, I am sure this country will be convulsed,—I am sure there will be very astonishing commotions, if those acts are not repealed, and that very speedily too, after the Parliament have got well together. But, as I said before, I do not pretend to know this people as well as those who were bred, and have always dwelt among them. Indeed, I have been confirmed more and more every day, that the commonalty in this country are no more like the commonalty in America, than if they were two utterly distinct and unconnected people.'

"'Very true, Mr Quincy,' replied Governor Pownall; 'your observation is certainly just. You have formed a right judgment, and you will see more reason to strengthen your opinion every day you live in the island.'

"Governor Pownall presented me with two of his late productions, one to be sent to Dr Cooper, which I shall do, if I am able, by this opportunity. I have written you that I shall be in Philadelphia in May next, if the acts are not repealed. I have made that determination, because I think I shall be able to do some good there. In conversation we can say and do more than by whole folios of writing. But my being there at that time is so uncertain, that I would not upon any account have my friends omit sending their letters of intelligence to me here. Such letters are of amazing service; with them I can do more good than you would think possible if you had never experienced the effect.

"Adieu. May the great Father of spirits inspire you! Act worthy of yourselves, and you must be successful and happy.

"P. S. I intend to send you Burke's Speech published this day. It will be read in America with avidity and applause. I am well informed that Mr Hayley, on receiving a large parcel of letters from America without *one order* enclosed, merely said,—'I find there is not even an inclination in Boston to smuggle now.'

"A certain Mr ———, lately arrived from Boston, said, 'A few more troops will be sufficient to enforce all the measures of the ministry.'

"I have neither room nor time for comment."

TO MRS QUINCY.

London, January 12, 1775, *Twelve at night.*

"My very dear Friend,

"I have been all this day toiling for my oppressed country. I have just closed my advices to the southward. I should not now resume the pen, having written you very largely to-day and yesterday, had I not been just gratified with yours and my good friend James Lovell's favours of November and December. Yours, dated 18th of November and 9th of December; his, November 25th and December 7th. Thank him most heartily for his zeal and industry in the cause of his country, and his affection and good wishes for me. Show him my letters; tell him to consider them as addressed to him,—and *command* him to persevere in his way of well-doing.

"If you are satisfied that what you wrote me relative to the speeches of Major Paddock and ———— is really true, in fact, please to convey word to Major P——, and assure him in my name, that I have '*dared* to show my head in London;'—that I have *dared* to enter into the presence of Lord North and Lord Mansfield,—and what he may think more, on two days successively to stand before the throne of a king; literally within the reach of his royal sceptre, and the sword of justice; neither one nor the other dazzled or terrified me. Even the eloquence of a sovereign did not so confound my judgment, but that before the royal charm was over, I was able to recollect and remind a friend who stood near me, of the memorable saying of Henry Marten to

Edward Hyde ;—'*I do not think one man wise enough to govern us all.*'

" Nay, the splendour of royal robes, the pomp of state attendants, or the glitter of a diadem, never once so fascinated my understanding, or beguiled my heart, as that I did not realize the solemn and eternal truth, delivered by the illustrious Milton ;—' The trappings of a monarchy will set up a commonwealth.'

" You may tell —————, that I am not yet ' hanged,' and whether he or I shall first ' dangle on a gibbet,' is a matter altogether problematical. But whether he or I deserve it most, I am willing to submit to a jury of freeholders in his own vicinity ; and if he will move for sentence upon their verdict, I will agree not to move in arrest of judgment.

" Politics, you see, so wholly engross my time, that I have no time to write about those affections that are very deep in my heart. I know you will excuse the indulgence. Write by every possible way some little memorandum of the dates of letters received. It will gratify me much to hear of the safe arrival of any of my letters. * * * Tell my friends that my health and spirits still continue high. As to my sentiments and opinions, my integrity and firmness,—they must judge of those by my conduct.

"Yours &c.

"Do not think I forget my children because I do not speak of them. * * * * * * *

"*January* 13*th.* Since writing the above last night, Governor Pownall hath this morning called upon me, and, I having Mr Brand Hollis with me, he had only time to say,—' You will have terrible news from Boston soon; the matter is decided before this time!'

"This day Mr George Green informed me that Governor Hutchinson carried Messrs Blowers, Bliss, and Ingersol, the morning after their arrival, to Lord North. He also informed me that Mr —— had said in the coffee-house, that 'if administration did not enforce the present measures, it was all over with them.' Another person, lately from America, said, that 'a few more regiments would do the business.' Mr Inspector Williams also told me this moment, that he had seen Mr Peters's representation to the Privy Council, 'and it is,' added Mr Williams, ' the most bitter, abominable thing I ever saw ;—the bishops have taken it up, and the Connecticut charter will be snapped this session.' Mr Williams has promised to procure me a copy of the above paper, and if he does, I shall send it by this opportunity. I have every moment something I want to communicate. My attention is ever awake, and my time employed."

JOURNAL CONTINUED.

"January 13th. Received visits from Governor Pownall, Mr Brand Hollis, and others. Received letters from Mrs Quincy and my father. Wrote to Mrs Quincy, and to J. Lee Esq. Sent the above letters, as well as those of Sheriff Lee and Dr Baillie enclosed, by Captain Gordon, who sails in Col. Lee's employ.

TO MRS QUINCY.

London, January 14, 1775.

"My best Friend,

"I was this moment closing my advices to you, when I received from Mr Blowers your letter of October 15th, November 3d and 18th,— and my father's of November 3d. I am so fatigued with writing &c., that I *can write no more*. The person by whom I send this, goes in ten minutes. Thank my friends most heartily for their letters. Don't let them think I neglect their favours; they must consider my letters to you as addressed to them all. I am so hurried I have no other way. * * * * *

" I have acknowledged to you the receipt of all the letters I have received. I have told you all that I most wish you to know, excepting how much I am yours. * * * * * *

" My health was never better. I have as yet had no symptom of a seasoning."

JOURNAL CONTINUED.

" January 15th. Dined with Mr Edward Dilly.

" January 16th. Received Dr Warren's letter* of November 21, 1774, by Mr Williams Jun. Dined with Mr Brand Hollis, in company with Dr Priestley, Dr Franklin, Dr Price, and others.

" January 17th. Dined with Mrs Stevenson, with a number of ladies and gentlemen, in celebration of Dr Franklin's birthday, who made one of the festive company, although he this day enters the seventieth year of his age.

---

* See page 204.

" January 18th. Spent this day and evening at St James's in attending the celebration of the Queen's birthday at the drawing and ball room. The dresses were splendid and magnificent, much beyond any thing I had ever before seen. The Queen appears amiable and is very affable. The young Prince of Wales resembles his mother in countenance and air very much. The *Bishop* of Osnaburgh is a very handsome *boy*. The little princes are comely enough.

" January 19th. Attended the House of Commons and heard debates between North, Burke, and Mr Eden, &c. Spent the evening at the London coffee-house with Dr Franklin, Priestley, Price, Calder, and many others.

" January 20th. Attended the debates in the House of Lords. Good fortune gave me one of the best places for hearing, and taking a few minutes.

" Lord Chatham rose like Marcellus,—' *Viros supereminet omnes.*' He seemed to feel himself superior to those around him. His language, voice, and gesture were more pathetic, than I ever saw or heard before, at the bar or senate. He seemed like an old Roman senator, rising with the dignity of age, yet speaking with the fire of youth. The illustrious sage stretched forth his hand with the decent solemnity of a Paul, and rising with his subject, he smote his breast with the energy and grace of a Demosthenes.

"This great and astonishing character opened with some general observations on the importance and magnitude of the present American quarrel (as he called it). He enlarged upon the dangerous and ruinous events that were coming upon the nation in consequence of the present dispute, and the measures, already begun and now carrying on by His Majesty's ministers. He arraigned their conduct with great severity and freedom. He then proceeded—

"'My Lords, these papers from America, now laid by administration for the first time before your lordships, have been, to my knowledge, five or six weeks in the pocket of the minister. And notwithstanding the fate of this kingdom hangs upon the event of this great controversy, we are but this moment called to a consideration of this important subject. My Lords, I do not wish to look into one of these papers. I know their contents well enough already. I know that there is not a member in this house but is acquainted with their purport also. There ought therefore to be no delay in entering upon this matter. We ought to proceed to it immediately. We ought to seize the first moment to open the door of reconciliation. The Americans will never be in a temper or state to be reconciled—they ought not to be—till the troops are withdrawn. The troops are a perpetual irritation to these people; they are a bar to all confidence, and all cordial reconcilement. I therefore, my Lords, move, ' That an humble address be presented to His Majesty, most humbly to advise and beseech His Majesty, that in order to open the way towards an happy settlement of the dangerous troubles in America, by beginning to allay ferments and soften animosities there, and above all, for preventing in the mean time any sudden and fatal catastrophe at Boston, now suffering under the daily irritation of an army before their eyes, posted in their town, it may graciously please His Majesty that immediate orders may be despatched to General Gage for removing His Majesty's forces from the town of Boston, as soon as the rigour of the season, and other circumstances indispensable to the safety and accommodation of the said troops, may render the same practicable.

"' The way must be immediately opened for reconciliation. It will soon be too late. I know not who advised the present measures: I know not who advises to a perseverance and enforcement of them; but this I will say, that whoever advises them, ought to answer for it at his utmost peril.

" ' I know that no one will avow that he advised, or that he was the author of these measures; every one shrinks from the charge. But somebody has advised His Majesty to these measures, and if His Majesty continues to hear such evil counsellors, His Majesty will be undone. His Majesty may indeed wear his crown, but, the American jewel out of it, it will not be worth the wearing.

" ' What more shall I say? I must not say the king is betrayed; but this I will say, the nation is ruined. What foundation have we for our claims over America? What is our right to persist in such cruel and vindictive measures against that loyal, respectable people? They say, you have no right to tax them without their consent. They say truly. Representation and taxation must go together; they are inseparable. Yet there is scarcely a man in our streets, though so poor as scarcely to be able to get his daily bread, but thinks he is the legislator of America.

" ' "*Our American subjects*," is a common phrase in the mouths of the lowest orders of our citizens; but property, my Lords, is the sole and entire dominion of the owner : it excludes all the world besides the owner. None can intermeddle with it. It is a unity, a mathematical point. It is an atom ; untangible by any but the proprietor. Touch it, and the owner loses his whole property. The touch contaminates the whole mass, the whole property vanishes. The touch of another annihilates it ; for whatever is a man's own, is absolutely and exclusively his own.

" ' In the last Parliament, all was anger—all was rage. Administration did not consider what was practicable, but what was revenge. *Sine clade victoria* was the language of the ministry last sessions, but every body knew, an ideot might know, that such would not be the issue. But the ruin of the nation was a matter of no concern, if administration might be revenged. The Americans were abused, misrepresented, and traduced, in the most atrocious manner, in order to give a colour, and urge on the most precipitate, unjust, cruel, and vindictive measures that ever disgraced a nation.

" Gnossius hæc Rhadamanthus habet durissima regna;
Castigatque, auditque dolos."

" ' My Lords, the very infernal spirits—they chastise, *castigatque : sed auditque*—my Lords—the very spirits of the infernal regions *hear*, before they punish.

" ' But how have this respectable people behaved under all their grievances ? With unexampled patience, with unparalleled wisdom. They chose delegates by their free suffrages; no bribery, no corruption, no influence there, my Lords. Their representatives meet, with the sentiments and temper, and speak the sense of the continent. For genuine sagacity, for singular moderation, for solid wisdom, manly spirit, sublime sentiments, and simplicity of language, for every thing respectable and honourable, the congress of Philadelphia shine unrivalled. This wise people speak out. They do not hold the language of slaves; they tell you what they mean. They do not ask you to repeal your laws as a favour ; they claim it as a right—they demand it. They tell you they will not submit to them ; and I tell you, the acts must be repealed ; they will be repealed ; you cannot enforce them. The ministry are checkmated ; they have a move to make on the board ; yet not a move, but they are ruined.

"'Repeal, therefore, my Lords, I say. But bare repeal will not satisfy this enlightened and spirited people. What! repeal a bit of paper! repeal a piece of parchment! That alone will not do, my Lords. You must go through the work—you must declare you have no right to tax—then they may trust you ; then they will have some confidence in you.

"'I have heard a noble Lord speak, who seemed to lay some blame on General Gage. I think that honourable gentleman has behaved with great prudence and becoming caution. He has entrenched himself, and strengthened his fortifications. I do not know what he could do more. His situation puts me in mind of a similar transaction in the civil wars of France, when the great Condé, on one side, and Marshall Turenne, on the other, with large armies, lay many weeks very near each other. Turenne, conscious of the terrible consequences of victory to himself and country, though the armies were several days in sight of each other, never came to a battle. On his return to the court of France the Queen asked him, "Why, Marshall, I think you lay several days in sight of your enemy, and you might have been up with him at any time; pray why did you not take him?" The General very shrewdly replied, "Should I have taken him, please your majesty, I was afraid all Paris would have taken me." My Lords, there are three millions of whigs;—three millions of whigs, my Lords, with arms in their hands, are a very formidable body. It was the whigs, my Lords, that set His Majesty's royal ancestors on the throne of England. I hope, my Lords, there are yet double the number of whigs in England that there are in America. I hope the whigs of both countries will join, and make a common cause. Ireland is with the Americans to a man. The whigs of that country will, and those of this country ought to think the American cause their own. They are allied to each other in sentiment and interest, united in one great principle of defence and resistance, against tyranny and oppression. They ought therefore, and they will, run to embrace and support their brethren. The cause of ship-money was the cause of all the whigs of England. You shall not take my money, without my consent, is the doctrine and the language of whigs; it is the doctrine and voice of whigs in America, and whigs here. It is the doctrine, in support of which I do not know how many names I could—I may call in this

House,—among the living, I cannot say how many I could—to join with me, and maintain these doctrines with their blood;—but among the dead, I could raise an host innumerable! And, my Lords, at this day there are very many sound, substantial, honest whigs, who ought and who will consider this American controversy, as a great common cause.

"'My Lords, consistent with the preceding doctrines, and with what I ever have, and shall continue to maintain, I say, I shall oppose America whenever I see her aiming at throwing off the navigation act, and other regulatory acts of trade, made *bonâ fide* for that purpose, and wisely framed, and calculated for reciprocity of interest and the general extended welfare and security of the whole empire. It is suggested such is their design; I see no evidence of it. But to come at a certain knowledge of their sentiments and designs on this head, it would be proper first to do them justice. Treat them as subjects, before you treat them as aliens, rebels, and traitors.

"'My Lords, deeply impressed with the importance of taking some healing measures at this most alarming, distracted state of our affairs, though bowed down with a cruel disease, I have crawled to this House to give you my best counsel, and experience, and my advice is " to beseech His Majesty &c. &c." This is the best I can think of. It will convince America that you mean to try her cause in the spirit, and by the laws of freedom and fair inquiry, and not by codes of blood. How can she now trust you, with the bayonet at her breast? She has all the reason in the world now to believe you mean to her death or bondage. Thus entered on the threshold of this business, I will knock at your gates for justice without ceasing, unless inveterate infirmities stay my hand. My Lords, I pledge myself never to leave this business. I will pursue it to the end in every shape. I will never fail of my attendance on it at every step and period of this great matter, unless nailed down to my bed by the severity of disease. My Lords, there is no time to be lost; every moment is big with dangers. Nay, while I am now speaking, the decisive blow may be struck, and millions involved in the consequence. The very first drop of blood will make a wound, that will not easily be skinned over. Years, perhaps ages, may not heal it. It will be *immedicabile vulnus :* a wound of that rancorous, malignant, corroding, festering nature, that in all probability it will mortify the whole body. Let us then, my Lords, set to this business in earnest! not take it up by bits and scraps, as formerly, just as exigencies pressed, without any regard to general relations, connexions, and dependencies. I would not by any thing I have said, my Lords, be thought to encourage America to proceed beyond the right line. I reprobate all acts of violence by her mobility. But when her inherent constitutional rights are invaded, those rights she has an equitable claim to enjoy, by the fundamental laws of the English constitution, and which are engrafted thereon by the unalterable laws of nature; then I own myself an American, and feeling myself such, shall, to the verge of my life, vindicate those rights against all men who strive to trample upon or oppose them.'"

———

" It surpasses all description how such wisdom and such eloquence affected a right honourable and right *reverend* senate of modern Britain! But we may conjecture how such an union would have touched,—to what deeds it would have moved, and to what noble darings it would have inspired a senate of ancient Sparta, or an assembly of old Romans. Indeed, from the effects of this speech on the great audience without the bar, and from my own emotions and feelings, the miracles of ancient eloquence, the blaze of genius, and the burst of thought, with which Grecian and Roman orators have been said to work wonders in the senate and the field, no longer appeared fabulous.

" Lord Camden (undoubtedly the first common lawyer in England) spoke next on the side of America, and in support of the motion. He equalled Lord Chatham in every thing but that fire and pathos, which are the *forte* of his lordship. In learning, perspicuity, and pure eloquence, probably no one ever surpassed Lord Camden.

" His lordship opened briefly upon the nature of property, the right of taxation, and its inseparability from representation.

" ' My Lords, I will not enter into the large field of collateral reasoning applicable to the abstruse distinctions touching the omnipotence of Parliament. The declaratory law sealed my lips, and I have been silent. But this I will say, not only as a statesman, politician, and philosopher, but as a common lawyer,—my Lords, you have no right to tax America. I have searched the matter;—I repeat it, my Lords, you have no right to tax America;—the natural rights of man, and the immutable laws of nature, are all with that people. Much stress is laid upon the supreme legislative authority of Great Britain, and so far as the doctrine is directed to its proper object, I accede to it. But it is equally true, according to all approved writers on government, that no man, agreeably to the principles of natural or civil liberty, could be divested of any part of his property without his consent. Every thing has been staked on the single position that the authority of Parliament must be obeyed; but this general, unconditional, unlimited assertion, I am far from thinking applicable to every possible case that may arise in the turn of times. For my part, I imagine, that a power resulting from a trust arbitrarily exercised, may be lawfully resisted; whether the power is lodged in a collective body, or single person; in the few, or the many. However modified, makes no difference; whenever the trust is wrested to the injury of the people,— whenever oppression begins, all is unlawful and unjust; and resistance, of course, becomes lawful and right. But some lords tell us seriously that administration must reduce the Americans to obedience and submission; that is, you must make them absolute and infamous slaves, and then—what?—we will, say they, give them full liberty. Aye!—is this the nature of man? No, my Lords; I would not trust myself, American as I am, in this situation; I do not think I should, in that case, be myself for giving them their liberty. No, if they submitted to such unjust, such cruel, such degrading slavery,—I should think they were made for slaves, that servility was suited to their nature and genius. I should think they would best serve this country as their slaves,—that their servility would be for the benefit of Great Britain; and I should be for keeping such Cappadocians in a state of servitude, such as was suited to their constitution, and might redound much to our advantage.

"'My Lords,—some noble lords talk much of resistance to acts of Parliament. King, Lords, and Commons, are fine sounding names;—but, my Lords, acts of Parliament have been resisted in all ages. King, Lords, and Commons may become tyrants as well as others;—tyranny in one or more, is the same;—it is as lawful to resist the tyranny of many as of one. Somebody once asked the great Mr Selden in what law book, in what records, or archives of state, you might find the law for resisting tyranny. " I don't know," said Mr Selden, " whether it is worth your while to look deeply into the books upon this matter; but I'll tell you what is most certain, that it has always been the ' custom of England,' and the ' custom of England' is the law of the land."

" ' There is a gentleman, whom I need not name, his works are well received, and well known, who avoids stating any rules when resistance is lawful, and he lays down the revolution as the only precedent. He says, that the various circumstances, events, and incidents, that may justify, cannot be defined ; but the people at large will judge of their welfare and happiness, and act accordingly. The same writer says, that whenever a case, exactly similar in all its parts and circumstances occurs, when a case shall run upon all fours with that, then the law seems to be settled that resistance is lawful. I do not pretend to quote his words ; I think his meaning is very much as I have stated it. But, undoubtedly, in cases in many respects dissimilar, but in equal degree tyrannical and oppressive, resistance may be lawful, and the people in all ages, countries, and climes, have at times known these things, and they have, and they will for ever act accordingly.'

"Lord Shelburne in the course of his argument said, 'My Lords, we know,—we all know, that justice and injustice, right and wrong, are not at all considered in the course of our Parliamentary proceedings. We all know, that nothing is debated in Parliament for information or conviction, but for mere form. Every thing is considered in the cabinet, and brought into Parliament not for consideration, but for the sanction of the legislature, and the screening the counsellors of the king. The measures of the Parliament are the measures of the minister, and the measures of this minister are very often those of his commissioner.'

"The Marquis of Rockingham also supported the motion. Lords Littleton, Suffolk, Gower, Townsend, Rochford, and Weymouth, spoke in opposition. I omit stating what their lordships said, lest I should be suspected by any who may see this journal, of an unfair report of their speeches. But a very remarkable saying of Lord Gower I cannot omit. His Lordship said, 'My Lords, I am for *enforcing* these measures,—and' (with great *sneer* and *contempt*) 'let the

Americans sit talking about their natural and divine rights! their rights as men and citizens! their rights from God and nature!'

"The Duke of Richmond, in the course of his speech, said, 'Some nobles seem to think that regular troops can easily vanquish raw soldiers. But, my Lords, discipline was intended only as a substitute for what the Americans have already,—attachment to their cause,—virtue to inspire,—a common cause,—their all, to keep them to their duty. Americans will keep to their duty, without discipline. They will keep to their standard without fear of discipline in case they desert it. My Lords, Americans have the substance of what discipline is only the shadow. Discipline is only the substitute for a common cause, to attach through fear, and keep to their ranks and standard those who would otherwise desert them. But, my Lords, suppose you succeed, you cannot enforce these acts; you cannot force a form of government upon any people. You may spread fire, sword, and desolation, but that will not be government. You must change your places as you make your march of destruction. When you leave one place to subdue another, your government is gone.'

"' You cannot force men to serve in office. You cannot force men to be counsellors, judges, or sheriffs. You cannot compel jurors to sit on trial. You cannot force juries to present offences;—in short, no people can ever be made to submit to a form of government they say they will not receive.'

"The house divided on the question about ten, after the preceding debates.

"Contents, eighteen; non-contents, seventy-seven, including proxies.

"The Duke of Richmond, Lord Shelburne, and Lord Camden, pledged themselves to attend at all hazards, and at all times, as Lord Chatham had done.

"Went from the debates to visit Hugh Baillie LL. D., a Scotch gentleman, of very liberal sentiments, and a most zealous partizan of America. I supped, and returned to my lodgings, and spent most of the night and morning in entering the preceding speeches.

"January 21st. Spent the morning with Dr Franklin. Dined at the exchange coffee-house with Messrs Bromfield and Williams, and went for the first time to the serious opera of Armida in the evening. Some parts of the music exquisitely fine, the dancing elegant indeed, but in general a poor entertainment for an Englishman.

"January 22d. Wrote to William Phillips Esq.—to Mrs Quincy (a very long letter containing Chatham's speech),—and to Josiah Quincy Esq. Dined and spent the evening with Dr Franklin.

TO JOSIAH QUINCY ESQ.

"*London, January* 22, 1775.

"Honoured and dear Sir,

"I intend to say nothing more in this letter than that I am in health and spirits, having never had an ill day since my arrival in this island. I am here doing my duty. Last Friday was a day of great happiness to me; I heard a Chatham, and a Camden speak, for hours, on the concerns of my country.

"This letter is intended to contain nothing but what the spies of the ministry may be willing to let pass; and having gratified their own curiosity, I wish they may be candid and generous enough to let my friends gratify theirs also.

"Your affectionate and obliged
"JOSIAH QUINCY JUN."

JOURNAL CONTINUED.

"January 23d. Attended a long debate in the House of Commons on American affairs. Speakers for the Americans: Burke, Johnston, Charles Fox, T. Townsend, Lord J. Cavendish, Captain Lutterell, Alderman Sawbridge, &c.—eighty-two. Against the Americans: Sir William Meredith, Lord North, Lord Clare, Sir George Macartney, Sir G. Eliot, Lord Stanley, &c.—total one hundred and ninety-seven.

"This debate and division, show that if King, Lords, and Commons can subdue America into bondage against the almost universal sentiment, opinion, wish, and hope of the Englishmen of this island, the deed will be done.

"This night, for the first time since my arrival, I was taken very ill with a fever and spasms.

"January 24th. Visited by Dr Fothergill, who prescribed for my disorder. Was this day to have dined at Mr Towgood's with Dr Price, Dr Franklin, Dr Jeffries, and Dr Priestley, but my illness prevented that pleasure.

"January 25th. Visited by Dr Fothergill, who peremptorily refused his fee.

"Received invitations to dine on Friday at Mrs Huron's, Kensington, &c. and on Sunday with Mr Hollis. Ill health obliged me to decline both.

"Dined with Lord Shelburne, in company with Lord Tankerville, Drs Franklin, Price, Priestley, Counsellors Dunning, Lee, Leigh, and several others. After a very elegant entertainment, his Lordship laid before us copies of the papers from America, now lying before the two Houses for their consideration.

"January 26th. Visited by Dr Fothergill, and confined to my home all day. Mr Williams watched with me this night.

"January 27th. Visited by Dr Fothergill, who again refused his fee, saying, 'I consider this as a public cause, to which we must all contribute.' Waited upon by Mr Alderman Sawbridge, who spent an hour and a half with me in conversation on American and Parliamentary concerns. Went out to reside with Mr Bromfield, at Islington, while in my present feeble state of health. Received by this amiable family, and treated with the greatest hospitality and kindness. It is now the third of February, during which time I have been treated in the most friendly and hospitable manner.

"February 3d. This day Dr Fothergill visited me, and gave me new prescriptions.

"February 6th. Every day since I have been at Islington, I have received the greatest evidences of the number and attachment of my friends—who are many and affectionate.

"February 9th. Visited by Dr Fothergill, who again absolutely refused his fees. Every day visited by more or less of my many friends, and great numbers send daily to inquire after my health, whom I never saw.

"February 24th. This day the celebrated Dr Burgh (author of 'Political Disquisitions'), who has seen none but his own family for many months, took a double dose of opium to allay the pain of his disease, and sent for me in, and I spent about an hour with him.

"February 26th. Rode out for the fourth time on horseback about twelve or fourteen miles. Evidently better when I am in the open air, and the motion of the horse not fatiguing. My friends redouble in the number and frequency of their visits, as the time for my departure for America draws nigh. Among many others this past week, I have been visited by Drs Price, Priestley, Franklin, Messrs Rogers, Towgood, Sheriff Lee, Arthur Lee, &c. &c.

"It is a good deal against my own private opinion and inclination, that I now sail for America. I have had no letter from there since they knew of my arrival. I know not what my next letters may contain. Besides the fine season is now coming on here, and Dr Fothergill thinks Bristol air and water would give me perfect health.

" On the other hand, my most intimate friends (except Mr Bromfield) insist upon my going directly to Boston. They say, no letters can go with safety, and that I can deliver more information and advice *vivâ voce*, than could or ought to be written. They say, my going now must be (if I arrive safe) of great advantage to the American cause.

" February 27th. Went to London * * *

" February 28th. Went to Fulham in a post chaise with Mr Bromfield, and dined with Mr Abraham Dupuis, partner with Mr Thomas Bromfield, a very amiable, sensible friend of liberty.

" March 1st. On this day I had about an hour and a half of private conversation with Dr Franklin, on the subject of the present situation of American affairs, and what course America, and especially New England, ought now and during the spring and summer to hold.

"I wish I might with propriety enter his discourse.

"March 2d. William Lee Esq., late Sheriff, came and spent three hours with me in conversation on American affairs. N. B. Gen. Con.—Vote of credit for the raising and supporting —— for the defence of the liberties of America, in whatever part attacked. A proper person to France and Spain.

"Supposes Boston ought to be abandoned—urges me much to attend the congress at Philadelphia.

"This day, Thomas Rogers Esq., banker near the Exchange, politely presented me with all Dr Price's works, in three volumes, elegantly bound.

"March 3d. This day being the day before my departure, I dined with Dr Franklin, and had three hour's private conversation with him. Dissuades from France or Spain. Intimate with both the Spanish and French ambassador, the latter a shrewd, great man. By no means take any step of great consequence, unless on a sudden emergency, without advice of the continental congress. Explicitly, and in so many words, said, that only New England could hold out for ages against this country, and if they were firm and united, in *seven years* would conquer them.

"Said, he had the best intelligence that the manufacturers were bitterly feeling, and loudly complaining of the loss of the American trade. Let your adherence be to the non-importation and non-exportation agreement a year from next September, or to the next session of Parliament, and the day is won.

"Received this day from my friend, Thomas Brand Hollis Esq., a present of eight valuable books, and eight pamphlets.

"Received also two books and two pamphlets from that most worthy and extraordinary character, the Reverend Theophilus Lindsey, being the whole of his works.

"Had great satisfaction in reading my reports of the debates of the House of Lords, to one or two friends who heard them. They thought them exceedingly correct, and were amazed at the blunders, omissions, and misrepresentations of the printed accounts."

At this date, the Journal abruptly terminates. During the remainder of his residence in London the habitual activity of his pen ceased, either through inability consequent on sickness, or occupation while preparing for his homeward voyage. In obedience to the wishes of his political friends, contrary to the advice of his physician, and in opposition to his own declared opinion that his recovery depended upon his remaining in England, he embarked for Boston, on the sixteenth of March 1775.

The following extracts from a letter written by him while in the English channel describe the state of his health and his feelings, at the commencement of this voyage.

TO THOMAS BROMFIELD ESQ., LONDON.

"*March* 16, 1775.
"*March* 18. *Going into Plymouth Harbour.*
" Dear Bromfield,
" Paper being scarce, I am obliged to take the remains of a letter I was beginning to you two days since, when the boat put off and left the ship. The sea runs high and I can scarcely write legibly. * * * * * * * * *

A word as to my health. My cough is far from better, though in the day time I am troubled a very trifle with it.

"I wrote you I had been ill-used and deceived. I discover every day more instances of it.

"If we reach into Plymouth to night, I shall have a thousand minds to go to Bristol. I am perplexed much what I ought to do. The sea runs so high, I must only wish you and yours, what my heart does every day, as its duty and delight, the best of blessings.

JOSIAH QUINCY JUN.

This letter, the last he ever wrote, was found among his papers; the ship not having touched at Plymouth, or any other British port. The full import of these expressions—"I have been ill-used, and deceived,"—cannot now be known. They probably referred to the want of comfortable arrangements, and suitable preparations for his accommodation on board the vessel. The only information his friends could obtain on this subject, was derived from one of the inferior officers of the ship, to whom they were indebted for all that is known of the incidents of a voyage full of privation and suffering. After being five weeks at sea, the wished-for shore yet at a distance, he became convinced that his fate was inevitable,— and prepared to submit himself to the will of

Heaven with heroic calmness and christian resignation.

Under the oppression of disease and amidst the daily sinking of nature, his friends, his family, and above all, his country, predominated in his affections. He repeatedly said to the seaman, on whose attentions he was chiefly dependant, that he had but one desire and one prayer, which was, that he might live long enough to have an interview with Samuel Adams, or Joseph Warren;—that granted, he should die content. This wish of the patriot's heart, Heaven, in its inscrutable wisdom, did not grant.

As he drew towards his native shore, the crisis he had so long foreseen arrived. The battle of Lexington was fought. According to his prediction, " his countrymen sealed their faith and constancy to their liberties with their blood." But he lived not to hear the event of that glorious day.

While yet the ship was three days' sail from land, exhausted by disease, and perceiving his last hour approach, he called the seaman to the side of his birth, and being himself too weak to write, dictated to him a letter full of the most interesting and affecting communications to his family and nearest friends. This letter still exists among his papers, in the rude hand writing of an illiterate sailor.

The following extracts, being of a general nature, are here inserted, in the language which he dictated.

"*At Sea, April* 21, 1775.

" Foreseeing that there will be many inexplicable circumstances in the way of my friends, to account for many things relating to my conduct, I should have been glad, if God had spared my life, to converse with them once more. But this, his holy Providence seems fully settled to deny. Some few matters I have prevailed with a friend on board to minute for their information.

My going to America at this time was very considerably against my inclinations, especially as Doctor Fothergill was of opinion that Bristol waters would be of great advantage to me. But he did not dissuade me from going to America, but advised it very strongly in preference to my staying in London, or its environs.

" The most weighty motive of all that determined my conduct, was the extreme urgency of about fifteen or twenty most stanch friends to America, and many of them the most learned and

respectable characters in the kingdom, for my immediately proceeding to Boston. Their sentiments what ought to be the conduct of Boston, and of the continent, at this, and the approaching season, I had heard very often in the social circle; and in what things they differed I perfectly knew. It appeared of high importance that the sentiments of such persons should be known in America. To commit their sentiments to writing, was neither practicable nor prudent at this time. To the bosom of a friend they could intrust what might be of great advantage to my country. To me that trust was committed, and I was, immediately upon my arrival, to assemble certain persons, to whom I was to communicate my trust, and had God spared my life, it seems it would have been of great service to my country.
* * * * * * * * * * * * * *
* * * * * * * * * * * * * *
* * * * Ever since I have been out, almost every thing has been different from what I expected. Instead of pleasant weather, the most inclement and damp, which removes me entirely from the deck, and when I was flattered with the hope of getting into port six days ago, I am yet here, as distant from it as when the encourage-

ment was given me. Had Providence been pleased that I should have reached America six days ago, I should have been able to converse with my friends. I am persuaded that this voyage and passage are the instruments to put an end to my being. His holy will be done!"

"Mr Quincy is so low, that he probably will not be able to read a word of the foregoing, but it is to be hoped it will be intelligible with a little pains."

Such is the last notice of the close of the life of Josiah Quincy Jun. On the twenty-sixth of April 1775, within sight of that beloved country which he was not permitted to reach; neither supported by the kindness of friendship, nor cheered by the voice of affection, he expired;— not, indeed, as, a few weeks afterwards, did his friend and co-patriot, Warren, in battle, on a field ever memorable and ever glorious; but in solitude, amidst suffering, without associate, and without witness; yet breathing forth a dying wish for his country, desiring to live only to perform towards her a last and signal service.

A few hours after his death, the ship with his lifeless remains, entered the harbour of Gloucester, Cape Ann.

His arrival had been anticipated with anxious solicitude, and the intelligence of his death was received with an universal sorrow. By his family and immediate friends, the event was mourned as the extinction of their brightest hope. His contemporaries, faithful to his virtues, and deeply sensible of his services, early associated his name with those most honoured and most beloved of the period in which he lived. It was his lot to compress events and exertions, sufficient for a long life, within the compass of a few short years. To live forever in the hearts of his countrymen, and by labour and virtue to become immortal in the memory of future times, were the strong passions of his soul. That he was prohibited from filling the great sphere of usefulness for which his intellectual powers seemed adapted and destined, is less a subject of regret, than it is of joy and gratitude that he was permitted, in so short a time, to perform so noble a part, and that to his desire has been granted so large a portion of "that imperishable meed," which, beyond all earthly reward, was the object of his search and solicitude.

The distracted state of the country, and the military force concentrated within and about Boston, immediately after the battle of Lexington, interrupted communication and denied to his family the consolation of paying the last sad tribute to his remains. Many of his nearest connexions were dispersed by the siege of Boston. His wife had been detained in the town by the dangerous illness of both their children. Their only daughter died on the thirteenth of April, 1775. After this event, with her only remaining child, she had sought the protection of her parents at their place of refuge at Norwich in Connecticut.

The inhabitants of Gloucester, upon whom devolved the melancholy duty, in performing his funeral rites, testified at once their own respect for his memory, and the public sympathy for his loss.

In his will dated " February 28, 1774," after enumerating various legacies and tokens of remembrance to his friends and relations, the following clause occurs :—" I give to my son, when he shall arrive to the age of fifteen years, Algernon Sidney's works,—John Locke's works,—Lord Bacon's works,—Gordon's Tacitus,—and Cato's Letters. May the spirit of liberty rest upon him!"

His literary and political manuscripts were entrusted to his wife, during the minority of his son, and through her careful execution of the trust they remain in perfect preservation. In case of his son's dying a minor, he bequeathed two thousand pounds sterling to Harvard University, for the purpose of founding a professorship of Moral Philosophy, Law, and Oratory.

The executors named in this will are Francis Dana, Jonathan Jackson, John Adams, William Phillips Jun., and John Lowell. The selection of these individuals not only shows the high place they held in his esteem, but the judgment with which he discriminated ability and worth. The general voice of society has long since confirmed his opinion, and these names in the progress of years have become synonymous with whatever is upright and honourable. The trust was fulfilled with characteristic judgment and integrity by his brother-in-law, William Phillips jun.

The letter dictated by Mr Quincy in the last moments of his life, contained a direction that his remains should be deposited in a tomb which he ordered to be built at Braintree.

As soon as the theatre of the war had been transferred to the other colonies, and Massachusetts was left in comparative tranquillity, that request was complied with by his father, and his remains were removed from Gloucester to the burial ground of Braintree, (now Quincy.)

After the death of his widow in 1798, a monument was erected to their memory, on which is the following inscription, written by John Quincy Adams.

Sacred
To the memory
of
JOSIAH QUINCY Jun.
Of Boston, Barrister at Law.
Brilliant talents, uncommon eloquence,
And indefatigable application,
Raised him to the highest eminence in his profession.
His early, enlightened, inflexible attachment
To the Cause of his Country,
Is attested by monuments more durable than this,
And transmitted to posterity
By well known productions of his genius.
He was born, the 23d of February, 1744;
And died the 26th of April 1775,
His mortal remains are here deposited, with
Those of Abigail, his wife, daughter of William Phillips Esq.
of Boston,
Born the 14th of April 1745. Died the 25th of March 1798.

STRANGER,

In contemplating this monument, the frail tribute
Of filial gratitude, and affection,

Glows thy bold breast with patriotic flame?
Let his example point the paths of fame!
Or seeks thy heart, averse from public strife,
The milder graces of domestic life?
Her kindred virtues let thy soul revere,
And o'er the best of mothers drop a tear.

OBSERVATIONS

ON THE

ACT OF PARLIAMENT

COMMONLY CALLED

THE

BOSTON PORT-BILL;

WITH

THOUGHTS

ON

CIVIL SOCIETY

AND

STANDING ARMIES.

By JOSIAH QUINCY, Jun'r.

BRITONS *arise!* - - - - - - - - - - - - - - -
And show you have the Virtue to be mov'd.
POPE.

NULLA FIDES, pietasq; viris, qui CASTRA sequuntur,
VENALESQUE MANUS : ibi fas, ubi maxima merces.
LUCAN.

Our necks are under PERSECUTION.
LAM. v. 5.

What MAN can do against them, *not afraid,*
Though to THE DEATH ; against such CRUELTIES
With *inward consolation* recompenc'd :
And oft supported so, *as shall amaze*
Their PROUDEST PERSECUTORS.   MILTON.

They that be slain by THE SWORD are better than they
that be slain *with hunger.*   LAM. iv. 9.

BOSTON: *N. E.*

PRINTED FOR AND SOLD BY EDES AND GILL, IN
QUEEN-STREET,   1774.

To the Freeholders and Yeomanry of my Country.

The virtue, strength, and fortitude of a state generally reside in the Freeholders of the nation. In you, gentlemen, as the landed interest of the country, do I place my confidence, under God, at this day.

To you, gentlemen, therefore, I dedicate this temporary work, as a testimony of that great respect and warm affection, with which

I am

Your friend and countryman,

Josiah Quincy Jun.

Boston, May 14, 1774.

PREFACE.

THE statute of the 14th George 3d, received in the last ships from London, (entitled "An Act to discontinue, in such manner, and for such time, as are therein mentioned, the landing and discharging, the lading or shipping of goods, wares, merchandize, at the town, and within the harbour of Boston, in the Province of Massachusetts Bay, in North America,") gave rise to the following Observations. They will appear thrown together in haste; and as the writer was out of town on business, almost every day the sheets were printing off, no doubt many errors of the press escaped correction.

The inaccuracies of a sudden production from one of infirm health, perplexed with various avocations, will receive a mild censure: more material faults, friends may be prone to forgive; but from enemies—public or private—we are never to expect indulgence or favour.

OBSERVATIONS.

In times of public calamity, it is the duty of a good citizen to consider. If his opportunities or advantages, for knowledge and reflection, are greater than those of mankind in general, his whole duty will remain undischarged, while he confines his thoughts to the compass of his own mind. But if danger is added to the calamity of the times, he who shall communicate his sentiments on public affairs with decency and frankness, merits attention and indulgence, if he may not aspire to approbation and praise.

Whoever attends to the tenor and design of the late act of the British Parliament for the blockade of this harbour, and duly considers the extensive confusion and distress this measure must inevitably produce; whoever shall reflect upon the justice, policy, and humanity of legislators, who could deliberately give their sanction to such a procedure,—must be satisfied, that the man, who shall openly dare to expose their conduct, hazards fatal consequences. Legislators, who could condemn a whole town unheard, nay uncited to answer; who could involve thousands in ruin and misery, without suggestion of any crime by them committed; and who could so construct their law, as that enormous pains and penalties would inevitably ensue, notwithstanding the most perfect obedience to its injunctions; I say, that legislators, thus formed as men, thus principled as statesmen, would undoubtedly imagine the attainder and death of a private individual, for his public animadversions, a less extraordinary act of power.* But all exertions of duty have their

---

* Since this treatise was advertised in the public papers, as being in the press, the author hath received, from the British coffee-house, an anonymous letter, in which he is represented as being " in imminent hazard of the loss of life and confiscation of estate." " You will," says the writer, " very probably get into the hands of a power, from which no power you can look to, will be able to deliver you." There is, says the writer, " but one expedient left to save you :"——" Employ, for God's sake, those rare talents, with which," saith the artful flatterer, " he hath blessed you, in convincing the people that they have nothing to do, but to submit, and make their peace with government :—You may,"continues he, " by this means probably make your peace, and ward off the punishment that hangs over your head. It is barely possible, that government may still continue its great lenity, and overlook your offences." The reader is left to his own reflections.

hazard :—if dread of parliamentary extravagance is to deter from public energies, the safety of the commonwealth will soon be despaired of; and when once a sentiment of that kind prevails, the excesses of present enormities so rapidly increase, that strides, at first appearance exorbitant, will soon be found—but the beginning of evils. We therefore consider it as a just observation, that the weight and velocity of public oppressions are ever in a ratio proportionate to private despondency and public despair.

He who shall go about to treat of important and perilous concerns, and conceals himself behind the curtain of a feigned signature, gives an advantage to his adversaries; who will not fail to stigmatize his thoughts, as the notions of an unknown writer, afraid or ashamed to avow his sentiments; and hence they are deemed unworthy of notice and refutation. Therefore I give to the world both my sentiments and name upon the present occasion, and shall hear with patience him, who will decently refute what is advanced, and shall submit with temper to that correction and chastisement which my errors deserve.

The act now under consideration opens with a recital, that " dangerous commotions and insurrections have been fomented and raised in Boston —by divers ill-affected persons, to the subversion of His Majesty's government, and to the utter destruction of the public peace, and good order of the said town; in which commotions and insurrections certain valuable cargoes of teas, being the property of the East India Company, and on board certain vessels lying within the bay or harbour of Boston, were seized and destroyed; and in the present condition of said town and harbour, the commerce of His Majesty's subjects cannot be safely carried on there, nor the customs payable to His Majesty be duly collected."

Two questions naturally arise out of this preamble: the first, whether the facts set forth are true; and secondly, whether upon a supposition of their truth, they are a sufficient foundation for the subsequent parts of the statute, or will warrant the disabilities, forfeitures, pains, and penalties, enacted and inflicted on the subject?— Both inquiries seem intimately to concern the honour and justice of the British legislature. And however unimportant the judgment of Americans may now appear to that august body, yet surely the judgment of Europe and future ages is not unworthy their high consideration. Removed from the eye of royalty, the piety of a sovereign may cease to pity miseries it doth not behold; remote from the cries of public justice, and the efforts of popular despair, lords and commons may remain unaffected, for a season, with American convulsions; yet justice and humanity must soon excite those operations in America and Europe, which hereafter will move even the senate of Britain. True knowledge and real virtue perhaps were never more diffused than on this northern continent; refined humanity (it is boasted) was never more predominant than in Europe at this day. Can it be supposed, that this virtue will be discordant and inactive; that this knowledge will omit to unfold public wrongs, or that such humanity will cease to interpose?

That commotions were in Boston; that East India tea was destroyed, are facts not controverted. But that such commotions were naturally to be expected; that they were such as statesmen must have foreseen, and a father of his country, who foresaw, would prevent, rather than punish, is equally true. The sentiments of all Americans relative to the tea act are no secret, their fervor in the common cause equally known; and their probable intemperance in consequence of the arrival of India teas, it required no profound skill in men and politics to predict. Nay the British papers were full, and the senate echoed, with predictions similar to those which are now fulfilled. It was not difficult for Englishmen in Britain to tell how Englishmen in America would conduct on such occasions. What shall we then say? Shall we impute to those, who are dignified as "the wisest and most august," the barbarous project—deliberately to ensnare, that they might superlatively punish? The calm deliberation of premeditated malice seems rather more characteristic of a private bosom, than a public body. But Governor Hutchinson (the representative of His Majesty in this province), when treating upon an act of the Massachusetts government imposing a tax or duty upon goods of the inhabitants of other colonies, hath assured us, that "in all ages and countries, by bodies and communities of men such deeds have been done as most of the individuals of which such communities consisted, acting separately, would have been ashamed of:"*—an observation that his Excellency might have imbibed from that prince of

---

* Mass. Hist. Vol. ii. p. 156.

historians, Dr Robertson. " To abandon usurped power, to renounce lucrative error, are sacrifices, which the virtue of individuals has, on some occasions, offered to truth ; but from any society of men, no such effort can be expected. The corruptions of society, recommended by common utility, and justified by universal practice, are viewed by its members, without shame or horror; and reformation never proceeds from themselves, but is always forced upon them by some foreign hand."* " Cæsar, Lepidus, and Antony," says Plutarch, " show, that no beast is more savage than man, when possessed of power equal to his passion." If the sentiments of Dr Robertson are just, have we not cause to fear from very powerful states and legislators an equal ferocity ? And it is an observation of the illustrious Lord Clarendon, that it is the nature of man, rather to commit two errors, than to retract one. When elevated characters commit a second error, it carries the air of an intended discovery, how little they feel for the first, how much they despise the people, how much they are above shame, fear, and amendment. But to heighten cruelty by wantonness,

---

* Hist. Scotland, Vol. i. p. 167.

to render it more pungent by insult, are such exorbitances, as seldom disgrace the records of mankind. But whenever such instances occur, they strikingly verify that eternal truth recorded in the House of Lords,—" It is much easier to restrain liberty from running into licentiousness than power from swelling into tyranny and oppression."* Can it add dignity to this noble sentiment, or weight to this important truth, to say, that among the illustrious personages who subscribed it with their hands and transmitted it to posterity, we find a " Chesterfield" and " Cobham," a " Strafford" and a " Bathurst," a " Haversham" and " Gower ?"

But to return. Are popular commotions peculiar to Boston? Hath not every maritime town in England been repeatedly affected by them? Are they not incident to every commercial and populous city? Whence then is it, that Boston is devoted to such unexampled treatment? But it may be said, Boston, as a town, hath aided, abetted, and participated in these tumults. Where is the evidence of it? I presume the Lords and Commons of Great Britain had none; for they

---

* Lord's Prot. Edit. 1767. Vol. ii. p. 141. Anno 1736.

do not suggest it ; I presume they did not believe it, because they have not intimated it. And had they been furnished with such evidence, had they believed the fact, surely it is an imputation unworthy of their dignity, to say, that they would not have given that matter in the preamble of the statute, as the ground of their extraordinary procedure. But the records of Boston, and known facts, prove that the inhabitants discountenanced and disavowed all riot and disorder. I am thus warranted in saying, that the mere occurrences expressed in the act, is that matter which the British legislature have judged worthy the most unparalleled penal severities. Whether this judgment be right, is a subject interesting to a citizen of the town to inquire ; it is a subject on which a man will speak feelingly ; on which an Englishman will speak freely and openly.

Previous to further observations, it may be necessary to say, that the town of Boston had, as a town, cautiously and wisely conducted itself; not only without tumult, but with studied regard to established law. This the rolls of the town verify, and a hundred witnesses can confirm.

At the last town-meeting relative to the East India tea and its consignees, it was largely debated whether it should be an instruction to the committee, who were appointed to wait on those gentlemen, to insist on their peremptory answer, —whether they would send back the tea; and after long debate on the question, it passed by a very large majority in the negative. And the greatest enemy of the country cannot point out any one step of the town of Boston, in the progress of this matter, that was tumultuous, disorderly, and against law. This also is an additional reason, why we must conclude that the mere temporary events which took place in Boston, without any illegal procedure of the town, in the matter of the tea, are, in the judgment of the British senate, an adequate foundation for the last act received from that powerful body.

The first enacting clause of the statute now in view, annihilates all commercial transactions within two certain points of the harbour of Boston, upon pain of the forfeiture of " goods, wares, and merchandise, and of boat, lighter, ship, vessel, or other bottom; and of the guns, ammunition, tackle, furniture, and stores, in or belonging to the same;" " and of any barge, hoy, lighter, wherry, or boat, into which any goods &c. are laden," &c.

The next paragraph, " in case any wharfinger, &c. or any of their servants shall take up or land, or knowingly suffer to be taken up or landed, or shall ship off, or suffer to be water-borne, at or from any of their said wharves, &c. goods &c." enacts a forfeiture and loss of such " goods &c. and treble the value thereof, to be computed at the highest price of such sort of goods, &c. together with the vessels and boats, and all the horses, cattle, and carriages, whatsoever, made use of in the shipping, unshipping, landing, removing, carriage, or conveyance of any of the aforesaid goods," &c.

The next clause provides, " that if any ship &c. shall be moored or lie at anchor, or be seen hovering within said bay, &c. or within one league from the said bay, &c. it shall and may be lawful for any Admiral, or commissioned officer of His Majesty's fleet or ships of war, or for any officer of His Majesty's customs, to compel such ship or vessel to depart to some other port or harbour, or to such station as the said officer shall appoint, and to use such force for that purpose as shall be found necessary : and if such ship or vessel shall not depart accordingly within six hours after notice for that purpose given by such person as aforesaid, such ship or vessel, together with all the goods laden on board thereon, and all the guns, ammunition, tackle, and furniture shall be forfeited and lost, whether bulk shall have been broken or not."

Let us here pause for a moment; let us give time for one single reflection; let us give space for one pulse of the veins—one emotion of the heart. And who can think, but those exalted characters and that generous prince, styled the father of all his people—who united to this terrible act, had many reflections, many feelings of humanity, while they were solemnly consigning thousands—if not millions—to ruin, misery, and desperation?

The persons in whom this authority is vested are not confined to the ports or harbours on this continent: the vessel and cargo may be ordered to what harbour, port, or station of the whole world, the officer pleases—if he appoint a continental station, it is grace and favour;—and what may be the price of that purchase, who can tell? what scope for malice and ill-will; for pride and haughtiness; for avarice and power to wanton and insult, till the one is satiated and the other wearied!

Who are the persons to whom such unbounded, such enormous power is entrusted? Power is known to be intoxicating in its nature, and, in proportion to its extent, is ever prone to wantonness. Power and authority, says Plutarch, awaken every passion, and discover every latent vice. What a cogent temptation is here placed to insnare the most virtuous? But if there be one depraved passion in the bosom, as power gives scope and opportunity, how soon will it be called forth into licentious exercise? Shall I be thought going too far, shall I trespass upon the bounds of truth and decency, if I say, that some of His Majesty's commissioned officers, in his fleet, or ships of war; some officers of his customs, are not altogether worthy of such high confidence and trust? Are there not inferior commissioned officers in the King's ships; are there not many of the lower officers of the customs, who have neither strength of understanding nor integrity of heart to wield such a mighty power? Nay, may not I add, that some few (into whose hands peradventure, the estate of a good subject and opulent merchant may chance to fall) are destitute of all sense, mental and humane? While contemplating this subject,—while the mind is active, and heart warm,—how apt are we to forget, that the illustrious Houses, who gave their sanction to this astonishing law, are dignified as learned and venerable; and the Prince that gave his *fiat*, denominated—" The wisest and best of Kings ?"

Declining an entrance upon matters heretofore discussed by abler heads, I have omitted all observation on the right and policy of the claims and laws of Great Britain over the colonies ; upon the same principle I waive entering that copious field which is presented, by that part of the present act, which provides for the recovery of all forfeitures and penalties in the courts of admiralty,—whose extended jurisdiction hath been matter of very great grievance, heart-burnings, and complaint; whose judges hold their commissions by the tenure of will and pleasure ; and whose large salaries are a most powerful incentive to the desire of—well-pleasing all on whom they depend.

Another passage in this statute makes utterly void all contracts, " for consigning, shipping, or carrying any goods &c. to or from the harbour of Boston, which have been made or entered into, or which shall be made or entered into, so long as the act continues in force, relating to any ship which shall arrive at said town or harbour after the first day of June."

Jurisprudents and the sages of the law for centuries have taught, that retrospective or *post facto* statutes, were not only militant with the principles of sound morals, but those also of political wisdom. But the Parliament, who by the bold figure of common lawyers are styled omnipotent, here enforce a different doctrine. The English colonist, replete with loyalty to his sovereign; the descendant from Britain, animated by love for a mother country, represses the excursions of his understanding and passions : but the subject or native of another state will feel no such restraint. He has contracted to send his merchandise to this port, expects his returns in the commodities of the country—in compliance with his obligations, his treasures are moving with hazard upon the ocean, with hopes warm for gain. The ship (in which peradventure he hath risked his life as well as fortune), after many a toil and jeopardy, reaches the destined port. But how are his hopes baffled—how will he rage and exclaim, vast have been his expenses to prepare for his adventure, and equally great his expectations from the Boston merchant! What guilt hath he contracted, what crime hath he committed, that he also should be involved in the calamitous consequences of this unexampled statute? Buoyed up for a moment, perhaps, with a vain expectation, that he may have a remedy on his contract against the merchant here;—how will this supposed foreigner sink with a ten-fold despondency; how will he rise again with adequate indignation, when he discovers all remedy gone;—his contract declared by the law, "utterly void, to all intents and purposes whatsoever!" Here again, love for a parent country, love for a parent king, checks the current of reason, and restrains the career of passion.

Having taken this view, before we proceed further, it is natural once more to ask, whence arose this extraordinary stride of legislation? what is it, that the town of Boston hath done? what new and unheard of crimes have the inhabitants committed, to justify the enacting of such disabilities, forfeitures, pains, and penalties? Punishments that descend indiscriminately on all, ought to have the sanction of unerring wisdom and almighty power, or it will be questioned, if not opposed. The present vengeance falls indiscriminately on the acknowledged innocent, as well as the supposed guilty. Surely the evil is of a very malignant and terrible nature, that can require such an extraordinary remedy. Admit for a moment, that the inhabitants of Boston were charged as high criminals; the highest criminals are not punishable, till arraigned before disinterested judges, heard in defence, and found guilty of the charge. But so far from all this, a whole people are accused, prosecuted by they know not whom; tried they know not when; proved guilty they know not how; and sentenced in a mode, which for number of calamities, extent and duration of severity, exceeds the annals of past ages, and, we presume in pity to mankind, will not mark any future era in the story of the world.

What will be the real consequences of this astonishing measure, and what those intended and expected by the planners of it, are very different considerations. A Machiavel may plan, and his schemes prove abortive; an Alva may be sent to execute, and his army be defeated. The circle of the arts and sciences, like the ball of empire, hath held a western course. From Chaldea and Egypt to Greece and Rome, and thence to the western provinces of Europe. Chaldea and Egypt had their magi, their law-givers, and heroes, when Greece and Rome swarmed with petty feudatories and barbarians; Greece and Rome flourished in literature, when Gaul, Germany, and Britain were uncivilized, rude, and ignorant. Wise and sagacious politicians have not been able to stay the rotation of this revolving scientific circle, any more than mighty potentates to repel the velocity of the flying ball of empire:—superior to human powers, like blazing stars, they hold their destined course, and play their coruscations as they run their race.

The expectations of those who were the fautors of the present measures, must have been to bring down superlative distress, discord, confusion, despair, and perdition upon a multitude. How then will our amazement increase, when we shall hear that the hard fate of this multitude cannot be avoided? Let the inhabitants comply with the requisitions of the statute; let them be implicitly obedient to its injunctions;—what is the evil they will escape? what is the boon they may hope to attain? Hope and fear are said to be the hinges of government. Legislators have therefore considered it as sound policy, never to drive the subject into acts of despair, by causing punishments to appear as inevitable, on the first promulgation of a law. When a legislative body ordaineth penalties to take place in cases of performance or non-performance of particular matters, they surely will take due care, that sufficient notice is given of their public will, and sufficient time to comply with their mandates; so that obedience may not only proceed from principles of regard to the lawmakers, but motives of personal safety to the subject himself. This seems not more consonant to political wisdom, than to nature and equity. But let us now suppose, that upon the first intimations of the present law, Boston had been as prone to obey the edict of a British court, as the Turk to comply with the mandate of the Divan; let us imagine them as servile, as fawning as a court dependant to a minister of state;—nay, if there be any thing in nature yet more humble and more base, let Boston (in idea for a short moment) be that humble, servile, base, and fawning something: What doth it all avail? The first time the inhabitants of this town had any intimation of the will of the British Parliament, was on the tenth of May, and the act is to take place on the first of June; and thence to continue in full force, until it shall sufficiently " appear to His Majesty, that full satisfaction hath been made by or on behalf of the inhabitants of the said town of Boston, to the united company of merchants of England, trading to the East Indies, for the damage sustained by the said company by the destruction of their goods sent to the said town of Boston, on board certain ships or vessels as aforesaid; and until it shall be certified to His Majesty in council by the Governor, or Lieutenant Governor, of the said province, that reasonable satisfaction hath been made to the officers of His Majesty's revenue, and others who suffered by the riots and insurrections above mentioned, in the months of November and December in the year 1773, and in the month of January in the year 1774."

Satisfaction could not be made to the East India company, if all Boston had the will and power to do it, till the town had time and opportunity to call a meeting, assemble, consult, and determine upon the measure. Great bodies are not calculated for speedy decision, any more than velocity of motion. The resolution formed, time must be given for despatches to England, application to the East-India company, an adjustment with them upon the nice point of "full satisfaction :"—that accomplished, time must be given for making the matter "sufficiently appear to His Majesty." Let any one consider but for a moment, what a length of time must inevitably elapse before all this can be accomplished: nay, may it not well be questioned, considering the parties and all persons concerned and the circumstances of this affair, whether such accomplishment be practicable? But is this all that is to be done and effected before relief can be given to this distressed land? Far otherwise. "The Governor, or Lieutenant Governor, must also first certify to His Majesty in council, that reasonable satisfaction hath been made to the officers of His Majesty's revenue, and others, who suffered by the riots and insurrections above mentioned." No person is particularly designated to be the judge between the subject and the officers of His Majesty's revenue. No provision being expressly made, touching this point, how probable that litigation might arise concerning it? If we say that the Governor, or Lieutenant Governor, is the implied judge of this matter; how is the question to be brought before him, how tried, and how adjusted? These also are points not settled in a moment. Long indeed would be the period before the subject in Boston would be able to ascertain and make such satisfaction, and as long before the person here pointed out would make his certificate, that it was plenary and reasonable. Governor Bernard lately filled the chair of government, while Mr Hutchinson was second in command. Governor Hutchison now fills the chair, and the office of Lieutenant Governor is vacant. How long would it be before the inhabitants of Boston would acquiesce in the decision of either of these gentlemen? How little probability is there, considering the sentiments, the past and present conduct of these gentlemen, that they would speedily give the required certificate? If it hath been found difficult to touch the tender feelings of the American and native, how long would it take to excite generous sentiments in the Briton and stranger?

But these are all preparatories to the obtaining any ease or relief from the pressure of this penal law. The prerequisites to the restoration of public felicity are here not only improbable, but when considered all together and in the present crisis of public affairs, are they not impracticable? But, yet worse, being accomplished, it could in no way prevent the misery and calamities of this British edict. The space given for the subject to stay this torrent of evils is so short, that it is impossible for him, exerting his utmost energies, to prevent being overwhelmed. (But what mortals are unable to prevent—Heaven may stay or divert.)

An avenue seems to be opened by the benignity of our British fathers; but when attempted, affords no way of escape. My veneration for Britain is so great, that I will not suppose the great council of the nation intended to flatter with a false hope, that cruel disappointment might heighten the poignancy of suffering—the anguish of despair. But surely the fathers of a people will consider, what are like to be the sentiments and conduct of men driven to distraction by a multitude of inevitable evils, and consigned to despair from the terms of their deliverance?

Wonder was excited on the first view of the present law; our astonishment hath been increasing in the progress of our survey. A period is not yet put to our admiration. The faculties of sensation are yet to be further stretched.

The civilian and statesman, the moralist and sage, had heretofore delivered those maxims of truth and those rules of government, which wise legislators have ever observed, and the bulk of mankind yet honour and revere. To know the laws of the land already in force, previous to the publication of a new code, or in the technical phraseology of a common lawyer, " to know how the law stood before we make a new statute," hath been considered as an indispensable accomplishment of a good legislator. But that illustrious Parliament, whose power is distinguished with the appellation of " omnipotent," seem not to have exercised this important knowledge ;—though we do not hence rashly infer, that they are destitute of information, because all who are vested with omnipotence of power are ever inspired with proportionate wisdom.

It must again be noticed, that no relief is to be had, " until full satisfaction hath been made by or on behalf of the inhabitants of the said town of Boston." Now to suppose that any in England or Europe would make satisfaction " on behalf" of said inhabitants was unnatural, if not absurd; but what is more to the point, it was certainly unparliamentary. The remaining alternative is,—that satisfaction must be made by Boston.

Every person knows, that towns in this Province cannot raise or appropriate any monies, but by the express provisions and direct authority of law. It is a matter of equal notoriety, that all town assessments of money are expressly confined, by the 4 Wm. & Mar. c. 13, to the " maintenance and support of the ministry, schools, the poor, and defraying of other necessary town charges :" a law which received the royal approbation, almost a century ago.

Will any now say, that the monies appointed to be paid to the East India house come within the words of "necessary town charges?" When did the town contract the debt, or how are they subject to the payment of it? Had the parliament seen fit to enact, that monies requisite to satisfy the India merchants, should be so considered; two questions (not of quick decision) might then have arisen;—the one touching the validity and obligatory force of the statute; the other, whether it would then come within the intent and design of the Province law. For, past doubt, our Provincial legislators had no such charge (as the one here supposed) in view, when they made the law of William and Mary; and in this way therefore the matter could not be brought within its provision. Parliament must then make a new act to enable and empower Boston to pay the India company, before the town can comply with the terms of relief of their trade. In the mean while, what is to be the situation of Boston and the inhabitants of the globe with whom they have such extensive connexions? But it is very apparent, that the Parliament have not as yet enacted the payment of this satisfaction as a town charge. They have only placed it in the option of the town to make that payment, or submit to the consequences. That payment, we affirm, they cannot make without a breach of the law of the land. New and unheard-of, therefore, is the state of this people. They must sustain the severest afflictions, they must stand the issue of distracting remedies, or violate one of the most known and practised laws of the land! Let us search the history of the world; let us inspect the records of a Spanish inquisition; let us enter the recesses of an Ottoman court; nay, let us traverse the regions of romance and fable;—where shall we find a parallel?

" When the Hungarians were called rebels first, they were called so for no other reason than this," says the elegant Lord Bolingbroke, " that they would not be slaves." But for Britons, when they would not venture to call their children rebels, that they should treat them as worse than rebels, was reserved to distinguish an age of vaunted light, humanity, and knowledge,—the era of a King, who prides himself as born and bred a Briton!

To complain of the enormities of power, to expostulate with over-grown oppressors, hath in all ages been denominated sedition and faction; and to turn upon tyrants, treason and rebellion. But tyrants are rebels against the first laws of Heaven and Society: to oppose their ravages is an instinct of nature—the inspiration of God in the heart of man. In the noble resistance which mankind make to exorbitant ambition and power, they always feel that divine afflatus, which, paramount to every thing human, causes them to consider the Lord of Hosts as their leader, and his angels as fellow-soldiers. Trumpets are to them joyful sounds, and the ensigns of war, the banners of God. Their wounds are bound up in the oil of a good cause; sudden death is to them present martyrdom, and funeral obsequies resurrections to eternal honour and glory,—their widows and babes, being received into the arms of a compassionate God, and their names enrolled among David's worthies:—greatest losses are to them greatest gains; for they leave the troubles of their warfare to lie down on beds of eternal rest and felicity.

There are other parts of the act now before us, which merit notice; particularly that relative to the prosecution of suits in the ordinary courts of law, " for any thing done in pursuance of the act;"

by which the defendant is enabled " to plead the general issue, and give the act, and the general matter, in evidence ;" whereupon it follows, that " if it shall appear so to have been done, the jury shall find for the defendant;" who, by an after clause, is to " recover treble costs." From this passage some have been led to conclude, that the appearance of this matter was to be to the judge; and that if it had that appearance to him, and he should direct the jury accordingly, however it might appear to the jury, they must follow the directions of the judge, and acquit the defendant. But this is a construction, which, as the words do not necessarily carry that meaning, I will not permit myself to suppose the design of the law. However the late donations of large salaries by the crown, to the justices of our Superior Courts, who are nominated by the Governor, and hold their commission *durante beneplacito*, have not a little contributed to the preceding apprehension.

Another passage makes provision for " assigning and appointing such and so many open places, quays, and wharfs, within the said harbour, creeks, havens, and islands, for the landing, discharging, lading, and shipping of goods, as his Majesty, his heirs, or successors, shall judge necessary and expedient;" and also for " appointing such and so many officers of the customs therein, as his Majesty shall think fit; after which it shall be lawful for any person or persons to lade or put off from, or to discharge and land upon, such wharfs, quays, and places, so appointed within the said harbour, and none other, any goods, wares, and merchandise whatsoever." By which the property of many private individuals is to be rendered useless, and worse than useless; as the possession of a thing aggravates the misfortune of those who are deprived of a capacity to enjoy. But if the property of some few is to be rendered nothing worth, so that of many others is to be openly invaded. But why should we dwell upon private wrongs, while those of the multitude call for all our attention?

If any should now say, we are a commercial people, commercial plans can only save us; if any think that the ideas of the merchant are at this day to give spring to our nerves and vigour to our actions; if any say, that empire in this age of the world, is only founded in commerce:—let him show me the people emancipated from oppression by commercial principles and measures: let him point me that unexplored land, where trade and slavery flourish together. Till then, I must hold a different creed; and believe—that though commercial views may not be altogether unprofitable, that though commercial plans may do much, they never can do all. With regard, then, to how much the merchant, the artificer, the citizen, and the husbandman may do, let us no longer differ. But let every one apply his strength and abilities to that mighty burden, which, unless removed, must crush us all. Americans have one common interest to unite them; that interest must cement them. Natural allies, they have published to the world professions of reciprocal esteem and confidence, aid and assistance; they have pledged their faith of mutual friendship and alliance. Not only common danger, bondage, and disgrace; but national truth and honour conspire to make the colonists resolve to—stand or fall together.

Americans never were destitute of discernment; they have never been grossly deficient in virtue. A small share of sagacity is now needful to discover the insidious art of our enemies; the smallest spark of virtue will on this occasion kindle into flame.

Will the little temporary advantage held forth for delusion, seduce them from their duty ? Will they not evidence at this time, how much they despise the commercial bribe of a British ministry; and testify to the world that they do not vail to the most glorious of the ancients, in love of freedom and sternness of virtue? But as to the inhabitants of this province, how great are the number, how weighty the considerations to actuate their conduct? Not a town in this colony, but have breathed the warmest declarations of attachment to their rights, union in their defence, and perseverance to the end. Should any one maritime town (for more than one I will not believe there can be), allured by the expectations of gain, refuse to lend their aid; entertaining the base idea of building themselves upon the ruins of this metropolis, and, in the chain of future events, on the destruction of all America;—what shall we say?—hours of bitter reflection will come, when their own feelings shall excite consideration; when remembrance of the past, and expectation of the future, shall fill up the measure of their sorrow and anguish. But I turn from the idea, which blasts my country with infamy—my species with disgrace.

The intelligent reader must have noticed, that

through the whole of the act of Parliament, there is no suggestion that the East India company had made any demand for damage done to their property:—if the company supposed they had received injury, it doth not appear whom they consider as guilty, and much less, that they had alleged any charge against the town of Boston. But I presume that if that company were intitled to receive a recompense from the town, until they prosecuted their demand they are supposed to waive it. And we cannot but imagine, that this is the first instance, where Parliament hath ordered one subject to pay a satisfaction to another, when the party aggrieved did not appear to make his regular claim; and much more uncommon is it, for such recompense to be ordered without ascertaining the amount to which the satisfaction shall extend.

But if the East India company were now made easy, and Boston reduced to perfect silence and humiliation; how many " others" are there, who would suggest, that they " suffered by the riots and insurrections abovementioned," and demand " reasonable satisfaction" therefor. The singular texture, uncertainty, looseness, and ambiguity of this phrase in the statute seems so calculated for dispute, such an eternal bar to a full compliance with the requisitions of the act, and of course to render permanent its evils, that I cannot speak upon the subject without trespassing upon those bounds of respect and decency, within the circle of which I have endeavoured to move.

Here, waiving further particular consideration of that subject which gave origin to this performance, I shall proceed to an equally interesting subject—that of standing armies and civil society.

THE faculty of intelligence may be considered as the first gift of God; its due exercise is the happiness and honour of man; its abuse, his calamity and disgrace. The most trifling duty is not properly discharged without the exertion of this noble faculty; yet how often does it lie dormant, while the highest concernments are in issue? Believe me, my countrymen, the labor of examining for ourselves, or great imposition, must be submitted to; there is no other alternative: and unless we weigh and consider what we examine, little benefit will result from research. We are at this extraordinary crisis called to view the most melancholy events of our day: the scene is unpleasant to the eye, but its contemplation will be useful, if our thoughts terminate with judgment, resolution, and spirit.

If at this period of public affairs, we do not think, deliberate, and determine like men—men of minds to conceive, hearts to feel, and virtue to act,—what are we to do?—to gaze upon our bondage? while our enemies throw about firebrands, arrows, and death, and play their tricks of desperation with the gambols of sport and wantonness.

The proper object of society and civil institutions is the advancement of " the greatest happiness of the greatest number." The people (as a body, being never interested to injure themselves and uniformly desirous of the general welfare) have ever made this collective felicity the object of their wishes and pursuit. But strange, as it may seem, what the many through successive ages have desired and sought, the few have found means to baffle and defeat. The necessity of the acquisition hath been conspicuous to the rudest mind; but man, inconsiderate that, " in every society, there is an effort constantly tending to confer on one part the height of power, and to reduce the other to the extreme of weakness and misery,"* hath abandoned the most

---

* Marquis Beccaria.

important concerns of civil society to the caprice and control of those, whose elevation caused them to forget their pristine equality, and whose interest urged them to degrade the best and most useful below the worst and most unprofitable of the species.* Against this exertion, and the principle which originates it, no vigilance can be too sharp, no determination too severe.

But alas! as if born to delude and be deluded—to believe whatever is taught, and bear all that is imposed—successive impositions, wrongs, and insults awaken neither the sense of injury nor spirit of revenge. Fascinations and enchantments, chain and fetters, bind in adamant the understanding and passions of the human race. Ages follow ages, pointing the way to study wisdom,—but the charm continues.

Sanctified by authority and armed with power, error and usurpation bid defiance to truth and

---

* "The modes of government which have been imposed on credulous man, have been not only deficient in producing the just ends of government, viz. the full and impartial security of the rights of nature; but also, have been rather formidable and dangerous cabals against the peace, happiness, and dignity of society." Macaulay's Observations on Burke's Thoughts, &c. Edit. 5. p. 10.

right, while the bulk of mankind sit gazing at the monster of their own creation :—a monster,* to which their follies and vices gave origin, and their depravity and cowardice continue in existence.

"The greatest happiness of the greastest number" being the object and bond of society, the establishment of truth and justice ought to be the basis of civil policy and jurisprudence. But this capital establishment can never be attained in a state where there exists a power superior to the civil magistrate and sufficient to control the authority of the laws. Whenever therefore the profession of arms becomes a distinct order in the state, and a standing army part of the constitution, we are not scrupulous to affirm, that the end of the social compact is defeated, and the nation called to act upon the grand question consequent upon such an event.

The people who compose the society (for whose security the labour of its institution was performed, and of the toils its preservation daily sustained),

---

* " This (standing army) is a monster, that will devour all your liberties and properties—there is a time for all men to speak, and now, when our liberties are at stake, duty to God, our prince, and country forbid to be silent." Sir John Hotham's speech in Parliament 1673. Grey's Debates, vol. ii. p. 391.

the people, I say, are the only competent judges of their own welfare, and, therefore, are the only suitable authority to determine touching the great end of their subjection and their sacrifices. This position leads us to two others, not impertinent on this occasion, because of much importance to Americans :—

That the legislative body of the commonwealth ought to deliberate, determine, and make their decrees in places where the legislators may easily know from their own observation the wants and exigencies, the sentiments and will, the good and happiness of the people; and the people as easily know the deliberations, motives, designs, and conduct of their legislators, before their statutes and ordinances actually go forth and take effect :—

That every member of the legislature ought himself to be so far subject in his person and property to the laws of the state, as to immediately and effectually feel every mischief and inconvenience resulting from all and every act of legislation.

The science of man and society, being the most extended in its nature, and the most important in its consequences, of any in the circle of erudition, ought to be an object of universal attention and study. Was it made so, the rights of mankind would not remain buried for ages under systems of civil and priestly hierarchy, nor social felicity overwhelmed by lawless domination.

Under appearances the most venerable and institutions the most revered; under the sanctity of religion, the dignity of government, and the smiles of beneficence, do the subtle and ambitious make their first encroachments upon their species. *Watch* and *oppose* ought therefore to be the motto of mankind. A nation in its best estate—guarded by good laws, fraught with public virtue, and steeled with martial courage—may resemble Achilles: but Achilles was wounded in the heel. The least point left unguarded the foe enters:—latent evils are the most dangerous—for we often receive the mortal wound, while we are flattered with security.

The experience of all ages shows that mankind are inattentive to the calamities of others, careless of admonition, and with difficulty roused to repel the most injurious invasions. "I perceive," said the great patriot Cicero to his countrymen, "an inclination for tyranny in all Cæsar projects and executes."* Notwithstanding this friendly cau-

---

* Plut. Life of Cæsar.

tion, not "till it was too late did the people find out, that no beginnings, however small, are to be neglected."* For that Cæsar, who at first attacked the commonwealth with mines, very soon opened his batteries.† Encroachments upon the rights and property of the citizen are like the rollings of mighty waters over the breach of ancient mounds; slow and unalarming at the beginning; rapid and terrible in the current; a deluge and devastation at the end. Behold the oak, which stretcheth itself to the mountains, and overshadows the vallies, was once an acorn in the bowels of the earth. Slavery, my friends, which was yesterday ingrafted among you, already overspreads the land, extending its arms to the ocean, and its limbs to the rivers. Unclean and voracious animals, under its covert, find protection and food;—but the shade blasteth the green herb, and the root thereof poisoneth the dry ground, while the winds which wave its branches scatter pestilence and death.

Regular government is necessary to the preservation of private property, and personal security. Without these, men will descend into barbarism, or

---

* Plut. Life of Cæsar. † Ib.

at best become adepts in humiliation and servility; but they will never make a progress in literature or the useful arts. Surely a proficiency in arts and sciences is of some value to mankind, and deserves some consideration. What regular government can America enjoy with a legislative a thousand leagues distant, unacquainted with her exigencies, militant in interest, and unfeeling of her calamities? What protection of property—when ministers under this authority shall overrun the land with mercenary legions? What personal safety, when a British administration—(such as it now is, and corrupt as it may be)—pour armies into the capital and senate-house, point their artillery against the tribunal of justice, and plant weapons of death at the posts of our doors?*

Thus exposed to the power, and insulted by the arms of Britain—standing armies become an object of serious attention. And as the history of mankind affords no instance of successful and confirmed tyranny, without the aid of military forces, we shall not wonder to find them the *desiderata* of princes, and the grand object of modern policy. What though they subdue every generous passion,

---

* All this, and much more, hath Boston been witness to.

and extinguish every spark of virtue—all this must be done, before empires will submit to be exhausted by tribute and plundered with impunity.

Amidst all the devices of man to the prejudice of his species, the institution of which we treat hath proved the most extensively fatal to religion, morals, and social happiness. Founded in the most malevolent dispositions of the human breast, disguised by the policy of state, supported by the lusts of ambition, the sword hath spread havock and misery throughout the world. By the aid of mercenary troops, the sinews of war, the property of the subject, the life of the commonwealth have been committed to the hands of hirelings, whose interest and very existence depend on an abuse of their power. In the lower class of life, standing armies have introduced brutal debauchery and real cowardice; in the higher orders of state, venal haughtiness and extravagant dissipation. In short, whatever are the concomitants of despotism, whatever the appendages of oppression, this armed monster hath spawned or nurtured, protected or established;—monuments and scourges of the folly and turpitude of man.

Review the armament of modern princes :— what sentiments actuate the military body? what characters compose it? Is there a private sentinel of all the innumerable troops that make so brilliant a figure, who would not for want of property have been driven from a Roman cohort, when soldiers were the defenders of liberty?*

Booty, and blind submission, is the science of the camp. When lust, rapacity, or resentment, incites, whole battalions proceed to outrage. Do their leaders command—obedience must follow. "Private soldiers," said Tiberius Gracchus from the Roman rostrum, "fight and die to advance the wealth and luxury of the great."† "Soldiers," said an eminent Puritan, in his sermon, preached in this country more than a hundred and thirty years ago, "are commonly men who fight themselves fearlessly into the mouth of hell for revenge, a booty, or a little revenue:—a day of battle is a day of harvest for the devil." Soldiers, like men, are much the same in every age and country.

> "Heroes are much the same, the point's agreed,
> From Macedonia's madman to the Swede."

What will they not fight for,—whom will they not fight against? Are these men, who take up

---

* See Rousseau's Social Comp. 202.
† Plut. Life of Tib. Grac.

arms with a view to defend their country and its laws? Do the ideas or the feelings of the citizen actuate a British private on entering the camp?* Excitements, generous and noble like these, are far from being the stimuli of a modern phalanx. The general of an army, habituated to uncontrolled command, feels himself absolute; he forgets his superiors,† or rather despises that civil authority, which is destitute of an energy to compel his obedience. His soldiers (who look up to him as their sovereign, and to their officers as magistrates) lose the sentiments of the citizen, and contemn the laws. Thus a will and a power to tyrannize, become united; and the effects are as inevitable and fatal in the political, as the moral world.

The soldiers of Great Britain are by the mutiny act deprived of those legal rights which belong to the meanest of their fellow-subjects, and even to the vilest malefactor.‡ Thus divested of those

---

* See 1 Black. Com. p. 307.

† " It is grown a principle among the army (an ill nursery for young men), that Parliaments are roots of rebellion." Sir John Hotham in the House of Commons, 1673. Grey's Debates in Parliament, Vol. ii. p. 203.

‡ Lds. Prot. Vol. i. p. 280. Anno 1717.

rights and privileges which render Britons the envy of all other nations, and liable to such hardships and punishments as the limits and mercy of our known laws utterly disallow ; it may well be thought they are persons best prepared and most easily tempted to strip others of their rights, having already lost their own.* Excluded, therefore, from the enjoyments which others possess, they envy and hate the rest of the community, and indulge a malignant pleasure in destroying those privileges to which they can never be admitted.† How eminently does modern observation verify that sentiment of Baron Montesquieu, " A slave living among freemen will soon become a beast.‡

A very small knowledge of the human breast, and a little consideration of the ends for which we form into societies and commonwealths, discover the impropriety and danger of admitting such an order of men to obtain an establishment in the state ; the annals and experience of every age show, that it is not only absurdity and folly, but distraction and madness. But we in this

---

* See Lds. Prot. Vol. i. p. 283. Anno 1717.
† Montesq. Sp. Laws, 15, 12 ; and 1 Black. Com. 416.
‡ See Sp. Laws, 348. 2 Edit.

region of the earth have not only to dread and struggle with the natural and common calamities resulting from such military bodies, but the combined dangers arising from an army of foreigners, stationed in the very bowels of the land. Infatuated Britons have been told, and as often deceived, that an army of natives would never oppress their own countrymen. But Cæsar and Cromwell, and an hundred others, have enslaved their country with such kind of forces. And who does not know that subalterns are implicitly obedient to their officers; who, when they become obnoxious are easily changed; as armies, to serve the purposes of ambition and power, are soon new modelled. But as to America, the armies which infest her shores, are in every view foreigners, disconnected with her in interest, kindred, and other social alliances; who have nothing to lose, but every thing to gain, by butchering and oppressing her inhabitants. But yet worse;— their inroads are to be palliated, their outrages are to receive a sanction and defence from a Parliament whose claims and decrees are as unrighteous, as the administration is corrupt; as boundless as their ambition, and as terrible as their power. The usurpation and tyranny of the

Decemviri of Rome are represented as singularly odious and oppressive; but even they never assumed what Britain, in the face of all mankind, hath avowed and exercised over the colonies;— the power of passing laws merely on her own authority. "Nothing that we propose," said they to the people, "can pass into a law without your consent. Be yourselves, ye Romans, the authors of those laws on which your happiness depends."

"The dominion of all great empires degrades and debases the human species."* The dominion of Britain is that of a mighty empire. Her laws waste our substance, her placemen corrupt our morals, and her armies are to break our spirits. Yes, are they not to do more? "To spoil, to slaughter, and to commit every kind of violence; and then to call the manœuvre by a lying name, —government; and when they have spread a general devastation, call it peace."† In the barbarous massacres of France, in the 16th century, the very hangmen refused obedience to the cruel

---

* See Dr Robertson's Hist. Charles V. vol. i. p. 3.
† Part of a noble speech recorded by Tacitus (Vita Agric.), of an old Britain to his followers, exciting them to free their country, then a province of Rome, from the yoke of bondage.

mandates of the French monarch, saying, they were legal officers, and only executed those the laws condemned. Yet history bears testimony that the soldiers performed the office which the hangman refused.* Who then can be at a loss for the views of those who were so fond of introducing and tenacious of obtaining similar peace-officers in this obnoxious capital?† But let all such,—yes, let Great Britain consider the nature of mankind; let her examine carefully the history of past events, and attend to the voice of experience.

In the same age we have just mentioned, the Low Countries, then subject to the crown of Spain, being persecuted by the court and church of that kingdom, rose up to resist their oppressors. Upon which in the year 1567, the Duke of Alva was sent, and entered the country with a well appointed army, ten thousand strong; in order to quell and punish the insurgents. Terrified with these martial operations, the towns suffered

---

* See the life of Theod. Agrip. D'Aubigne, p. 38.
† Whoever wants information of the spirit, cruelty, and rapine of soldiers quartered in populous cities, let them peruse the first book of the elegant and instructive history, written by the masterly hand of Tacitus.

the open breach of their charters, and the people submitted to the most humiliating infraction of their liberties; while Alva, being invested with the government, erected the court of twelve, called The Council of Blood, and caused great numbers to be condemned and executed on account of the insurrections. Universal complaints ensued on this disuse of the ordinary courts of law and the introduction of the army; but complaints were in vain, and all murmurs despised. The people became enraged; but without a leader, they were over-awed. "The army," says Sir William Temple, "was fierce and brave, and desirous of nothing so much as a rebellion of the country." All was seizure and process, confiscation and imprisonment, blood and horror, insolence and dejection, punishments executed and meditated revenge. But though the multitude threatened vengeance, the threats of a broken and unarmed people excited contempt and not fear. Alva redoubled his impositions and ravages; his edicts were published for raising monies without the consent of the state, and his soldiers were called to levy the exactions by force. But the event showed, that the timidity and tameness of mankind, like every thing human, will have a period. The patience of the miserable sufferers came to an end; and those commotions began, which deluged a great part of Europe with blood, and finally freed the United Provinces from the yoke of Spain and the Inquisition. What conflicts too sharp, what horrors too dreadful to endure, for such a happy deliverance,—such a glorious issue? Thus " the first period of the Low-Country troubles," says the same ingenious writer, " proved to King Philip (of Spain) a dear experience, how little the best conduct and boldest armies are able to withstand the torrent of a stubborn and enraged people, which ever bears all down before it, till it comes to be divided into different channels by arts, or by chance; or till the springs, which are the humours that fed it, come to be spent, or dry up of themselves." *

During several centuries, history informs us, that no monarch in Europe was either so bold, or so powerful, as to venture on any steps towards the introduction of regular troops. At last, Charles the Seventh of France, seizing a favourable opportunity in 1445, executed that which his

---

* See Temple's Obs. upon the United Provinces, pp. 15, 16, 17, 19.

predecessors durst not attempt, and established the first standing army known in Europe. Lewis the Eleventh, son and successor of Charles, finding himself at the head of his father's forces, was naturally excited to extend the limits of his ancestors, in the levies of money and men. Charles had not been able to raise upon his subjects two millions, but the army he left his successor enabled him to levy nearly five. The father established an army of about seventeen hundred, which "he kept in good order, and placed for the defence of the realm;" but this army, though thus disciplined and stationed, enabled the son to maintain "in continual pay a terrible band of men of arms, which gave the realm," says the historian, Philip de Comines, "a cruel wound, of which it bled many years." *
How regular, correspondent, and uniform are the rise and progression of military calamities in all ages! How replete with instruction,—how full of admonition, are the memorials of distant times; especially when contracted into the view, and held up in comparison with the present.

---

* Sixth Book of the Hist. of Ph. de Comines, p. 206. London Edit. 1614.

Charles and Lewis having set the example, all the neighbouring crowned heads soon followed, and mercenary troops were introduced into all the considerable kingdoms of the continent. They gradually became the only military force that was employed or trusted. "It has long been," says the learned Dr Robertson, "the chief object of policy to increase and support them, and the great aim of princes or ministers to discredit and to annihilate all other means of national activity or defence."* Who will wonder at this, who reflect, that absolute monarchies are established, and can only be supported by mercenary forces? Who can be surprised, that princes and their subalterns discourage a martial spirit among the people, and endeavour to render useless and contemptible the militia, when this institution is the natural strength, and only stable safeguard, of a free country? †
"Without it, it is folly to think any free government will ever have security and stability." ‡ A

---

* Hist. Charles V. vol. i. p. 95. See also Macauly's Hist. of England, vol. ii. p. 165. Sir John Phillips' Speech in the British House of Commons, 1744. Debates of the Commons, vol. ii. p. 61.

† "Our trained bands are the truest and most proper strength of a free nation." Eikonoklastes of John Milton.

‡ Hume 278.

standing army in quarters will grow effeminate and dissolute; while a militia, uniformly exercised with hard labor, are naturally firm and robust. Thus an army in peace is worse than a militia; and in war, a militia will soon become disciplined and martial. But "when the sword is in the hands of a single person, as in our constitution, he will always," says the ingenious Hume, "neglect to discipline the militia,* in order to have a pretext for keeping up a standing army. It is evident," says the same great character, "that this is a mortal distemper in the British government; of which it must at last inevitably perish." † What a deformed monster is a standing army in a free nation! Free, did I say! what people are truly free, whose monarch has a numerous body of armed mercenaries at his heels? who is already absolute in his power,—or

---

* Of a like opinion was Sir Thomas Lee, in Charles the Second's reign. See Grey's Debates, vol. ii. p. 391.

In order to discourage the train bands in Charles the First's time, the court found means to enhance the price of powder; and it was accordingly complained of in Parliament as " a great grievance." See Rush. Coll. vol. i. p. 33. Let us not be surprised, if any like artifice should be practised in our day. † Hume 279.

by the breath of his nostrils may in an instant make himself so?

No free government was ever founded, or ever preserved its liberty, without uniting the characters of citizen and soldier in those destined for the defence of the state. The sword should never be in the hands of any but those who have an interest in the safety of the community, who fight for their religion and their offspring,—and repel invaders that they may return to their private affairs and the enjoyment of freedom and good order. Such are a well regulated militia composed of the freeholders, citizens, and husbandmen, who take up arms to preserve their property as individuals, and their rights as freemen. Such is the policy of a truly wise nation, and such was the wisdom of the ancient Britons. The primitive constitution of a state in a few centuries falls to decay; errors and corruptions creep gradually into the administration of government, till posterity forget, or disregard, the institutions of their remote ancestors. In ancient time, the militia of England was raised, officered, and conducted, by common consent. Its militia was the ornament of the realm in peace, and for ages continued the only and sure defence in war. Was the king himself general of an army, it was by the consent of his people. Thus when the Romans visited the island of Britain, Cassibelan was the prince and chief commander in war; but it was by the election of the great common council. *Summa belli*, says Cæsar, *communi concilio, Cassibelano traditur*. Nor will this seem strange, when we consider that it was the first state maxim with the Druids, *Ne loqui de republicâ, nisi per concilium*; not even to speak upon a matter of state but in council. Nor is it to be wondered that such politicians informed Cæsar, that they had been so long accustomed to liberty, that they knew not the meaning of tribute and slavery; and sent him word that they had as good blood as he, and from the same fountain. Surely a message that was received by a Roman, may be sent to a British Cæsar. These were those venerable Druids, who had inspired the Gauls, of whom Cæsar reports this memorable boast: "We can call or appeal to such a great common council, as all the world cannot resist." Tacitus, speaking of our Saxon ancestors, relates, *Reges ex nobilitate, duces ex virtute in iisdem conciliis eliguntur*. The great council, or the Parliament of the state, had, not only the appointment of the *principes militiæ*, but the conduct of all military forces, from the first erection of the standard to its lodgment in the citadel ; for, as the same noble writer informs, it was their general custom, not to entrust any man with the bearing of arms, *antequam civitas suffecturum probaverit.* Such was the security of the people from the calamities of a standing army : happy indeed, if their successors could boast a similar provision ; —Britain would not now be groaning under oppression, nor her distant children struggling for their freedom.

A spirited nation thus embodied in a well disciplined militia will soon become warlike ; and such a people, more fitted for action than debate, always hasten to a conclusion on the subject of grievances and public wrongs, and bring their deliberations to the shortest issue. With them "it is the work of but one day, to examine and resolve the nice question, concerning the behaviour of subjects towards a ruler who abuses his power."*

Artful dissemblings and plausible pretences are always adopted in order to introduce regular troops. Dionysius became the tyrant of Syracuse,

---

* See Dr Robertson's Hist. of Scotland, vol. i. p. 204, 205.

the most opulent of all the Grecian cities, by feigning a solicitude for the people and a fear of his own person. He humbly prayed only a guard for his protection: they easily granted, what he readily took—the power of plundering by military force and entailing his sovereignty by a devise of his sword. Agathocles, a successor to the Dionysian family and to the command of the army, continued the military tyranny, and butchered the enslaved people by centuries.

Cardinal Ximenes, who made the first innovation of this kind in Spain, disguised the measure under the pious and popular appearance of resisting the progress of the Infidels. The Nobles saw his views and excited opposition in the chief towns of the kingdom. But by dexterously using terror and entreaty, force and forbearance, the refractory cities were brought to compliance. The nobles, thus driven to desperate resolutions by the Cardinal's military movements, at a personal interview, were warm and intemperate; when the arch-prelate insensibly led them towards a balcony from which they had a view of a large body of troops under arms, and a formidable train of artillery. "Behold," says he, pointing to these, and raising his voice, " the powers which I have received from his Catholic majesty. With these I govern Castile, and with these I will govern it." Nobles and people discovered it was now too late for resistance :—to regret past folly and dread future calamities was the remaining fate of the wretched Castilians. After the Romans quitted the island of Britain, the first appearance of a standing army was under Richard the Second. The suppression of his enemies in Ireland calling him out of England, his subjects seized the opportunity and dethroned him.

Henry the Seventh, a character odious for rapacity and fraud, was the first king of England who obtained a permanent military band in that kingdom. It was only a band of fifty archers :— with the harmless appellation of *yeomen of the guards*. This apparently trivial institution was a precedent for the greatest political evil that ever infested the inhabitants of Britain. The ostensible pretext was the dignity of government—" the grandeur of majesty : "—* the alteration of the constitution and an increase of power was the aim of the prince. An early " oppugnation of the king's authority," though no doubt his favourite subalterns would have styled it "ill-timed," † had easily

---

* See Rapin. † See the late Governor Bernard's Speeches.

effected that disbanding of the new-raised forces, which being a little while delayed, no subsequent struggles have accomplished. The wisdom of resistance at the beginning has been repeatedly inculcated by the wise and liberal-minded of all nations, and the experience of every age hath confirmed their instruction. But no precept, or example, can make the bulk of mankind wise for themselves. Though cautioned (as we have seen)* against the projects of Cæsar, the smiles of his benignity deceived the Roman Commonwealth, till the increase of his power bid defiance to opposition. Celebrated for his generosity and magnificence, his complacency and compassion,† the complaisant courtier made his way into the hearts of his countrymen. They would not believe, though admonished by the best of men and first of patriots,‡ that the smiling Cæsar would filch away their liberties;—that a native—born and bred a Roman—would enslave his country—the land of his fathers—the land of his birth—the land of his posterity.§ But the ambitious Cæsar aiming

---

* See before, p. 398. † See Sallust.
‡ M. T. Cicero. See Plut. Life of Cæsar.
§ A similar infatuation hath, oftener than once, prevailed in this Province: an instance of which we have in the time

at authority, and Cæsar armed and intoxicated with power, appear in very different characters. He who appeared with the mildness of a fine gentleman, in his primeval state, in an advanced station conducted with the sternness of a tyrant. Opposed by a tribune of the people in taking money out of the public treasury against the laws, Cæsar, with an army at his heels, proclaimed, "arms and laws do not flourish together." " If you are

---

of Governor Dudley. This gentleman " after he had been agent for the country, tacked about, and joined with the instruments that overthrew the charter, and accepted an illegal and arbitrary commission from King James, by which he held the government, until the arrival of Sir Edmund Andross; and then was (as president of the council, and Chief Judge of the territory) a chief tool of all the ensuing barbarous and infamous administration." " After his appointment to the government, his conduct was of the same texture with his former life: (it was his son Paul, who wrote to England that this country would never be worth living in, for lawyers and gentlemen, till the charter is taken away.")—Yet such was the delusion at that day, " some of the Council would firmly believe charitably of him, because his family and interest were here, and therefore thought it unreasonable to believe he would do any thing that should hurt his country." See a book published in London, about 1708, intitled, "The deplorable state of New England, by reason of a covetous and treacherous Governor and pusillanimous Counsellors." p. 3 & 9, &c.

not pleased," added the usurper, "with what I am about, you have nothing to do but to withdraw. Indeed war will not bear much liberty of speech. When I say this, I am departing from my own right. For you and all I have found exciting a spirit of faction* against me are at my disposal." Saying this, he approached the doors of the treasury; as the keys were not produced, he sent his workmen to break them open.† This is the complaisant Cæsar—renowned for his amiable qualities: by his easy address he deceived, and by his arts enslaved his countrymen,—and prepared the way for a succeeding Nero to spoil and slaughter them. Singular and very remarkable have been the interpositions of Providence in favour of New England :—the permission of an early carnage in our streets, peradventure, was to awaken us from the danger—of being politely beguiled into security and fraudfully drawn into bondage ;—a state that sooner or later ends in rapine and blood. Shall we be too enthusiastic, if we attribute to the Divine influence that unexpected

---

* Justice was faction in ancient Rome, as well as modern Britain. See Macauly's Hist. 405. Montagu's Rise and Fall of the Ancient Repub. 275.

† Plut. Life of Cæsar.

good which hath so often in our day been brought out of premeditated evil? Few, comparatively, of the many mischiefs aimed against us, but what have terminated in some advantage, or are now verging to some happy issue. If the dexterity of veteran troops has not excited envy, if their outrage hath not provoked revenge, their military discipline hath set a well-timed example, and their savage fury been a well improved incentive. The lusts of an enemy may touch a sensibility of mind, and his very pride pique the virtue of the heart.

Fleets which appeared formidable, and armies which threatened destruction, have either vapoured away with empty parade, or executed their mischievous designs with rashness and folly. To compensate the insult and repair the injury, Providence hath caused these armaments to scatter much wealth and diffuse abroad a martial passion:—a passion, which hath proved so contagious, that our militia are advanced a century, at least, in discipline and improvements. Where are the people who can compose a militia of better men, more expert in the use of arms and the conduct of the field, than we can now call forth into action? A militia who, a few years ago, knew near as much of the science of Algebra, as of the art military. Thus hostile invasions have roused among us the genius of war :—that genius, which, under God, will conduct us with safety and honour—with triumph and glory.

Surely we may say of our adversaries ;—In the net, which they hid, is their own foot taken, and they are snared in the wickedness of their own hands. Our enemies, the last ten years, have been employed to weave a spider's web and hatch the eggs of a cockatrice :—consuming their own bowels by what they have weaved ; and destroyed by what they have brought forth. Thus Goliah is killed with his own sword, Haman hanged upon his own gallows.* Marvellous were the doings of God in the eyes of our fathers ;—nor less astonishing are his works in the days of their progeny.†

---

* Thus also the Bishop of Verdun, who was the modern contriver of a new species of state-prison (for which many have cursed him), was, by the righteous dispensation of Providence, first put into it himself, and confined " in the cruel prison" fourteen years. Phil. de Com. Hist. p. 216.

† It was an observation applied by the first settlers of New England to their great consolation, that when wicked men are nearest their hopes, godly men are farthest from their fears, because the insolence and cowardice of the wicked usually engage God to defeat their design.

Charles the Second told his parliament, their "jealousy, that the forces he had raised were designed to control law and property, was weak and frivolous." * The cajolement took for a season, but his subjects having been abused by repeated violations of his most solemn vows, at last roused from their lethargy; and the king began to dread the severity of their vengeance. He therefore kept up a standing army, not only against law, but against the repeated resolutions of every Parliament of his reign. He found that corruption without force could not confirm him a tyrant, and therefore cherished and augmented his troops to the destruction of his people and the terror of his senators. "There go our masters," † was a common saying among the members of Parliament. "No law can restrain these people; houses are taken from us, our lives are in danger," said one member in Parliament. "Without betraying our trust," said Russel, "we must vote these standing forces a grievance. There are designs about the King, to ruin religion and property. Public business is the least of their concern. A

---

* Speech to both Houses, February 1672, and Grey's Deb. in Parl. vol. vii. p. 26.
† Johnson's Works, p. 312.

few upstart people, making hay while the sun shines, set up an army to establish their interest: I would have care taken for the future, that no army be raised for a cabal interest. A gentleman said, the last session, that this war was made rather for the army, than the army for the war. This government, with a standing army, can never be safe: we cannot be secure in this house; and some of us may have our heads taken off."*

Patriots harangued in vain;—the Commons voted the keeping up the army illegal and a grievance,—but while they thus did, they openly betrayed a dread of that army. " I would not give an alarm to those who have arms in their hands," said one member; " I cannot but observe that the House of Commons is now in fear of the army," said another.† Plain as it was for what end the army was kept up, the people slumbered.

The exigencies of the times called for something more than votes and paper resolutions. What was the consequence of this national cowardice and inactivity? " England saw herself engaged in the expense of 600,000 pounds sterling, to pay an army and fleet, which certainly, " says

---

* Grey's Debates, vol. ii. 219, 393.
† Grey's Debates in Parl. vol. vii. p. 71, 72, 73.

Rapin, "had not been prepared to make war with France, or for the security of England." Spirited resolves may please the ear ; senatorial eloquence may charm the eye, but these are not the weapons with which to combat standing armies ; these were not those, which freed this capital from stationed regiments ;—they are not those, which will ultimately——But I forbear : time will unfold, what 1 may not foretell.

The British court, never destitute of plausibilities to deceive, or inventions to inthrall the nation, appropriated monies, raised by Parliament for the purpose of disbanding the army, to their continuance ; * and uniformly pursued similar measures, till, in the year 1684, "the King, in order to make his people sensible of their new slavery, affected to muster his troops, which amounted to 4000, well armed and disciplined." † If Rapin denominated so small an armament, the "slavery of the subject under Charles the Second," what would he call the state of Britons under George the Third ? With 4000 troops, the kingdom, it seems, was reduced to servitude : but the spirit of the nation soon after rose. In 1685 complaint was made in

---

* See King's Speech, October 1678. † See Rapin.

Parliament, " that the country was weary of the oppression and plunder of the soldiers ;" " the army," it was said, " debauched the manners of all the people, their wives, daughters, and servants."* The grievance became intolerable,—and what was happy, it was not too mighty for opposition. James the Second had only 14, or 15,000 troops, and no riot act. The barbarities of a Kirk, and the campaign of a Jeffreys, could not pass with impunity. The revolution succeeded, and James abdicated his throne. Such was the fate of one, who vainly affected to play the despot with about fifteen regiments. Had he been encircled with an hundred, no doubt he had reigned an applauded tyrant—flattered, in his day, with that lying appellation, "the wisest and the best of kings."†

---

* Grey's Debates, vol. viii. p. 365, 366.

† " Patriæ Patri, Regum Optimo," was part of an inscription on the marble statue erected to Charles the Second, as worthless and odious a prince as any in the history of England. See Rapin, p. 734. fol. edit.—Even Richard the Third, generally represented both as a monster in person and disposition, hath however had panegyrists who affirm, that he was remarkably genteel, and the best of kings. See Barrington's Observations on the more ancient Statutes, p. 392, 393.

Thus that insolent tyrant, Henry the Eighth, who disgraced his species by repeated violations of his most solemn vows,

The army of the present king of Great Britain is larger than that with which Alexander subdued the East, or Cæsar conquered Gaul. " If the army we now keep up," said Sir John Phillips thirty years ago, in the House of Commons, " should once be as much attached to the crown as Julius Cæsar's army was to him, I should be glad to know where we could find a force superior to that army." * Is there no such attachment now existing ? † Surely the liberties of England, if not held at will, are holden by a very precarious tenure.

---

and the practice of open debauchery and riot; a despot, who, lost to the common feelings of humanity, made his laws more bloody than those of Draco or Dionysius, and caused a greater number of executions than any other King of England, is characterized on the Journals of the House of Lords, as a Prince of wondrous goodness and wisdom. See the same Observations, p. 461, 462, 472. Surely he who calls the reigning monarch " the wisest and best of kings," ought always to be suspected of burlesque and sarcasm, or something worse.

* See Debates in the House of Commons, vol. ii. p. 56, 57, 58.

† " By a numerous army and a severe riot act, you may indeed prevent mobs and riots among the people; but if this method be pursued for a long time, you will make your min-

The supreme power is ever possessed by those who have arms in their hands, and are disciplined to the use of them. When the Argives, conscious of a good title, disputed with Lysander about boundaries, the Lacedæmonian showed his sword, and vauntingly cried out, "He that is master of this, can best plead about boundaries."* The Mamertines of Messina declined appearance at the tribunal of Pompey, to acknowledge his jurisdiction, alleging in excuse, ancient privileges, granted them by the Romans. "Will you never have done," exclaimed Pompey, "with citing laws and privileges to men who wear swords?"† What boundaries will they set to their passions, who have no limits to their power? Unlimited oppression and wantonness are the never-failing attendants of unbounded authority. Such power a veteran army always acquire, and being able to riot in mischief with impunity, they always do it with licentiousness.

---

isters tyrants and your people slaves." Sir John Bernard's Speech in the British House of Commons, 1774. Debat. vol. ii. p. 118. *Qu.* If this method hath not been thus pursued? And *Qu.* Whether the prophecy is fulfilling, or already accomplished in Great Britain?

* Plut. Life of Lysander. † Plut. Life of Pompey.

Regular soldiers, embodied for the purpose of originating oppression, or extending dominion, ever compass the control of the magistrate. The same force which preserves a despotism immutable, may change the despot every day. Power is soon felt by those who possess it, and they who can command, will never servilely obey. The leaders of the army, having become masters of the person of their sovereign, degrade or exalt him at will.* Obvious as these truths may seem, and confirmed as they are by all history, † yet a weak or wicked prince is easily persuaded, by the creatures who surround him, to act the tyrant. A character so odious to subjects must necessarily be timid and jealous. Afraid of the wise and good, he must support his dignity by the assistance of the worthless and wicked. Standing armies are therefore raised by the infatuated prince; no sooner established, than the defence-

---

* " Whoever uses a mercenary army," says the great Lord Chancellor Bacon, " though he may spread his feathers for a time, he will mew them soon after; and raise them with what design you please, yet, like the West India dogs, in Boccaline, in a little time they will certainly turn sheep-biters."

† See Dr Sullivan's Lectures on the Laws of England, p. 56.

less multitude are their first prey. Mere power is wanton and cruel; the army grow licentious, and the people grow desperate. Dreadful alternative to the infatuated monarch! In constant jeopardy of losing the *regalia* of empire, till the caprice of an armed banditti degrade him from sovereignty,* or the enraged people wreak an indiscriminate and righteous vengeance. Alas! when will kings learn wisdom, and mighty men have understanding?

A further review of the progress of armies in our parent state, will be a useful, though not a pleasant employ. No particular reason or occasion was so much as suggested in the bill which passed the Parliament in 1717, for keeping on foot a standing army of 30,000 men in time of peace (a number since amazingly increased:) an act justly recorded in the Lord's Journal to be a precedent for keeping the same army at all times, and which, the protest of that day foretold, " must inevitably subvert the ancient constitution

---

* Sir Robert Atkins (afterwards Lord Chief Justice of the Common Pleas in England) said in Parliament (anno 1667), —" Six Emperors in five years had their heads tumbled down by a military government." Grey's Debates in Parl. vol. i. p. 23.

of the realm, and subject the subjects to arbitrary power." * To borrow the pointed turn of a modern orator,—what was once prophecy, is now history.

The powers given by the mutiny act which is now constantly passed every year, were repeatedly in former times " opposed and condemned by Parliament as repugnant to Magna Charta, and inconsistent with the fundamental rights and liberties of a free people."† In this statute, no provision is made for securing the obedience of the military to the civil power, on which the preservation of our constitution depends. A great number of armed men governed by martial law,‡ having it in their power, are naturally inclined not only to disobey, but to insult, the civil magistrate.§ The experience of what hath happened

---

* See Lords' Prot. vol. iii. p. 273.

† See same book, p. 279.

‡ " A law unknown to our constitution, destructive of our liberties, not endured by our ancestors, and never mentioned in any of our statutes, but in order to condemn it." Lords' Prot. vol. ii. p. 283.

§ Very notable instances of this have been seen in this province; which will be recorded to the eternal infamy of those who brooked the insult.

in England, as well as the memorials of all ages and nations have made it sufficiently apparent, that wherever an effectual provision is not made to secure the obedience of soldiers to the laws of their country, the military hath constantly subverted and swallowed up the civil power. What provision of this kind can the several continental legislatures make against British troops stationed in the colonies? Nay, if the virtue of one branch of government attempted the salutary measure, would the first branch ever give its consent? A governor must, he will, obey his master; the alternative is obvious;—the armies quartered among us must be removed, or they will in the end overturn and trample on all that we ought to hold valuable and sacred.

We have authority to affirm, that the regular forces of Great Britain consist of a greater number than is necessary for the guard of the king's person and the defence of the government, and therefore dangerous to the constitution of the kingdom. What then do these armaments, when established here, threaten to our laws and liberties? Well might the illustrious members of the House of Peers, in 1722, hold forth the danger of "a total alteration of the frame of our constitution, from a legal and limited monarchy to a despotic;" and declare, they were "induced to be of this judgement, as well from the nature of armies, and the inconsistency of great military power and martial law, with civil authority, as from the known and universal experience of other countries in Europe, which, by the influence and power of standing armies, in time of peace, have from limited monarchies, like ours, been changed into absolute." * The taxes necessary to maintain a standing army, drain and impoverish the land. Thus exhausted by tribute, the people gradually become spiritless, and fall an easy sacrifice to the reigning power.

Spirits, like Britons, naturally fierce and independent, are not easily awed or suddenly vanquished by the sword. Hence an augmentation of forces hath been pushed, when there was no design of bringing them into action against Englishmen in an open field. New forces have oftener than once been raised in England more for civil than military service; and as elections for a new Parliament have approached, this door has been opened to introduce a large body of

---

* See Lords' Prot. vol. i. pp. 337, 338.

commissioned pensioners.* What hath been the consequence? A constant majority of placemen meeting under the name of a Parliament, to establish grievances instead of redressing them,—to approve implicitly the measures of a court without information,—to support and screen ministers they ought to control or punish,—to grant money without right and expend it without discretion? Have these been the baneful consequences? Are these solemn truths? Alas! we tremble to think;—but we may venture to say, that when this is true of that legislative authority, which not only claims, but exercises, " full power and authority to make laws and statutes to bind the colonies and people of America in all cases whatsoever," † the forms of our constitution, creating

---

* See Lords' Prot. vol. ii. p. 162.

† See the declarative act of the British Parliament, anno 1766.—" From that period (Sir Robert Walpole's day) to the present time (1762), has proved a very remarkable one in the history of the British constitution;—no one instance can be produced in which the royal business has been retarded, through the scrupulousness of the people's representatives." Political Essays concerning the Present State of the British Empire.—" From the revolution to this day (1762), the measures of the crown have universally been the measures of Parliament." Ib. p. 46.

a fatal delusion, will become our greatest grievance.

The formalities of a free, and the ends of a despotic state, have often subsisted together. Thus deceived was the republic of Rome;—officers and magistrates retained their old names;—the forms of the ancient government being kept up, the fundamental laws of the commonwealth were violated with impunity, and its once free constitution utterly annihilated.* He who gave Augustus Cæsar the advice " that to the officers of state the same names, pomp, and ornaments, should be continued, with all the appearances of authority, without the power," † discovered an intimate acquaintance with mankind. The advice was followed, and Cæsar soon became senate, magistracy, and laws. Is not Britain to America what Cæsar was to Rome?

It is curious to observe the various acts of imposition, which are alternately practised by the great and subtle of this world on their subordinate and simple-minded brethren. Are a people free, new oppressions are introduced or shrouded under

---

* See hereafter.

† " Eadem magistratûm vocabula, sua consulibus, sua prætoribus species."

old names;—are they in present bondage, and begin to grow turbulent; new appellations must be adopted to disguise old burthens. A notable instance of this latter kind we find in the Parliament of Great Britain, (in 36 Ed. III, c. 2,) upwards of four hundred years ago. The royal prerogative, called *purveyance*, having been in vain regulated by many preceding statutes, still continued so intolerably grievous, that fresh murmurs and complaints called for a more adequate or better adapted provision. The British legislature, for this valuable purpose, therefore passed this very remarkable law, which, by way of remedy, enacted as follows, viz.—"That the hateful name of *purveyor*, shall be changed into that of *Acator*." Thus the nation were made to believe that the oppression ceased, because the name was altered. For the honour of government, as well as mankind, it is devoutly to be wished, that our laws and history contained no other record of such disgraceful practices. If any late acts of the British Parliament carry strong marks of a similar policy, it is surely not altogether unworthy the consideration of the members of that august body, —how far such disingenuous practices are consistent with the honour of their private characters, or the dignity of their public station.

The magic of sounds and appellations hath not ceased, and they work as much deception and abuse as ever. What valuable purpose does a wholly subordinate legislative serve (except to amuse with the shadow, while the substance is departed), if a remote state may legislate for and bind us " in all cases ? " To what end doth an American House of Representatives go through the forms of granting away monies, if another power, full as familiar with our pockets, may annihilate all they do; and afterwards, with a modern dexterity, take possession of our purses without ceremony, and dispose of the contents without modesty, without control, and without account ?*

---

* " If the king could at pleasure levy the necessary sums of money (for the expenses of the government &c.), he being sole judge of the necessity, both as to measure and quantity, as Charles the First claimed, in the case of ship-money, the state of the subjects would be precarious, and the king would be as absolute a monarch as the present king of France or Spain." Dr Sullivan's Lectures on the Laws of England, p. 189. What is it to America, whether the King or Parliament of Great Britain, or any other body, natural or political, is absolute master over her,—and where is the difference between French, Spanish, and English dragooning? In the reign of Charles the Second, a wooden shoe, such as the

It is curious and instructive to attend the course of debate in the British Commons for keeping up the army. At first even the highest courtiers would argue—that a standing army, in time of peace, was never attempted.* Soon after the court speakers urged for continuance of a numerous army for one year longer. At the end of several years after, the gentlemen throw aside the mask, and boldly declare such a number of troops must always be kept up. In short, the army must be continued till it becomes part of the constitution; and in later times members of the house have ventured to harangue for measures, none would have dared to lisp a few years before. The wise foresaw this, and the honest foretold it. " If we continue the army but a little while longer," said a celebrated member upwards of forty years ago, " it may be in the power of some gentlemen to talk in this house † in terms that will be no way

---

peasants wear, in France, was laid near the chair of the Speaker of the Commons House; the arms of England drawn at one end of it, and those of France at the other, with these words in the interval, *Utrum horum mavis accipe.* Grey's Debates, vol. ii. p. 223.

* See Sir Robert Carr's Harangue in Parliament, 1673. Grey's Debates, vol. ii. p. 220.

† Commons of Great Britain.

agreeable to the constitution or liberties of our country. To tell us, that the same number of forces must be always kept up, is a proposition full-fraught with innumerable evils, and more particularly with this, that it may make wicked ministers more audacious than otherwise they would be in projecting and propagating schemes which may be inconsistent with the liberties, destructive of the trade, and burthensome on the people of this nation. In countries governed by standing armies, the inclinations of the people are but little minded, the ministers place their security in the army, the humours of the army they only consult, with them they divide the spoils, and the wretched people are plundered by both." Who that now reconsiders this prophetic language, in conjunction with the events of his own time, but will cry out—The speaker felt the impulse of inspiration!

"Whoever," says the justly celebrated Dr Blackstone, "will attentively consider the English history may observe, that the flagrant abuse of any power, by the crown or its ministers, has always been productive of a struggle, which either discovers the exercise of that power to be contrary to law, or, if legal, restrains it for the future." *

The ingenious commentator seems here to have particular reference to periods prior to the revolution. But will the learned judge say, that since that era there have been no flagrant abuses of power by the crown or its ministers? Have not repeated struggles arisen in consequence of such abuses, which did not terminate in the happy issue so characteristic of Englishmen? Let any one peruse the journals of Parliament, especially those of the house of peers: let him carefully review the British and American annals of the present century, and answer truly to those questions. The natural inquiry will be—Whence then is it, that such abuses have become so numerous and flagrant, and the struggles of Britons so unsuccessful? Will not the question receive an ample solution in the words of the same great lawyer?— "There is a newly acquired branch of (royal) power; and that not the influence only, but the force of a disciplined army, paid indeed ultimately by the people, but immediately by the crown; raised by the crown, officered by the crown, commanded by the crown." †

---

* 3 Bla. Com. p. 135. † 1 Bla. Com. pp. 336, 337.

We are told, by the same learned author, that " whenever the unconstitutional oppressions, even of the sovereign power, advance with gigantic strides and threaten desolation to a state, mankind will not be reasoned out of the feelings of humanity, nor will sacrifice their liberty by a scrupulous adherence to those political maxims, which were established to preserve it."* But those who cannot be reasoned out of their feelings, are easily repressed by the terror of arms from giving tokens of their sensibility; and states, ancient and modern,—(yes, Britain will bear me witness!)—who would disdain to sacrifice their freedom to political institutions, have tremblingly stood aloof, while it was dragged to the altar under the banners of a royal army.

The policy and refinements of men clothed with authority often deceive those who are subject to its control; and thus a people are often induced to waive their rights, and relinquish the barriers of their safety. The fraud, however, must at last be discovered, and the nation will resume their ancient liberties, if there be no force sufficient to screen the usurper and defend his domination. The sword alone is sufficient to subdue that spirit,

---

* 1 Bla. Com. 245.

which compels rulers to their duty, and tyrants to their senses. Hence, then, though a numerous standing army may not be absolutely requisite to depress a kingdom into servitude, they are indispensably necessary to confirm an usurpation.

A large army and revenue are not easily and at once forced upon a free people. By slow degrees and plausible pretences, as we have seen in England, the end is accomplished. But when once a numerous body of revenue and military men, entirely dependant on the crown, are incorporated, they are regardless of any thing but its will: and where that will centres, and what such power can effect, is a matter of no doubtful disputation.

The present army of a prince is always composed of men of honor and integrity, as the reigning monarch is ever the best of kings. In such an army, it is said, you may trust your liberties with safety : in such a king, you may put your confidence without reserve ;—the good man has not a wish beyond the happiness of his subjects! Yet let it be remembered, that under the best of kings, we ought to seize the fleeting opportunity, and provide against the worst. But admitting that from this rare character—a wise and good monarch—a nation have nothing to fear ; yet they have every thing to dread from those who would clothe him with authority, and invest him with powers incompatible with all political freedom and social security.* France, Spain, Denmark, and Sweden, in modern times have felt the baneful effects of this fatal policy. Though the latter state are said to have this excellent institution, that the commissions to their military officers all run, *quam diu se bene gesserint :* a regulation which ought to be the tenure of all offices of public trust, and may be of singular utility in states which have incorporated a standing army as a part of the constitution of government.

An invasion and conquest by mere strangers and foreigners are neither so formidable nor disgraceful as the establishment of a standing army under color of the municipal law of the land. Thus Roman armies were more terrible to the Roman

---

* "Galba had the greatest integrity of heart: but in the court of Galba appeared all the extortion of Nero's reign:—and as the rapacity and other excesses of his ministers were imputed to him, Galba was no less hated, than if he had committed them himself." Plut. Life of Galba.—See also, to the same point, Gord. Disc. on Tacitus, vol. iii. p. 19, 35, 38, 79. A Monarch justly dignified with the appellation of "the wisest and best of kings," will surely receive some advantage by attentively contemplating an instance so replete with instruction.

colonies, than an "enemy's army."* Valor has scope for action against an open enemy, but the most precious liberties of a kingdom are massacred in cold blood by the disciplined Janizaries of the state, and there is little hope of a general resistance. The natural, inherent right of the conquered is to throw off the yoke, as soon as they are able; but subjects enslaved by the military forces of their own sovereign, become spiritless and despondent ; and scaffolds and axes, the gibbet and the halter, too often terrify them from those noble exertions which would end in their deliverance by a glorious victory or an illustrious death.

Yet in full peace, without any just apprehensions of insurrections at home or invasions from abroad, it was the mischievous policy of the English ministry, in 1717, to procure an allowance of nearly double the forces to what had ever before been established by the sanction of Parliament in times of public tranquillity. Well might many of the nobility of Britain conceive, that as so many forces were no ways necessary to support, they had reason to fear danger to the constitution, which

---

* See Gordon's Disc. on Sallust, vi. § 3. p. 128.

was never entirely subverted but by a standing army. * The English military bands have since been much augmented ;—and whether this disgraceful subversion has already taken place, or is still verging to its accomplishment, may be resolved, after a further inspection into memorials of the present age.

More than half a century since, the discerning members of the House of Lords discovered the tendency of these extraordinary armaments to be no other, than to overthrow the civil power of the kingdom, and to turn it into a military government.† A very short period after this, many of the same noble house bore open testimony, that they were " justly jealous, from the experience of former times, that the crown itself, as well as the liberties of the people, might be found at the disposal of a standing army at home." ‡

But as if one standing army was not enough to ruin a nation of Englishmen, a new kind of forces was raised against the Commonwealth. The officers employed in the customs, excise, in other branches of the revenue, and other parts

---

* Lords' Prot. vol. i. p 282.
† See Lords' Prot. vol. i. p. 315, anno 1721.
‡ See Lords' Prot. vol. ii. 80.

of public service, compose in effect a second standing army in England, and in some respects are more dangerous, than that body of men, properly so called. The influence which this order have in the elections of members to serve in Parliament, hath been too often felt in Great Britain to be denied. And we have good authority to say, "that examples are not hard to find, where the military forces have withdrawn to create an appearance of a free election, and the standing civil forces of this kind have been sent to take that freedom away." * Is a House of Commons, thus chosen, the representative of the people,—or of the administration,—or of a single minister? †

As Lewis the Eleventh of France, was the first monarch in Europe, who reduced corruption to a system, so the era of its establishment in England may be fixed at the reign of Charles the Second. Britain, then for the first time, saw corruption, like a destroying angel, walking at noonday. Charles pensioned his Parliament, and by it extinguished, not only the spirit of freedom, but the sentiments of honour and the

---

* See Lords' Prot. vol. ii. p. 83.

† See same book and page. The reader is desired to read again p. 433, and the note at p. 434. See also hereafter p. 449.

feelings of shame. Since the age of Charles, the science of bribery and corruption hath made amazing progress. Patriots of the last century told their countrymen what it threatened,—the worthies of this day ought rather to tell what hath been effected.

Near fifty years ago, there were more than two hundred persons holding offices or employments under the crown in the House of Commons.* Since that time this body like the military (and for the same purposes) has received very notable additions. Is it to be wondered, then, as we verge nearer to our own times, we should hear the most august assembly in the kingdom declaring to the whole world, that " the influence of the crown is almost irresistible, being already overgrown and yet increasing ;" †—that " the most valuable rights of the nation are subverted by arbitrary and illegal proceedings :" ‡—that "a flagrant usurpation " is made upon the subject, " as highly repugnant to every principle of the constitution, as the claim of ship-money by King Charles the First, or that of the dispensing

---

* See Lords' Prot. p. 66, anno 1729.
† See Lords' Prot. Feb. 8, 1760. Suppl. to Lords' Prot. p. 9.
‡ See same book, p. 12, Jan. 1770.

power by King James the Second." * Finally, considering all that we have seen in the course of our review, could any thing else be expected, than what forty of the House of Lords openly protest " they have seen with great uneasiness ; —a plan, for a long time systematically carried on, for lowering all the constitutional powers of the kingdom, rendering the House of Commons odious, and the House of Peers contemptible." †

Here let us pause, my fellow citizens, and consider :—hath the execrable plan thus systematically and for a long time pursued, at last taken effect ? Are all the constitutional powers of Great Britain so lowered in the estimation of the people, that their representatives are detested, and their nobility despised ? Is their King possessed of power sufficient to make fear a substitute for love ? Has he an army at his absolute command, with which no force in his empire is able to cope ? Judge ye, my countrymen, of these questions, upon which I may not decide; —judge, for yourselves, of the political state of that kingdom, which claims a right of disposing of our all,—a right of laying every burden that

---

* See Lords' Protest, p. 22, 23, Feb. 1770.
† See Supplement to Lords' Prot. p. 29, anno 1770.

power can impose,*—a right of overrunning our soil and freeholds with mercenary legions, and still more mercenary placemen and dependants. Thus luxury and riot, debauchery and havock, are to become the order and peace of our cities, and the stability and honour of our times. To this and like hopeful purposes, we find " the fullest directions sent to the several officers of the revenue, that all the produce of the American duties, arising, or to arise, by virtue of any British act of Parliament, should from time to time be paid to the deputy paymaster in America, to defray the subsistence of the troops, and any military expenses incurred in the colonies."† Highly favoured Americans! you are to be wasted with taxes and impositions, in order to satisfy the charges of those armaments which are to blast

---

* " It will be proper to lay on the Americans every burthen which the hand of power can impose, if they should attempt to become manufacturers." Conduct of Administration examined, 1767. p. 62. Thus Americans are to be treated, for an attempt only to do, what is their duty as soon as possible to effect, and what no power on earth can restrain, without violating the laws of God and nature.

† Lords' Prot. vol. ii. p. 291, 1766. By the Lords who entered their protest against the repeal of the American stamp-act.

your country with the most terrible of all evils,—universal corruption, and a military government. *

The reigns of past and present great monarchs, when compared, often present a striking similitude. The Emperor Charles the Fifth, having exalted the royal prerogative (or the influence of the crown) on the ruins of the privileges of the Castilians, allowed the name of the Cortes (or the Parliament) to remain; and the formality of holding it thus continued, he reduced its authority and jurisdiction to nothing, and modelled it in such a manner, that "it became," says Dr Robertson, " rather a junto of the servants of the

---

* Englishmen in the reign of Henry the Fourth had the virtue and courage to " declare it in Parliament as the undoubted right of the kingdom, not to be charged with aught for the defence of the realm, or safeguard of the seas, but by their own will and consent in Parliament." The Rights of the Kingdom, p. 146, edit. 1682. Had Britons in the age of Geo. III. been as considerate of the spirit of their laws and constitution, or attentive to that old rule,—to do as you would be done by,—they would not have charged America with a large revenue for " the subsistence of troops, and military expenses," without consulting its local Parliament, and against the will of its Commons; more especially since it was the position of that able, though most arbitrary prince, Edward the First of England, touching martial affairs,—*Quod omnes tangit, ab omnibus approbetur.*

crown, than an assembly of the representatives of the people."* The success of Charles in abolishing the privileges of the Commons, and in breaking the power of the nobles of Castile, encouraged an invasion of the liberties of Arragon, which were yet more extensive.

Attend, Americans! reflect on the situation of your mother country, and consider the late conduct of your brethren in Britain towards this continent. " The Castilians (once high-spirited and brave in the cause of freedom) accustomed to subjection themselves, assisted," says the same illustrious historian, " in imposing the yoke on their more happy and independent neighbours."† Hath not Britain (fallen from her pristine freedom and glory) treated America, as Castile did Arragon? Have not Britons imposed on our necks the same yoke which the Castilians imposed on the happy Arragonese? Yes! I speak it with grief,—I speak it with anguish,—Britons are our oppressors: I speak it with shame,—I speak it with indignation,—*we are slaves.*

As force first fixes the chains of vassalage, so cowardice restrains an enslaved people from burst-

---

* Hist. of Charles V. vol. iii. p. 434. † Ib.

ing asunder their bonds. But the case perhaps is not desperate till the yoke has been so long borne, that the understanding and the spirits of the people are sunk into ignorance and barbarism, supineness and perfect inactivity. Such, I yet trust, is not the deplorable state of the land of my nativity. How soon it may be—we shall tremble, when we reflect that the progress of thraldom is secret, and its effects incredibly rapid and dreadful.* Hence we see nations, once the freest and most high-spirited in Europe, abject in the most humiliating condition. The oath of allegiance to their king exhibits the true standard of all just subjection to government, and testifies a genuine sense and spirit. " We who are each of us as good, and who are altogether more powerful than you, promise obedience to your government, if you maintain our rights and liberties ; if not, not."† When a people, endowed with such understanding, sentiments, and virtue, have fallen into a disgraceful vassalage,—what have we in this land, at this time, reason to fear?

---

* " The loss of liberty," says that sagacious politician, Tacitus, " is ever accompanied with the loss of spirit and magnanimity." Vita Agric.

† Dr Robertson's Hist. Charles V. vol. i. p. 153.

The same Athenians, who insulted and bid defiance to a Philip of Macedon, crouched and cowered at the feet of an Alexander. Romans, who with righteous indignation expelled royalty and the Tarquins, bore with infamy and shame the ravages of succeeding kings and emperors. Englishmen, who rose with a divine enthusiasm against the first Charles, disgracefully submitted to the usurpation of a Cromwell, and then with unexampled folly and madness restored that odious and execrable race of tyrants, the house of Stewart. Examples like these, ought to excite the deepest concern;—at this day, they ought to do more,—to inspire fortitude and action.

Providence from the beginning hath exercised this country with singular trials. In the earliest periods of our history, New England is seen surrounded with adversaries, and alternately vexed with foes, foreign and domestic. Fierce as her enemies were from abroad, and savage as the natives of America were within,—her worst enemies will be found those of her own household.

Our fathers " left their native country with the strongest assurance that they, and their posterity should enjoy the privileges of free, natural-born English subjects."* Depending upon these assurances, they sustained hardships scarcely paralleled in the annals of the world.† Yet compassion, natural to the human breast, did not restrain internal foes from involving them in new calamities; nor did that disgrace and contempt, which suddenly fell upon the conspirators, damp the ardour of their malignity.

So early as 1633 (not fourteen years after the first arrival at Plymouth), "the new settlers were in perils from their own countrymen."‡ In this, the infant state of the country, while exposed to innumerable hardships, vexed with hostilities from Europe, and the depredations of savages, there existed men, who "beheld the Massachusetts with an envious eye."§ The characteristics of the first conspirators against this province were secrecy and industry: they had effected the mischief before the people knew of their danger. Morton in his letter to Jeffreys of the first of May, 1634, writes that "the Massachusetts patent, by an order of Council, was brought in view, and the

---

* See Hutch. Hist. vol. i. pref. p. 4.
† See same Hist. p. 19, 45. Appendix, p. 538.
‡ Same Hist. p. 31.
§ Ib. p. 31.

privileges well scanned."* But by whom? very like some of more modern fame: an archbishop, and the privy council of Charles the First! Excellent assay-masters for New-England privileges,—most renowned judges of the rights and liberties of mankind! They first discover the Charter " to be void,"† and then no doubt advise to the issuing of the commission found by my Lord Barrington in the 31st volume of Mr Petyt's Manuscript,—" a commission directed to the archbishop of Canterbury, the Lord Chancellor, and other Lords of the privy council, by which they are empowered to prepare laws for the better government of the colonies," "which were afterwards to be enforced by the king's proclamation." ‡

This was considered as a master-stroke of policy, and the public conspirators of the day displayed the plumage of triumph with that spirit and ostentation, § which have descended to their successors. But how easy is it with Providence, to disappoint the projects and humble the pride of man! Laud and his master, in the subse-

---

* Hutch. vol. i. p. 31.   † Same page.
‡ Barr. Obs. on the more Anc. Statutes, p. 146, note.
§ See Morton's Let. before cited.

quent periods of history, are found too busied with their own concerns, to attend much to those of others. Hence this extraordinary commission was never executed, and the plan set on foot within three years after, " for revoking the patent of the Massachusetts," * proved abortive. Literary correspondences inimical to the province, commenced with Archbishop Laud,† in 1638.‡ But in the pious language of our fathers, " the Lord delivered them from the oppressor ; " § " against all men's expectations they were encouraged, and much blame and disgrace fell upon their adversaries." ‖ Yet notwithstanding, " a spirit full of malignity against the country (not very long after) much endangered both its civil and religious liberties." ¶

---

* Hutch. Hist. vol. i. p. 48, 51.

† Laud was the favourite character selected for a correspondent by the American letter-writers of the last century ; in the next age mankind will be as well acquainted with the genius and spirit of some more modern British correspondents, as they now are with the temper of that renowned prelate.

‡ Hutch. Hist. vol. i. p. 86.   § Morton's Memo. p. 15.

‖ Same book, p. 35.   See also, Collect. of Orig. Papers, &c. p. 52.   ¶ Morton's Memo. p. 96, 187.

More than a century ago, "the great privileges of New England were matter of envy,"* and accordingly complaints multiplied to Cromwell,† no doubt for the benevolent purpose of abridging what were called English liberties. "All attempts to the prejudice of the colony being to no purpose" ‡ with the Protector, the adversaries of the province were despondent, until the restoration of Charles the Second gave new hopes; when " petitions and complaints were preferred against the colony to the king in council, and to the Parliament." §

" False friends and open enemies " now became the terror of the country,‖ while new foes brought new charges to render it obnoxious. ¶ " The great men and natives of the country made their complaints also to the king."** The consequences were such as might be expected. " Four persons were sent over from England, one of them the

---

* Hutch. Hist. p. 194. † Ib. p. 192, 194.
‡ Ib. p. 194. § Ib. p. 211. ‖ Ib. p. 220.
¶ Ib. p. 224, 225.
** Appen. to Hutch. Hist. No. 15. Another native of New England, as we have seen, about the year 1705, wrote to England, that " this country would never be worth living in for lawyers and gentlemen, until the charter was taken away."

known and professed enemy of the country, with such extraordinary powers, that our ancestors with grief complain they were to be subjected to the arbitrary power of strangers proceeding not by any established law, but by their own discretion."*
—How astonishingly uniform, how cruelly consistent has been the conduct of Britain from that day to the present!

Amid all these severe trials, the inhabitants of New England conducted with a virtue and piety worthy remembrance and imitation. "They appealed to God,—they came not into this wilderness to seek great things for themselves, but for the sake of a poor and quiet life;"—they testified to their sovereign, that "their liberties were dearer to them than their lives."† "Evil-minded men continue, however, to misrepresent them," ‡ and what is almost incredible, "the distresses of the colony, during a war which excited compassion in some, yet these very distresses were improved by others to render the colony more obnoxious." §

---

* Hutch. Hist. p. 232.
† Ib. p. 232, 233.   Appen. No. 16, p. 542.
‡ Hutch. Hist. p. 242, 243.   § Ib. p. 308, anno 1676.

Although " this is certain, that as the colony was at first settled, so it was preserved from ruin without any charge to the mother country;"* yet " in the height of the distress of war, and whilst the authority of the colony was contending with the natives for the possession of the soil, complaints were making in England which struck at the powers of government."† With what ferocity have Americans been pursued from the earliest times? That demon of malevolence, which went forth at the beginning, still spirits up our adversaries and persecutes the country with unabated malice.

" Randolph, who, the people of New England said, went up and down seeking to devour them," ‡

---

* Hutch. Hist. p. 310. See also, in confirmation of the above, same Hist. 93—114. Vol. ii. p. 130, 204.

† Ib. 310, 311. " The dominion of the crown over this country before the arrival of our predecessors, was merely ideal. Their removal hither realized that dominion, and has made the country valuable both to the crown and nation, without any cost to either of them, from that time to this. Even in the most distressed state of our predecessors, when they expected to be destroyed by a general conspiracy and incursion of the Indian natives, they had no assistance from them." The Answer of the Council of the Province to Governor Hutchinson's Speech, 25th of Jan. 1773.

‡ Hutch. Hist. p. 319.

was the next active emissary against the province. " He was incessant and open in endeavouring the alteration of the constitution."* In his open enmity, he appears far less odious than those who have been equally inimical and equally indefatigable to the same purpose, with more cowardice, dissimulation, and hypocrisy. Eight voyages were made across the Atlantic in the course of nine years by this inveterate spirit, with hostile intentions to the government.† Nor will it be surprising to find him thus expose his life upon the ocean, when such services acquired " new powers." ‡ Have we not seen, in our own day, a similar policy adopted, and the same object operating as a motive to the like execrable conduct? Such has been the strange, though unhappily consistent, conduct of our mother country, that she has laid temptations, and given rewards and stipends to those, who have slandered and betrayed her own children. Incited probably by the same motive, Cranfield rose up as in a league with Randolph, and " infamously represented the colony as rogues and rebels." §

---

* Hutch. Hist. p. 335, 336.
† Ib. p. 329.   ‡ Ib. p. 329.   § Ib. p. 337.

Libels and conspiracies of this nature called for the interposition of authority : express laws were enacted for the prevention of like treasonable practices for the future ; and death being deemed the proper punishment for an enemy to his country, traitors to the constitution were to suffer that penalty. Thus a "conspiracy to invade the commonwealth, or any treacherous attempt to alter and subvert fundamentally the frame of polity and government, was made a capital offence." *

Did our laws now contain a like provision, public conspirators and elevated parricides would tremble for their heads, who do not shudder at the enormity of their crimes. There are characters in society so devoid of virtue and endued with ferocity, that nothing but sanguinary laws can restrain their wickedness. Even the distress and cries of their native country excite no compassion : reverence for fathers, and affection for children, cause no reluctance at measures which stain the glorious lineage of their ancestors with infamy, and blast their spreading progeny with oppression. That emanation from the deity which creates them intelligents, seems to cease its operation ; and

---

* Hutch. Hist. p. 442.

the tremendous idea of a God and futurity, excites neither repentance nor reformation.

Thus, my countrymen, from the days of Gardiner and Morton,* Gorges and Mason,† Randolph and Cranfield,‡ down to the present day, the inhabitants of this Northern region have constantly been in danger and troubles from foes open and secret, abroad and in their bosom. Our freedom has been the object of envy, and to make void the charter of our liberties the work and labour of an undiminished race of villains. One cabal having failed of success, new conspirators have risen, and what the first could not make " void," the next " humbly desired to revoke." § To this purpose one falsehood after another hath been fabricated and spread abroad with equal turpitude and equal effrontery. That minute detail which would present actors now on the stage, is the province of history. She, inexorably severe towards the eminently guilty, will delineate their characters with the point of a diamond ;—and thus blazoned in the face of day, the abhorrence

---

* Hutch. Hist. p. 31, 32, anno 1632.
† Ib. p. 51, anno 1636.
‡ Ib. p. 337. And Collec. of Orig. Papers, &c. p. 477, &c.
§ Ib. p. 31, 32, 35.

and execrations of mankind will consign them to an infamous immortality.

So great has been the credulity of the British Court, from the beginning, or such hath been the activity of false brethren, that no tale inimical to the Northern Colonies, however false or absurd, but what hath found credit with administration, and operated to the prejudice of the country. Thus it was told, and believed in England, that we were not in earnest in the expedition against Canada at the beginning of this century, and that the country did every thing in its power to defeat the success of it, and that the misfortune of that attempt ought to be wholly attributed to the northern colonies. While nothing could be more obvious, than that New England had exhausted her youngest blood and all her treasures in the undertaking; and that every motive of self-preservation, happiness, and safety must have operated to excite these provinces to the most spirited and persevering measures against Canada.*

The people who are attacked by bad men have a testimony of their merit, as the constitution which is invaded by powerful men, hath an evi-

---

* See Jer. Dummer's Letter to a Noble Lord, edit. 1712. p. 12, 13, &c.

dence of its value. The path of our duty needs no minute delineation;—it lies level to the eye. Let us apply then like men sensible of its importance and determined on its fulfilment. The inroads upon our public liberty call for reparation; the wrongs we have sustained, call for justice. That reparation, and that justice, may yet be obtained by union, spirit, and firmness. But to divide and conquer, was the maxim of the devil in the garden of Eden; and to disunite and enslave hath been the principle of all his votaries from that period to the present. The crimes of the guilty are to them the cords of association, and dread of punishment, the indissoluble bond of union. The combinations of public robbers ought, therefore, to cement patriots and heroes: and as the former plot and conspire to undermine and destroy the commonwealth, the latter ought to form a compact for opposition,—a band of vengeance.

What insidious arts, and what detestable practices have been used to deceive, disunite, and enslave the good people of this continent? The mystical appellations of loyalty and allegiance, the venerable names of government and good order, and the sacred ones of piety and public virtue, have been alternately prostituted to that abominable purpose. All the windings and guises, subterfuges and doublings, of which the human soul is susceptible, have been displayed on the occasion. But secrets which were thought impenetrable are no longer hid; characters deeply disguised are openly revealed: the discovery of gross impostors hath generally preceded, but a short time, their utter extirpation.

Be not again, my countrymen, "easily captivated with the appearances only of wisdom and piety —professions of a regard to liberty and of a strong attachment to the public interest."[*] Your fathers have been explicitly charged with this folly by one of their posterity. Avoid this and all similar errors. Be cautious against the deception of appearances. "By their fruits ye shall know them," was the saying of one who perfectly knew the human heart. Judge of affairs which concern social happiness by facts:—judge of man by his deeds. For it is very certain, that pious zeal for days and times, for mint and cummin, hath often been pretended by those who were infidels at bottom; and it is as certain, that attachment to the dignity of

---

[*] Hutch. Hist. vol. i. p. 53.

government, and the King's service, hath often flowed from the mouths of men who harboured the darkest machinations against the true end of the former, and were destitute of every right principle of loyalty to the latter. Hence, then, care and circumspection are necessary branches of political duty. And as "it is much easier to restrain liberty from running into licentiousness, than power from swelling into tyranny and oppression,"* so much more caution and resistance are required against the overbearing of rulers, than the extravagance of the people.

To give no more authority to any order of state, and to place no greater public confidence in any man, than is necessary for the general welfare, may be considered by the people as an important point of policy. But though craft and hypocrisy are prevalent, yet piety and virtue have a real existence: duplicity and political imposture abound, yet benevolence and public spirit are not altogether banished the world. As wolves will appear in sheep's clothing, so superlative knaves and parricides will assume the vesture of the man of virtue and patriotism.

* Lords' Prot. p. 141, anno 1736.

These things are permitted by providence, no doubt, for wise and good reasons. Man was created a rational, and was designed for an active being. His faculties of intelligence and force were given him for use. When the wolf, therefore, is found devouring the flock, no hierarchy forbids a seizure of the victim for sacrifice ; so also, when dignified impostors are caught destroying those whom their arts deceived and their stations destined them to protect,—the sabre of justice flashes righteousness at the stroke of execution.

Yet be not amused, my countrymen!—the extirpation of bondage, and the reestablishment of freedom, are not of easy acquisition. The worst passions of the human heart, and the most subtle projects of the human mind, are leagued against you ; and principalities and powers have acceded to the combination. Trials and conflicts you must, therefore, endure ;—hazards and jeopardies —of life and fortune—will attend the struggle. Such is the fate of all noble exertions for public liberty and social happiness. Enter not the lists without thought and consideration, lest you arm with timidity and combat with irresolution. Having engaged in the conflict, let nothing discourage your vigour, or repel your perseverance.

Remember that submission to the yoke of bondage is the worst that can befall a people after the most fierce and unsuccessful resistance. What can the misfortunes of vanquishment take away, which despotism and rapine would spare? "It had been easy," said the great lawgiver, Solon, to the Athenians,* "to repress the advances of tyranny, and prevent its establishment; but now it is established and grown to some height, it would be more glorious to demolish it." But nothing glorious is accomplished, nothing great is attained, nothing valuable is secured, without magnanimity of mind and devotion of heart to the service. Brutus-like, therefore, dedicate yourselves at this day to the service of your country; and henceforth live a life of liberty and glory. "On the ides of March," said the great and good man to his friend Cassius, just before the battle of Philippi,—"on the ides of March I devoted my life to my country, and since that time, I have lived a life of liberty and glory."

Inspired with public virtue, touched with the wrongs and indignant at the insults offered his country, the high-spirited Cassius exhibits an he-

---

* Plut. Life of Solon.

roic example :—" Resolved as we are," replied the hero to his friend,—" resolved as we are, let us march against the enemy; for though we should not conquer, we have nothing to fear.*

Spirits and genii, like these, rose in Rome—and have since adorned Britain : such also will one day make glorious this more western world. America hath in store her Bruti and Cassii—her Hampdens and Sydneys—patriots and heroes, who will form a band of brothers :—men who will have memories and feelings—courage and swords : —courage that shall inflame their ardent bosoms, till their hands cleave to their swords—and their swords to their enemies' hearts.

The author has felt exquisitely while writing upon the subjects of his consideration ; and the multitude and perplexity of his private business have denied him sufficient time to revise this publication. Under these circumstances, and being also several years on this side of the meridian of the age of man, there will be found, no doubt, many indiscretions and faults for those of riper years and cooler judgment to correct and censure.—The great Lord Chancellor Bacon hath told us of wise legislators, who have made their law upon the spur of the occasion :—a good citizen, deeply pricked by the spur of the times, is very apt to start with an over-hasty speed. The only excuse of the writer is, that as he at first assumed his pen from the impulses of his conscience, so he now publishes his sentiments from a sense of duty to God and his country.

---

* Plut. Life of Brutus.

APPENDIX.

Extract from the " Memoirs of Benjamin Franklin, written by himself."

"In 1755, war being in a manner commenced with France, the government of Massachusetts Bay projected an attack upon Crown Point, and sent Mr Quincy to Pennsylvania, and Mr Pownall (afterwards Governor Pownall) to New York to solicit assistance. As I was in the assembly, knew its temper, and was Mr Quincy's countryman, he applied to me for my influence and assistance: I dictated his address to them, which was well received. They voted an aid of ten thousand pounds to be laid out in provisions. But the Governor refusing his assent to their bill (which included this with other sums granted for the use of the crown), unless a clause were inserted exempting the proprietary estate from bearing any part of the tax that would be necessary; the assembly, though very desirous of making their grant to New England effectual, were at a loss how to accomplish it. Mr Quincy laboured hard with the Governor to obtain his assent, but he was obstinate. I then suggested a method of doing the business without the Governor, by orders on the trustees of the loan office, which, by law, the assembly had the right of drawing. There was indeed little or no money at the time in the office, and therefore I proposed that the orders should be payable in a year, and to bear an interest of five per cent. : with these orders I supposed the provisions might be easily purchased. The assembly with very little hesitation adopted the proposal, the orders were immediately printed, and I was one of the committee directed to sign and dispose of them. The fund for paying them was the interest of all the paper currency then extant in the province upon loan, together with the revenue arising from the excise ; which being known to be more than sufficient, they obtained credit, and were not only taken in payment for the provisions, but many monied people, who had cash lying by them, vested it in those orders, which they found advantageous, as they bore interest while upon hand, and might on any occasion be used as money. So that they were all eagerly bought up, and in a few weeks none of them were to be seen. Thus this important affair was by this means completed. Mr Quincy returned thanks to the assembly in a handsome memorial, went home highly pleased with the success of his embassy, and ever after bore for me the most cordial and affectionate friendship."

Dr Franklin to Josiah Quincy.

London, April 8, 1761.

Dear Sir,

I received your very obliging letter of Dec. 25, by the hand of your valuable son,* who had before favoured me now and then with a kind visit. I congratulate you on his account, as I am sure you must have a great deal of satisfaction in him. His ingenuous, manly, and generous behaviour in a transaction here with the Society of Arts, gave me great pleasure, as it was much to his reputation.

I am glad my weak endeavours for our common interest were acceptable to you and my American friends; I shall be very happy indeed if any good arises from them. The people in pow-

---

* Edmund Quincy.

er here do now seem convinced of the truth of the principles I have inculcated, and incline to act upon them; but how far they will be able to do so at a peace, is still uncertain, especially as the war in Germany grows daily less favourable to us. My kinsman, Williams, was but ill-informed in the account he gave you of my situation here. The Assembly voted me £1500 sterling, when I left Philadelphia, to defray the expense of my voyage, and negotiations in England, since which they have given nothing more, though I have been here near four years. They will, I make no doubt, on winding up the affair, do what is just, but they cannot afford to be extravagant, as that report would make them. * * * * * *

Pray make my best respects acceptable to your amiable family, and do me the justice to believe that no one more sincerely wishes a continuance of your happiness, than,

  Dear friend,
    Yours most affectionately,
      BENJAMIN FRANKLIN.

Thomas Hollis Esq. to Edmund Quincy, Boston.

Pall Mall, October 1, 1766.

Sir,

I beg you to accept my best acknowledgments for a long, curious, and interesting letter, dated July 25th, though written on a melancholy occasion, and for other matters which accompanied that letter. The death of that able, good, public man, Dr Mayhew, my old and much esteemed friend, has grieved me excessively. He seems to have died through overstrain of application and philanthropy. I pray God to soften the afflictions of his widow, that accomplished, excellent lady, and to endue her with fortitude equal to her loss. The resolution taken by her, not to publish any posthumous works of his, appears to me to be judicious.

I guess not distinctly at what the hint thrown out to you by the late worthy Doctor alluded. It is true I honoured and valued him exceedingly, and not long since repeatedly wrote to him, that I was his assured friend; which he would have experienced, particularly in case he had been ordered here on the stamp act, as was more than once whispered, with what truth I know not.

Not a book has been sent more to the college at Cambridge, as I recollect, through request or inclination of that excellent man, for he made no request of that sort, though it would have been complied with; nor will now be sent less that he is dead; nor did he or any one know in any degree, till lately, the plan adopted by me in regard to books intended to be presented to that college.

I confess to bear affection towards the people of North America; those of Massachusetts, and Boston in particular, believing them to be a good and brave people. Long may they continue such, and the spirit of luxury, now consuming us to the very marrow here at home, kept out from them! One likeliest means to that end will be, to watch well over their youth, by bestowing on them a reasonable, manly education, and selecting thereto the wisest, ablest, most accomplished men, that art or wealth can obtain; for nations rise and fall by individuals not by numbers, as I think all history proveth. With ideas of this kind have I worked for the public library of Cambridge in New England, neither caring too exactly to remember how the last best library in all America was lost there; nor sparing towards it expense, labour, or time. It is certain, the last winter I passed in town, against inclination, health, and conveniency, on account of the stamp act; and this summer with much preceding time—time, the most valuable of all things,—on account of that library. If any good hath followed from this procedure, or should follow from it, I shall be content. After sustaining a thirteen years' unremitted campaign, day, week, and month, year following year, successive to each other; altering, though not broken in constitution, yet verging, it may be towards a Mayhew's fate, without his magnanimity,—I now seek relaxation and quiet; and am going into Dorsetshire, where I have some estate, but no house, the ensuing winter or spring, it is probable to settle there. * * * * * * * * * * * I have not attended the meeting of the Society instituted for promoting "Arts and Commerce," in the Strand, for years past, something having happened there, which made me deem it right to keep away. But every other service in my power I gladly render to that noble society. The article relating to it in your letter, was copied and sent directly to Dr Templeman.

 I am with great respect, Sir,
   your much obliged and
    most obedient servant,
     THOMAS HOLLIS.

Dr Franklin to Josiah Quincy, Braintree.

London, February 26, 1775.

Dear Sir,

I received, and perused with great pleasure, the letter you honoured me with, by your amiable and valuable son. I thank you for introducing me to the acquaintance of a person so deserving of esteem for his public and private virtues. I hope for your sake, and that of his friends and country, that his present indisposition may wear off, and his health be established. His coming over has been of great service to our cause, and would have been much greater, if his constitution would have borne the fatigues of being more frequently in company. He can acquaint you so fully with the state of things here, that my enlarging upon them will be unnecessary. I most sincerely wish him a prosperous voyage, and a happy meeting with his friends and family; and to you, my old dear friend, and the rest of those you love, every kind of felicity; being, with the truest esteem and affection,

Yours,

BENJAMIN FRANKLIN.

P. S. Besides that the air of this city is found extremely prejudicial to his health, all our friends here are of opinion that your son's return at this time, when writing is so inconvenient, may be of singular service.

John Adams Esq. to Josiah Quincy, Braintree.

Philadelphia, July 29, 1775.

Dear Sir,

I had yesterday the honour of your letter of July the eleventh, and I feel myself much obliged by your kind attention to me and my family, but much more, by your care for the public safety, and the judicious and important observations you have made. Your letters, sir, so far from being "a burthen," I consider as an honour to me, besides the pleasure and instruction they afford me. Believe me, sir, nothing is of more importance to me, in my present most arduous and laborious employment, than a constant correspondence with gentlemen of experience, whose characters are known. The minutest fact, the most trivial event, that is connected with the great American cause, becomes important in the present critical situation of affairs, when a revolution seems to be in the designs of providence, as important as any that ever happened in the affairs of mankind.

We jointly lament the loss of a Quincy, and a Warren; two characters as great in proportion to their age, as any that I have ever known in America. Our country mourns the loss of both, and sincerely sympathizes with the feelings of the mother of the one, and the father of the other. They were both my intimate friends, with whom I lived and conversed, with pleasure and advantage. I was animated by them, in the painful, dangerous course of opposition to the oppressions brought upon our country, and the loss of them has wounded me too deeply, to be easily healed. *Dulce et decorum est pro patria mori.* The ways of heaven are dark and intricate, but you may remember the words, which, many years ago, you and I fondly admired, and which, upon many occasions, I have found advantage in recollecting.

" Why should I grieve, when grieving I must bear,
And take with guilt, what guiltless I might share ? "

I have a great opinion of your knowledge and judgment from long experience, concerning the channels and islands in Boston harbour; but I confess your opinion that the harbour might be blocked up, and seamen and soldiers made prisoners, at discretion, was too bold and enterprizing for me, who am not very apt to startle at a daring proposal; but I believe I may safely promise you powder enough, in a little time, for any purpose whatever. We are assured, in the strongest manner, of saltpetre and powder in sufficient plenty another year, of our own make. That both are made in this city, you may report with confidence, for I have seen both,—and I have seen a set of very large powder works, and another of saltpetre.

I hope, sir, we shall never see a total stagnation of commerce for any length of time. Necessity will force open our ports; trade, if I mistake not, will be more free than usual. Your friend, Dr Franklin, to whom I read your letter, and who desires his kind compliments to you, has been employed in directing the construction of row-gallies for this city. The Committee of Safety for this province have ordered twenty of them to be built; some of them are finished. I have seen one of them; it has twelve oars on each side. They rowed up the river the first time, four miles in an hour, against a tide which ran down four miles an hour. The congress have recommended to the colonies, to make provision for the defence of their navigation, in their harbours, rivers, and on their seacoasts. Of a floating battery I have no idea—am glad you are contriving one.

You tell me, sir, that General Lee complained that " he did not find things as the Massachusetts delegates had represented them." What General Lee could mean by this, sir, I know not. What particular he found different from the representation, I do not know; nor do I know which delegate from the Massachusetts, he received a mistaken representation from. I think he should have been particular, that he might not have run the risk of doing an injury. If General Lee should do injustice to two of the Massachusetts delegates, he would commit ingratitude at the same time; for to two of them he certainly owes his promotion in the American army, how great a hazard soever they ran in agreeing to it. I know him very thoroughly, I think, and that he will do great service in our army at the beginning of things, by forming it to order, skill, and discipline. But we shall soon have officers enough. * * * * Your friend and humble servant,

JOHN ADAMS.

Gen. Washington to Josiah Quincy, Braintree.

Cambridge, November 4, 1775.

Sir,

Your favour of the 31st ult. was presented to me yesterday. I thank you (as I shall do every gentleman) for suggesting any measure, which you conceive to be conducive to the public service; but in the adoption of a plan, many things are to be considered to decide upon the utility of it. In the one proposed by you, I shall not undertake to determine whether it be good, or whether it be bad; but thus much I can say, that if there is any spot upon the main, which has an equal command of the ship-channel to Boston harbour (and give me leave to add that Point Alderton is not without its advocates), in all other respects it must have infinitely the preference; because the expense of so many batteries as you propose, with the necessary defences to secure the channel, the communication, and a retreat in the dernier resort from the east end of Long Island, are capital objections. Not, I confess, of such importance as to weigh against the object in view, if the scheme is practicable. But what signifies Long Island, Point Alderton, Dorchester, &c.,

while we are in a manner destitute of cannon, and compelled to keep the little powder we have, for the use of the musketry. The knowledge of this fact is an unanswerable argument against every place, and may serve to account for my not having viewed the several spots which have been so advantageously spoken of. I am not without intentions of making them a visit, and shall assuredly do myself the honour of calling upon you. In the mean while, permit me to thank you most cordially for your polite invitation, and to assure you that I am, sir,

>Your most obedient
>>Humble servant,
>>>GEORGE WASHINGTON.

James Bowdoin to Josiah Quincy, Braintree.

Middleborough, January 29, 1776.

Dear Sir,

After looking over and calculating the papers Mr ———— came about, my eyes, and a pain in my breast consequent on writing, and which will oblige me to throw aside the pen entirely, would scarcely permit me to read, much less to attempt an answer to your very friendly letter of the 22d.

Your obervations on the friendships of this world are very just; the most of those friendships are mere varnish, and quickly end in disappointment; and even when they are sincere, from the transient nature of earthly felicity, and the accidents humanity is heir to, they can be but short-lived. In this, as in every thing else, the wisdom of our beneficent Creator is discernible; who, intending us for a superior state of existence, is disciplining and preparing us for it, by those very accidents and disappointments, which, in concurrence with other things, discover to us that real friendship and permanent felicity are to be expected in that state only. Hence, if we suffer not a wayward humour or false expectations to misguide us, we shall be induced to place our hopes, affections, and dependence there, upon objects worthy of them; but primarily and superlatively on that Being, whose friendship, like himself, is eternal and unchangeable; and who, by the mediation of our blessed Redeemer, will completely beatify the virtuous expectants of his kingdom.

In the mean time, notwithstanding past disappointments, we should endeavour to cultivate the social, friendly principle within us, the cul-

culture of which will not only yield a present satisfaction, but form a habit, which will introduce us with great advantage, to the acquaintance and friendship of kindred spirits in the future state. Good habits thus induced are as well calculated to introduce us to such an acquaintance there, as polished manners into good company here. Both of them seem to be the effect of education,—of education in an extended sense, including the whole of our progress in this state. Agreeably to which sense this world may be considered as a great school, in which mankind in different classes have different employments assigned them. Those that make the best, or any proficiency, will finally be honoured with the approbation of the great Preceptor, who will distinguish and advance them, according to their respective merits. But the greatest proficient will then find he has not got beyond the rudiments of science. His brightened intellect will discover to him new paths of science, of which, like the joys he participates, it never entered into the heart of man to form any conception; and which will afford him infinite matter for the improvement of his growing faculties, and for praise and thanksgiving to the adorable Creator to all eternity. May you and I be companions together in this glorious employment; and have an opportunity of cultivating a friendship, not like the friendships of this world, interrupted by many accidents, and oftentimes by the oppressive hand of despotism,—which has lately made some of us fugitives, and aims to make us vagabonds on the earth,—but, with the favour of our Creator, like our future selves, immortal, and always improving, " growing with our growth, and strengthening with our strength."

Pardon this reverie, as it was occasioned by the kind expressions of your obliging letter; and believe me to be with sincere esteem,
Dear Sir,
Your most obedient humble servant,
JAMES BOWDOIN.

Gen. Washington, to Josiah Quincy, Braintree.
Cambridge, March 24, 1776.
Sir,

I am favoured with your letter of the 21st instant. It came to hand this afternoon, and I thank you for the many kind and flattering expressions it contains. To obtain the applause of deserving men is a heart-felt satisfaction,—to merit it, is my highest wish. If my conduct, therefore, as an instrument in the late signal interposition of Providence, hath merited the approbation of this great country, I shall esteem it one of the most fortunate and happy events of my life. I acknowledge myself your debtor for the share you have bestowed on me of it. The continuance of the fleet in Nantasket roads affords matter for speculation; it surpasses my comprehension, and awakens all my suspicions. I have taken every step in my power, to guard against surprises; but the temper of your people seems to me to be apprehensive of no danger till it stares them in the face. I do not think there is cause to apprehend such marauding parties as you dread; if any stroke is aimed, it will be a capital one; for which reason I wish to be much upon my guard, and therefore have appointed guard-boats, look-outs, &c. There is one evil I dread, and that is their spies. I could wish, therefore, that the most attentive watch was kept, to prevent any intercourse with the ships and the main land; for this purpose, and to prevent suspected persons (for I have no doubt but that trusty soldiers, sergeants, and even commissioned officers in disguise will be sent out) from travelling about, I wish a dozen or more of honest, sensible, and diligent men were employed to haunt the communication, between Roxbury, and the different landing-places nearest the shipping, in order to question, cross-question, &c. all such persons as are unknown, and cannot give an account of themselves in a straight and satisfactory line. If you could hire men for this purpose, whilst the shipping continue where they now are, I would pay the wages you agree upon, and thank you for the trouble, as I think it a matter of some importance to prevent them from obtaining intelligence of our situation. The earliest information should also be communicated of any movements which may be discovered, and whether any of the shipping are getting out, as it were by stealth.

I am exceedingly sorry to hear of your indisposition, and heartily wish you a perfect restoration to health. I should be very happy to take you by the hand, before I bid adieu to the colony; but as my motions are regulated by those of the enemy, I cannot say when or where it can happen. In sincerity and truth, I remain,

 Dear Sir,
  Your most obedient and obliged servant,
   GEORGE WASHINGTON.

Gen. Washington to Josiah Quincy, Braintree.

New York, April 25, 1776.

Dear Sir,

Your favour of the seventh instant coming duly to hand, I thank you for the intelligence therein contained. It gives me pain, to find from your account that matters are taking a wrong bias in the politics of your government. I left five regiments (upon an average as strong as any in the service) to erect such works, and in such places, as should be deemed most conducive to the defence of the harbour. I did, as it was a government concern, leave the works which should be constructed for the defence of the harbour, to the adoption of the General Court, under the auspices of Colonel Gridley, whom I have been taught to view as one of the greatest engineers of the age. If things have gone wrong, I can only express my concern, and lament that time at so important a juncture should be wasted, and the best mode for the defence of the harbour neglected. My extreme hurry will only allow me, in addition to what I have said, to thank you most cordially for your friendly wishes, and to assure you, that I am with great truth and sincerity, Dear Sir,

Your most obedient
and obliged, humble servant,
GEORGE WASHINGTON.

Dr Franklin to Josiah Quincy, Braintree.

Saratoga, April 15, 1776.

Dear Sir,

I am here on my way to Canada, detained by the present state of the lakes, in which the unthawed ice obstructs navigation. I begin to apprehend that I have undertaken a fatigue that at my time of life may prove too much for me, so I sit down to write to a few friends by way of farewell.

I congratulate you on the departure of your late troublesome neighbours. I hope your country will now for some time have rest, and that care will be taken so to fortify Boston, as that no force shall be able again to get footing there. Your very kind letter of November 13th, enclosing Lord Chatham's and Lord Camden's speeches, I duly received. I think no one can be more sensible than I am of the favours of corresponding friends, but I find it impossible to answer as I ought. At present I think you will deem me inexcusable, and therefore I will not attempt an apology. But if you should ever happen to be at the same time oppressed with years and business, you may then extenuate a little for your old friend.

The notes of the speeches taken by your son, whose loss I shall ever deplore with you, are exceedingly valuable, as being by much the best account preserved of that day's debate.

You ask, " When is the continental congress by *general consent* to be formed into a supreme legislature ; alliances, defensive and offensive, formed ; our ports opened ; and a formidable naval force established at the public charge ? " I can only answer at present, that nothing seems wanting but that " general consent." The novelty of the thing deters some, the doubt of success, others, the vain hope of reconciliation, many. But our enemies take continually every proper measure to remove these obstacles, and their endeavours are attended with success, since every day furnishes us with new causes of increasing enmity, and new reasons for wishing an eternal separation ; so that there is a rapid increase of the formerly small party who were for an independent government.

Your epigram on Lord Chatham's remark has amply repaid me for the song. Accept my thanks for it, and for the charming extract of a lady's letter, contained in your favour of January 22d. I thought, when I sat down, to have written by this opportunity to Dr Cooper, Mr Bowdoin, and

Dr Winthrop, but I am interrupted. Be so good as to present my affectionate respects to them, and to your family.

Adieu, my dear friend, and believe me ever
>Yours most affectionately,
>>BENJAMIN FRANKLIN.

Dr Franklin to Josiah Quincy, Braintree.
>Passy, April 22, 1779.

Dear Sir,

I received your very kind letter by Mr Bradford, who appears a very sensible and amiable young gentleman, to whom I should with pleasure render any services in my power upon your much respected recommendation; but I understand he returns immediately.

It is with great sincerity I join you in acknowledging and admiring the dispensations of Providence in our favour. America has only to be thankful, and to persevere. God will finish his work, and establish their freedom; and the lovers of liberty will flock from all parts of Europe with their fortunes to participate with us of that freedom, as soon as peace is restored.

I am exceedingly pleased with your account of the French politeness and civility, as it appeared among the officers and people of their fleet. They have certainly advanced in those respects many degrees beyond the English. I find them here a most amiable nation to live with. The Spaniards are by common opinion supposed to be cruel, the English proud, the Scotch insolent, the Dutch avaricious, &c. but I think the French have no national vice ascribed to them. They have some frivolities, but they are harmless. To dress their heads so that a hat cannot be put on them, and then wear their hats under their arms, and to fill their noses with tobacco, may be called follies perhaps, but they are not vices. They are only the effects of the tyranny of custom. In short, there is nothing wanting in the character of a Frenchman, that belongs to that of an agreeable and worthy man. There are only some trifles surplus, or which might be spared.

Will you permit me, while I do them this justice, to hint a little censure on our own country people, which I do in good will, wishing the cause removed. You know the necessity we are under of supplies from Europe, and the difficulty we have at present in making returns. The in-

terest bills would do a good deal towards purchasing arms, ammunition, clothing, sail-cloth, and other necessaries for defence. Upon inquiry of those who present these bills to me for acceptance, what the money is to be laid out in, I find that most of it is for superfluities, and more than half of it for tea! How unhappily in this instance the folly of our people, and the avidity of our merchants, concur to weaken and impoverish our country! I formerly computed that we consumed before the war, in that single article, the value of £500,000 sterling annually. Much of this was saved by stopping the use of it. I honoured the virtuous resolution of our women in foregoing that little gratification, and I lament that such virtue should be of so short duration! Five hundred thousand pounds sterling, annually laid out in defending ourselves, or annoying our enemies, would have great effect. With what face can we ask aids and subsidies from our friends, while we are wasting our own wealth in such prodigality? With great and sincere esteem I have the honour to be,
 Dear Sir,
  Your most obedient servant,
   BENJAMIN FRANKLIN.

Dr Franklin to Josiah Quincy, Braintree.

Passy, September 11, 1783.

My Dear Sir,

Mr —— told me not long since, that you complained of my not writing to you. You had reason, for I find among your letters two unanswered. The truth is, I have had too much business to do for the public, and too little help allowed me ; so that it became impossible for me to keep up my private correspondencies. I promised myself more leisure when the definitive treaty of peace should be concluded. But that, it seems, is to be followed by a treaty of commerce, which will probably take up a good deal of time, and require much attention. I seize this interim to sit down and have a little chat with my friends in America.

I lament with you, the many mischiefs, the injustice, the corruption of manners, &c. that attended a depreciating currency. It is some consolation to me that I washed my hands of that evil, by predicting it in congress, and proposing means that would have been effectual to prevent it, if they had been adopted. Subsequent operations that I have executed, demonstrate that my plan was practicable. But it was unfortunately rejected. Considering all our mistakes and mismanagements, it is wonderful we have finished our affair so well and so soon! Indeed, I am wrong in using that expression—*We* have finished our affairs so well. Our blunders have been many, and they serve to manifest the hand of Providence more clearly in our favour, so that we may much more properly say, "These are thy doings, oh! Lord, and they are marvellous in our eyes!"

The epitaph on my dear and much esteemed young friend, is too well written, to be capable of improvement by any corrections of mine; your moderation appears in it, since the natural affection of a parent has not induced you to exaggerate his virtues.

How admirably constituted was his noble and generous mind. Having plenty of merit in himself, he was not jealous of the appearance of it in others. I shall always mourn his loss with you, a loss not easily made up to his country.
* * * * * * * * * * * *
* * * * * * * * * * I rejoice with you in the peace God has blessed us with, and in the prosperity it gives us a prospect of.

The Definitive Treaty was signed the third instant. We are now friends with England, and with all mankind!

May we never see another war! for in my opinion, there never was a good war, or a bad peace.

Adieu, and believe me ever,
My dear Friend,
Yours most affectionately,
BENJAMIN FRANKLIN.

THE END.